Questions, Exercises, Problems, and Cases to Accompany Financial Accounting

Rick Antle
Yale University

Stanley J. Garstka
Yale University

Kathleen Sevigny
Bridgewater State College

South-Western College Publishing
Thomson Learning™

5101 Madison Road Cincinnati, OH 45227-1490

Questions Exercises, Problems, and Cases to Accompany Financial Accounting, by Antle, Garstka, Sevigny
Publisher: Dave Shaut
Acquisitions Editor: Steve Hazelwood
Developmental Editor: Ken Martin
Production Editor: Tamborah Moore
Manufacturing Coordinator: Doug Wilke
Production House: Pre-Press Company, Inc.
Compositor: Pre-Press Company, Inc.
Printer: Globus Printing, Inc.

Printed in the United States of America
1 2 3 4 5 04 03 02 01

For more information contact South-Western, 5101 Madison Road, Cincinnati, Ohio, 45227 or find us on the Internet at http://www.swcollege.com

For permission to use material from this text or product, contact us by
*   **telephone: 1-800-730-2214**
*   **fax: 1-800-730-2215**
*   **web: http://www.thomsonrights.com**

ISBN: 0-324-10081-7

contents

Chapter one

Introduction to Financial Accounting

Questions . . . .

1. What is accounting?
2. a. What are economic concepts, accounting conventions, and institutional context?
   b. What is the relationship between these three elements and accounting?
3. Describe the three basic financial statements.
4. What is Novell's most valuable asset according to its balance sheet in Exhibit 1.1?
5. What is the largest source of expenses for Novell according to its income statement in Exhibit 1.2?
6. Which of Novell's financial statements shows the amount of cash collected from customers in the year ended October 31, 1998?
7. Did Novell sell any common stock during fiscal 1998? How do you know?
8. Give three examples of decisions that can be improved by examining accounting information.
9. According to Exhibit 1.4, how does Novell treat "highly liquid debt instruments purchased with a term to maturity of three months or less"? Can you provide a rationale for this treatment?
10. Do the financial statements contain exact numbers that reflect the value of future contingencies, such as pending litigation?
11. What is the financial value of an item? What factors help determine whether we can measure financial value?
12. What is an organization's wealth?
13. What is the accounting equation?
14. How does the accounting identity (Assets = Liabilities + Equities) differ from Einstein's famous equation $e = mc^2$? In particular, can the accounting equation fail to hold? Can Einstein's equation fail to hold? Why or why not?
15. What is an organization's "economic income" over a period?
16. Name three problems accountants face in practice in applying the concepts of financial value, wealth, and economic income.
17. What is accounting valuation?
18. What is recognition?
19. What is GAAP and who determines it?
20. What is an independent audit, and by whom is it conducted?
21. Do accounting reports reflect economic reality? Why or why not?

Cases and Projects . . . .

C1-1 Explore the Web

Many, but not all, companies make their financial reports accessible on the web. Often these reports can be found through a link called "shareholder information," or something similar. Select a company, go to its web site, and find its financial reports. Then view the financial reports to answer the following questions. (Do not print out the entire document.)

a. What is the name of the company?

b. Who are the company's auditors?

c. Are there any unusual statements in the auditors' report?

d. What is the date of the most recent balance sheet?

e. What period is covered by the most recent income statement?

f. What period is covered by the most recent statement of cash flows?

g. What are the company's major reported assets?

h. What are the major reported liabilities?

i. What are the major sources of revenues?

j. What are the major expenses?

k. What was the amount of the company's total assets at the beginning of the year?

l. What was the amount of the total assets at the end of the year?

m. What was the amount of the average total assets?

n. What was the net income for the year?

C1–2   EDGAR

The Securities and Exchange Commission (SEC) is an agency of the United States government. Its primary responsibility is the regulation of the markets for stocks and bonds. The SEC requires that companies whose shares are publicly traded file a variety of reports in electronic format. These reports are available to the public through the SEC's EDGAR (Electronic Data Gathering and Reporting) system, which is fully accessible through the World Wide Web.[4]

There are many types of required filings, but the ones of most interest to us are the 10-K and 10-Q reports. The 10-K is the primary form that carries a company's annual financial statements prepared in accordance with generally accepted accounting principles (GAAP). The 10-Q contains the company's quarterly GAAP-based financial statements.

Required

Choose one of the following companies:

- Dell Computer
- Navigant Consulting
- WalMart
- Perrigo

Find the company's most recent 10-K on the EDGAR web site. Then view the financial reports to answer the following questions. (Do not print out the entire document.)

a. Who are the company's auditors?

b. Are there any unusual statements in the auditors' report?

---

[4] The reports are stored as text files (*.txt) on the EDGAR web site. You can either download the files or view them straight from your browser, if you have configured your browser properly.

c. What does the company call its balance sheet? For example, is it a Balance Sheet, Statement of Financial Position, or some other name?

d. What is the date of the company's most recent balance sheet?

e What does the company call its income statement?

f. What period is covered by the company's most recent income statement?

g. What does the company call its statement of cash flows?

h. What period is covered by the company's most recent statement of cash flows?

i. What are the company's major reported assets?

j. What are the major reported liabilities?

k. What are the major sources of revenues?

l. In the footnotes to the financial statements, is there a description of the company's revenue recognition policies? If so, summarize them.

m. What are the major expenses?

n. What was the amount of the company's total assets at the beginning of the year?

o. What was the amount of the total assets at the end of the year?

p. What was the amount of the average total assets?

q. What was the amount of the net income for the year?

C1–3   Financial Disclosures in an Initial Public Offering

An initial public offering (IPO) is the first sale of shares in a company to the public. Several unusual IPOs occurred in September 1999. One of these was for shares in the World Wrestling Federation (WWF). Before its IPO, shares in the WWF were held by only a few members of one family. The following are excerpts from the WWF's Form 424B1, filed with the SEC on October 19, 1999. The entire form is available through the SEC's EDGAR database.

Our Operations
Our operations are organized around two principal activities:

- the creation, marketing and distribution of our live and televised entertainment, which includes the sale of advertising time on our television programs; and
- the marketing and promotion of our branded merchandise.

Live and Televised Entertainment
Live Events
In fiscal 1999, we held approximately 200 live events in approximately 100 cities in North America, including 18 of the 20 largest metropolitan areas in the United States. Attendance at our live events has increased approximately 109% over the last three years, from approximately 1.1 million people in fiscal 1997 to approximately 2.3 million people in fiscal 1999. Our live events provide the content for our television and pay-per-view programming.

Television Programming
We are an independent producer of television programming. Relying primarily on our in-house production capabilities, we produce seven shows consisting of nine hours of original programming 52 weeks per year. Four of our seven weekly television shows, including our two-hour

flagship show, Raw is War, are carried by the USA Network. We have enjoyed a 17-year relationship with the USA Network, which reaches approximately 75 million households in the United States. Two of our other shows are syndicated and are carried by approximately 120 stations nationwide. Our newest show, WWF SmackDown!, a two- hour program, has aired since August 1999 on the United Paramount Network, which can be seen in approximately 82 million households in the United States. Our brand of entertainment appeals to a wide demographic audience, and although it is principally directed to audiences aged 18 to 34, it has become most popular with males aged 18 to 34 and teenagers aged 12 to 17.

Pay-Per-View Programming

We have been pioneers in both the production and promotion of pay-per-view events since our first pay-per-view event, Wrestlemania, in 1985. By fiscal 1996, we had increased our pay-per-view offerings to 12 per year. Our events consistently rank among the pay-per-view programs achieving the highest number of buys.

New Media

We utilize the Internet to communicate with our fans and market and distribute our various products. Through our network of Internet sites, our fans can obtain our latest news and information, stay abreast of our evolving story lines, tap into interactive chat rooms to communicate with each other and our performers, purchase our webcast pay-per-view events, and purchase our branded merchandise. Our main site, wwf.com, is currently one of the Internet's most popular and most visited sites. We promote wwf.com on our televised programming, at our live events, in our two monthly magazines and in substantially all of our marketing and promotional materials.

Our Business Strategy

Some of the key elements of our strategy are to:

- Expand our television and pay-per-view distribution relationships;
- Increase the licensing and direct sale of our branded products;
- Grow our Internet operations;
- Form strategic relationships with other media and entertainment companies;
- Create new forms of entertainment and brands that complement our existing businesses; and
- Develop branded location-based entertainment businesses directly or through licensing agreements, joint ventures or other arrangements.

We cannot assure you that we will be able to achieve our business objectives, which will depend, in large part, on the continued popularity of our brand of sports entertainment and our success in expanding into new or complementary businesses in the face of a variety of risks as summarized under "Risk Factors."

Risk Factors

The failure to continue to develop creative and entertaining programs and events would likely lead to a decline in the popularity of our brand of entertainment.

The failure to retain or continue to recruit key performers could lead to a decline in the appeal of our story lines and the popularity of our brand of entertainment.

Our success depends, in large part, upon our ability to recruit, train and retain athletic performers who have the physical presence, acting ability and charisma to portray characters in our live events and televised programming. We cannot assure you that we will be able to continue to identify, train, and retain such performers in the future. Additionally, we cannot assure you that we will be able to retain our current performers when their contracts expire. Our failure to attract and retain key performers, or a serious or untimely injury to, or the death of, any of our key performers, would likely lead to a decline in the appeal of our story lines, and the popularity of our brand of entertainment, which would adversely affect our ability to generate revenues.

The loss of the creative services of Vincent McMahon could adversely affect our ability to create popular characters and creative story lines.

For the foreseeable future, we will heavily depend on the vision and services of Vincent McMahon. In addition to serving as chairman of our board of directors, Mr. McMahon leads the creative team that develops the story lines and the characters for our televised programming and our live events. Mr. McMahon is also an important member of the cast of performers. The loss of Mr. McMahon due to retirement, disability or death could have a material adverse effect on our ability to create popular characters and creative story lines. We do not carry key man life insurance on Mr. McMahon.

Because we depend upon our intellectual property rights, our inability to protect those rights could negatively impact our ability to compete in the sports entertainment market.

Our inability to protect our large portfolio of trademarks, service marks, copyrighted material and characters, trade names and other intellectual property rights could negatively impact our ability to compete.

Other parties may infringe on our intellectual property rights and may thereby dilute our brand in the marketplace. Any such infringement of our intellectual property rights would also likely result in our commitment of time and resources to protect these rights. We have engaged, and continue to engage, in litigation with parties that claim or misuse some of our intellectual property. We are involved in significant pending lawsuits relating primarily to the ownership of copyrights of some of the characters featured in our live and televised events and our home videos. Similarly, we may infringe on others' intellectual property rights. One or more adverse judgments with respect to these intellectual property rights could negatively impact our ability to compete.

Our insurance may not be adequate to cover liabilities resulting from accidents or injuries. We could incur substantial liabilities if pending material litigation is resolved unfavorably.

Use of Proceeds

The net proceeds to us from the sale of the shares being offered will be approximately $155.6 million, after deducting the underwriting discount and offering expenses.

The principal purposes of this offering are to increase our working capital, create a public market for our common stock and facilitate our future access to the public capital markets. Except for upgrading our television and post-production facility at an estimated cost of $12.0 million, we cannot specify with certainty the particular uses for the net proceeds to be received upon completion of this offering. Accordingly, our management will have broad discretion in applying the net proceeds. Pending any such use, we intend to invest the net proceeds in interest-bearing instruments.

Dividend Policy

We plan to retain all of our earnings, if any, to finance the expansion of our business and for general corporate purposes and do not anticipate paying any cash dividends on our Class A or Class B common stock in the foreseeable future.

Independent Auditors' Report

The Board of Directors and Stockholder of
World Wrestling Federation Entertainment, Inc.:

We have audited the accompanying combined balance sheets of World Wrestling Federation Entertainment, Inc. and related companies (the "Company") as of April 30, 1998 and 1999 and the related combined statements of operations, changes in stockholder's equity and cash flows for each of the three years in the period ended April 30, 1999. The combined financial statements include the accounts of World Wrestling Federation Entertainment, Inc., World Wrestling Federation Entertainment Canada, Inc. and Stephanie Music Publishing, Inc. These entities are under common ownership and management. These financial statements are the responsibility of the Company's management. Our responsibility is to express an opinion on these financial statements based on our audits.

We conducted our audits in accordance with generally accepted auditing standards. Those standards require that we plan and perform the audit to obtain reasonable assurance about whether the financial statements are free of material misstatement. An audit includes examining, on a test basis, evidence supporting the amounts and disclosures in the combined financial statements. An audit also includes assessing the accounting principles used and significant estimates made by management, as well as evaluating the overall financial statement presentation. We believe that our audits provide a reasonable basis for our opinion.

In our opinion, such financial statements present fairly, in all material respects, the combined financial position of the Company as of April 30, 1998 and 1999 and the combined results of its operations and its combined cash flows for each of the three years in the period ended April 30, 1999 in conformity with generally accepted accounting principles.

/s/ Deloitte & Touche LLP

Stamford, Connecticut
July 16, 1999
(October 1, 1999 as to Note 9 and
October 15, 1999 as to Note 10)

Notes to Combined Financial Statements (Excerpts)
(Dollars in thousands, except share and per share data)

2. Summary of Significant Accounting Policies

Cash and Cash Equivalents—Cash and cash equivalents include cash on deposit in overnight deposit accounts and certificates of deposit with original maturities of three months or less.

Accounts Receivable—Accounts receivable relate principally to amounts due the Company from cable companies for certain pay-per-view presentations and balances due from the sale of television advertising, videotapes and magazines.

Inventory—Inventory consists of merchandise sold on a direct sales basis, and videotapes, which are sold through wholesale distributors and retailers. Inventory is stated at the lower of cost (first-in, first-out basis) or market. Substantially all inventories are comprised of finished goods.

Property and Equipment—Property and equipment are stated at historical cost. Depreciation and amortization is computed on a straight-line basis over the estimated useful lives of the assets or, when applicable, the life of the lease, whichever is shorter. Vehicles and equipment are depreciated based on estimated useful lives varying from three to five years. Buildings and related improvements are amortized over thirty-one years, the estimated useful life. Maintenance and repairs are charged directly to expense as incurred.

World Wrestling Federation Entertainment, Inc.
Combined Balance Sheets
(Dollars in thousands)

	As of April 30		As of July 30
	1998	1999	1999 (unaudited)
ASSETS			
Current Assets:			
Cash and cash equivalents	$ 8,797	$ 45,727	$ 34,310
Accounts receivable (less allowance for doubtful accounts of $920 at April 30, 1999 and $776 (unaudited) at July 30, 1999)	21,221	37,509	34,737
Inventory, net	2,627	2,939	2,587
Prepaid expenses and other current assets	832	2,849	3,478
Assets held for sale	0	10,183	10,181
Total current assets	$33,477	$ 99,207	$ 85,293
Property and equipment, net	26,117	28,377	29,435
Other assets		2,604	2,786
Total assets	$59,594	$130,188	$117,514
LIABILITIES AND STOCKHOLDER'S EQUITY			
Current liabilities:			
Accounts payable	$7,878	$5,941	$1,857
Accrued expenses and other liabilities	12,412	25,821	26,247
Accrued income taxes	593	2,291	531
Deferred income	3,620	11,084	10,888
Current portion of long-term debt	709	1,388	1,797
Note payable to stockholder			32,000
Total current liabilities	$25,212	$ 46,525	$ 73,320
Long-term debt	11,685	11,403	10,741
Commitments and contingencies (Note 9)			
Stockholder's Equity:			
Common stock	568	568	568
Accumulated other comprehensive loss	(99)	(87)	(107)
Retained earnings	22,228	71,779	32,992
Total stockholder's equity	$22,697	$ 72,260	$33,453
Total liabilities and stockholder's equity	$59,594	$130,188	$117,514

See notes to combined financial statements.

Revenue Recognition—Revenues from live and televised entertainment are recorded when earned, specifically upon the occurrence or airing of the related event. Revenues from the licensing and sale of branded consumer products consist principally of royalty revenues, magazine subscription and newsstand revenues and sales of branded merchandise, net of estimated returns. Royalty revenues are recognized in accordance with the terms of applicable royalty and license agreements with each counter party. In certain situations the Company receives royalty advances from third parties which are deferred and recognized over the term

World Wrestling Federation Entertainment, Inc.
Combined Statements of Operations
(Dollars in thousands, except share and per share data)

	Fiscal year ended April 30			Three months ended	
	1997	1998	1999	July 31, 1998 (unaudited)	July 30, 1999 (unaudited)
Net revenues	$81,863	$126,231	$ 251,474	$39,042	$ 76,222
Cost of revenues	60,958	87,969	146,618	25,031	41,045
Selling, general and administrative expenses	25,862	26,117	45,559	8,305	13,970
Depreciation and amortization	1,729	1,676	1,946	418	659
Operating income (loss)	$ 6,686)	$ 10,469	$ 57,351	$ 5,288	$ 20,548-9
Interest expense	782	2,019	1,125	245	409
Other income, net	777	479	1,747	193	851
Income (loss) before income taxes	$ 6,691)	$ 8,929	57,973	5,236	20,990
Provision (benefit) for income taxes	(186)	463	1,943	175	714
Net income (loss)	$ 6,505)	$ 8,466	$ 56,030	$ 5,061	$ 20,276

UNAUDITED PRO FORMA INFORMATION (NOTE 3):

	1997	1998	1999	July 31, 1998	July 30, 1999
Historical income before income taxes			$ 57,973		$ 20,990
Pro forma adjustment other than income taxes			2,515		427
Pro forma income before income taxes			55,458		20,563
Pro forma provision for income taxes			22,227		8,064
Pro forma net income			$ 33,231		$ 12,499
Pro forma earnings per common share (basic and diluted)			$ 0.59		$ 0.22
Weighted average common shares outstanding			$56,667,000		$56,667,000

See Notes to Combined Financial Statements.

World Wrestling Federation Entertainment, Inc.
Combined Statements of Cash Flows
(Dollars in thousands)

	Year ended April 30,			Three months ended	
				July 31, 1998 (unaudited)	July 30, 1999 (unaudited)
	1997	1998	1999		
OPERATING ACTIVITIES:					
Net income (loss)	(6,505)	8,466	56,030	5,061	20,276
Adjustments to reconcile net income (loss)					
to net cash provided by operating activities:					
Depreciation and amortization	1,729	1,676	1,946	418	659
Provision for doubtful accounts	-	-	920	-	(144)
Provision for inventory obsolescence	-	-	1,530	-	-
Deferred income taxes	-	-	(483)	-	-
Changes in assets and liabilities:					
Accounts receivable	4,965	(8,848)	(17,208)	395	2,916
Inventory	(99)	(2,332)	(1,842)	(178)	352
Prepaid expenses and other current assets	114	(3)	(1,522)	(676)	(808)
Accounts payable	2,624	1,772	(1,937)	(5,450)	(4,085)
Accrued expenses and other liabilities	1,165	5,558	13,409	467	405
Accrued income taxes	(61)	360	1,698	(931)	(1,760)
Deferred income	(304)	(393)	5,105	3,896	(196)
Net cash provided by operating activities	3,628	6,256	57,646	3,002	17,615
INVESTING ACTIVITIES:					
Purchases of property and equipment	(892)	(1,294)	(3,756)	(907)	(1,717)
Purchase of hotel & casino	-	-	(10,878)	-	-
Proceeds from sale of property and equipment	43	-	-	-	-
Net cash used in investing activities	(849)	(1,294)	(14,634)	(907)	(1,717)
FINANCING ACTIVITIES:					
Proceeds (repayments) of short-term debt	1,350	(3,300)	-	-	-
Proceeds from long-term debt	285	12,000	1,563	-	-
Repayments of long-term debt	(975)	(4,478)	(1,166)	(196)	(252)
Repayments of capital lease obligations	(98)	(96)	-	-	-
S Corporation distributions	(2,365)	(2,152)	(6,479)	(510)	(27,063)
Net cash provided by (used in) financing activities	(1,803)	1,974	(6,082)	(706)	(27,315)
Net increase (decrease) in cash and cash equivalents	976	6,936	36,930	1,389	(11,417)
Cash and cash equivalents, beginning of period	885	1,861	8,797	8,797	45,727
Cash and cash equivalents, end of period	$1,861	$8,797	$45,727	$10,186	$34,310
Supplemental Cash Flow Information:					
Cash paid during the period for income taxes	162	106	644	560	2,611
Cash paid during the period for interest	602	2,063	1,143	319	272
Supplemental Non-Cash Information:					
Receipt of warrants	-	-	2,359	-	-
Issuance of note payable to stockholder	-	-	-	-	32,000

See Notes to Combined Financial Statements.

of the related agreements. Subscription revenues are initially deferred and earned pro-rata over the related subscription periods. Sales of merchandise and newsstand magazines are recorded when shipped to third parties.

Use of Estimates—The preparation of financial statements in conformity with generally accepted accounting principles requires management to make estimates and assumptions that affect the reported amounts of assets and liabilities and disclosures of contingent assets and liabilities at the date of the financial statements and the reported amounts of revenue and expenses during the reporting period. Actual results could differ from those estimates.

Valuation of Long-Lived Assets—The Company periodically evaluates the carrying value of long-lived assets when events and circumstances warrant such a review. The carrying value of a long-lived asset is considered impaired when indicators of impairment are present and undiscounted cash flows estimated to be generated by the asset are less than the asset's carrying amount. In that event, a loss is recognized based on the amount by which the carrying value exceeds the fair value of the long-lived asset. Fair value is determined primarily using the anticipated cash flows discounted at a rate commensurate with the risk involved.

3. Unaudited Pro Forma Information

The unaudited pro forma combined statement of operations information presents the pro forma effects on the historical combined statement of operations for the year ended April 30, 1999 and the three months ended July 30, 1999 of the additional compensation of $2,515 and $427, respectively to the chairman of the board of directors and to the chief executive officer pursuant to employment agreements that become effective upon the closing of the Offering. Additionally, it presents income taxes of $22,227 and $8,064 to give pro forma effect for the year ended April 30, 1999 and the three months ended July 30, 1999, respectively, due to the change in the Company's tax status from an S Corporation to a C Corporation, representing an overall effective tax rate of 40% and 39%, respectively.

Pro Forma Earnings Per Share (Basic and Diluted)

All share and per share information has been retroactively restated to reflect the 566,670-for-one stock split which became effective on October 15, 1999.

8. Income Taxes

Other than World Wrestling Federation Entertainment Canada, Inc., the Company is an S Corporation for U.S. federal income tax purposes. An S Corporation's income or loss and distributions are passed through to, and taken into account by, the corporation's stockholder in computing personal taxable income. Accordingly, no provision for U.S. federal income tax has been made in the accompanying historical combined financial statements. Income tax provision (benefit) in 1997, 1998 and 1999 was $(186), $463 and $1,943 respectively, and was comprised primarily of current state and foreign taxes.

Prior to or concurrent with the closing of the Offering, the Company will no longer be treated as an S Corporation and, accordingly, the Company will be subject to federal, foreign and state income taxes. See Note 3 regarding pro forma income taxes assuming the Company had not been an S Corporation.

9. Commitments and Contingencies

Contingencies

On May 13, 1991, William R. Eadie, a former professional wrestler who had been one of the Company's performers, filed a lawsuit in state court in Wisconsin against the Company and the Company's stockholder. The case was removed to the United States District Court for the District of Connecticut on August 7, 1991. The suit alleges that the Company reached a verbal agreement to compensate Eadie for the use of his ideas in connection with a wrestling tag team called "Demolition" and to employ him for life. Plaintiff is seeking $6,500 in compensatory damages and unspecified punitive damages. The Company has denied any liability and is vigorously contesting this action. In a similar action filed against the Company on April 10, 1992 in the United States District Court for the District of Connecticut, Randy Colley, a former professional wrestler who had been one of the Company's performers, also alleges that the Company breached an agreement to compensate him for disclosing his idea for a wrestling tag team called "Demolition." He is seeking unspecified compensatory and punitive damages. The Company has denied any liability and is vigorously defending this action. Colley's claims were consolidated for trial with those of Eadie in the action described above. The Company believes that both plaintiffs' claims are without merit. On May 20, 1998, a magistrate judge ruled that the plaintiffs' expert on damages could not testify at trial. Thereafter, the plaintiffs engaged a second expert on damages, whose report was filed on August 31, 1999. Discovery has not been completed, and no trial date has been scheduled. The Company believes that an unfavorable outcome in these actions may have a material adverse effect on its financial position or results of operations.

On August 28, 1996, James Hellwig, a former professional wrestler who had been one of the Company's performers, filed a suit against the Company in state court in Arizona alleging breach of two separate service contracts, defamation and unauthorized use of servicemarks and trademarks allegedly owned by him. Hellwig is also seeking a declaration that he owns the characters, Ultimate Warrior and Warrior, which he portrayed as a performer under contract with the Company. Pursuant to mandatory disclosure requirements filed with the court, Hellwig stated that he is seeking approximately $10,000 in compensatory damages and $5,000 in punitive damages, or such other amount as may be determined by the court or jury. The Company has denied all liability and is vigorously defending this action. The Company believes that Hellwig's claims are without merit. The Company has asserted counterclaims against him for breach of his service contracts and seeks rescission of an agreement by which the Company transferred ownership of the servicemarks to him. In addition, the Company filed a separate action in federal district court in Connecticut on March 11, 1998, seeking a declaration that the Company owns the characters, Warrior and Ultimate Warrior, under both contract and copyright law. Hellwig's motion to dismiss the federal case was denied, and the Company has since moved for summary judgment in the federal proceeding. In the state court proceeding in Arizona, on June 3, 1999, the Company moved for summary judgment on the two contract claims, the defamation claim, and the other claims of the plaintiff. On September 7, 1999, the Arizona court issued a summary judgment decision in the Company's favor on Hellwig's defamation claims. Hellwig had sought $100 in compensatory damages and $5,000 in punitive damages on this claim. The Arizona court also granted the Company's motion for summary judgment on Hellwig's claim for $4,000 damages for his failed business ventures. The court ruled Hellwig could not properly claim damages for the failed business ventures because the Company made no contractual commitment to fund his failed business ventures. Further, the court denied the Company's summary judgment motion with respect to his breach of the 1996 contract and at this time has not ruled upon the Company's fourth summary judgment motion with respect to his breach of the 1992 contract. The Company intends to move for summary judgment regarding Hellwig's royalty claims on the sale of videos and merchandise. The Company believes that the ultimate liability resulting from this suit, if any, will not have a material adverse effect on the Company's financial position or results of operations.

On June 21, 1996, the Company filed an action against WCW and Turner Broadcasting Systems, Inc. in the United States District Court for the District of Connecticut, alleging unfair competition and infringement of the Company's copyrights, servicemarks and trademarks with respect to two characters owned by the Company. The Company's claim that WCW, which contracted with two professional wrestlers who previously had performed under contract for the Company in the character roles of Razor Ramon and Diesel, misappropriated those characters in WCW's programming and misrepresented the reason that these former World Wrestling Federation professional wrestlers were appearing on WCW programming. During discovery proceedings, which were completed on October 16, 1998, WCW was twice sanctioned by the court for failure to comply with the court's discovery orders. The Company is seeking damages in the form of revenue disgorgement from WCW and has submitted expert reports supporting the Company's claim for substantial money damages. WCW and TBS have denied any liability.

On May 18, 1998, WCW filed an action against the Company in the United States District Court for the District of Connecticut and immediately moved to consolidate this action with the Company's pending action against WCW and TBS described above. WCW alleges that the Company diluted various marks owned by and/or licensed to WCW by disparaging those marks and also claims that the Company engaged in unfair competition when the Company aired its "Flashback" series of past World Wrestling Federation performances on USA Network without disclosing that some of the performers, at the time the series was subsequently broadcast, were then affiliated with WCW. The Company has denied any liability and is vigorously defending against this action. The Company has filed a counterclaim for abuse of process, which WCW has moved to dismiss. Discovery is ongoing, and the Company intends to move for summary judgment when discovery is concluded. The Company believes that WCW's claims are without merit. WCW has yet to state a claim for damages. The Company believes that the ultimate liability resulting from such proceeding, if any, will not have a material adverse effect on the Company's financial position, results of operations or prospects.

In addition, on December 11, 1998, WCW filed a suit against the Company in state court in Georgia alleging that the Company had breached an existing contract between the Company and High Road Productions, Inc., a film distribution company, and thereby allegedly interfered with a potential contract between High Road and WCW. WCW seeks unspecified money damages. The Company has denied all liability, believes that WCW's claims are without merit, and is vigorously defending against the suit. On April 2, 1999, the Company moved to dismiss and for judgment on the pleadings on the grounds that WCW's complaint fails to state a claim for tortious interference with business relations as a matter of Georgia law. A hearing on the motion was held on July 14, 1999, and on August 6, 1999 the judge granted the Company's motion and dismissed WCW's case.

On June 15, 1999, members of the family of Owen Hart, a professional wrestler performing under contract with the Company, filed suit in state court in Missouri against the Company, the Company's Chairman of the Board of Directors and the Company's President and Chief Executive Officer, and nine other defendants, including the manufacturer of the rigging equipment involved, individual equipment riggers and the arena operator, as a result of the death of Owen Hart during a pay-per-view event at Kemper Arena in Kansas City, Missouri on May 23, 1999. The specific allegations against the Company include the failure to use ordinary care to provide proper equipment and personnel for the safety of Owen Hart, the failure to take special precautions when conducting an inherently dangerous activity, endangerment and the failure to warn, vicarious liability for the negligence of the named individual defendants, the failure to properly train and supervise, and the provision of dangerous and unsafe equipment. Plaintiffs seek compensatory and punitive damages in unspecified amounts. On September 1, 1999, the Company filed its answer, affirmative defenses and cross-claim denying any liability for negligence and other claims asserted against the Company. The Company believes that it has meritorious defenses and intends to defend vigorously against the suit. On October 1, 1999, the Company filed a complaint in the United States District Court for the District of Connecticut. The Company is principally seeking a declaratory judgment with respect to the enforceability of certain contractual defenses, forum selection clauses, and other provisions of Owen Hart's contract with the Company. The defendants have not yet filed an answer. The Company believes that an unfavorable outcome of this suit may have a material adverse effect on the Company's financial position, results of operations or prospects.

On September 16, 1999, Nicole Bass, a professional wrestler affiliated with the Company, filed an action in the United States District Court for the Eastern District of New York alleging sexual harassment under New York law, civil assault and intentional infliction of emotional distress. Bass seeks $20,000 in compensatory damages and $100,000 in punitive damages. The Company has not been formally served with the complaint and has not conducted an extensive investigation of the allegations in the complaint. The Company believes that the claims are without merit and intend to vigorously defend against this action. Based on a preliminary review of the allegations and the underlying facts as the Company understands them, the Company does not believe that an unfavorable outcome in this action will have a material adverse effect on its financial condition or results of operations.

The Company is not currently a party to any other material legal proceedings. However, the Company is involved in several other suits and claims in the ordinary course of business, and it may from time to time become a party to other legal proceedings arising in the ordinary course of doing business.

Required:

a. What does the WWF call its income statement?

b. A company's *fiscal year* is the 12-consecutive-month period that it calls a year for financial purposes. The WWF's fiscal year runs from May 1 to April 30. Why, then, does it present a balance sheet as of July 30, 1999?

c. The company's total assets more than doubled from April 30, 1998, to April 30, 1999. Why?

d. The company's total assets declined from April 30, 1999, to July 30, 1999. Why?

e. Would the fall in the WWF's total assets inhibit investors' desire to buy shares?

f. Did the WWF earn a profit between April 30, 1999, and July 30, 1999? If so, how could its total assets have fallen?

g. Examine the auditors' report, the balance sheets, income statements (i.e., statements of operations), and cash flow statements. Aside from the name of the company, is there any information in these statements alone that tells you *how* the company earns a profit? That is, can you tell from the financials what business the company is in?

h. How does the WWF earn a profit? That is, what does it do?

i. Can you tell *just from the financial statements* what uses the company might find for amounts raised in the IPO?

j. How much does the company expect to raise in the IPO, and what are its plans for using those funds?

k. Can you tell *just from the financial statements* what major sources of risk face the company?

l. Give three major sources of risk for the WWF.

m. In its discussion of "Risk Factors," the company states that its "success depends, in large part, upon our ability to recruit, train and retain athletic performers who have the physical presence, acting ability and charisma to portray characters in our live events and televised programming." From an economic point of view, this ability is one of the WWF's biggest assets. Is it reported on the balance sheet?

n. The company states that Mr. Vincent McMahon leads its creative team, is a member of its cast of performers, and that the loss of his services could have a material adverse effect on the company. Is Mr. McMahon listed as an asset on the company's balance sheet?

o. The company states that it depends on its intellectual property rights. It has a large portfolio of trademarks, copyrighted material and characters, and trade names. Is the value of these assets shown on the company's balance sheets?

p. What is the average amount of total assets for the company in fiscal 1999?

q. What was the company's net income for fiscal 1999?

r. A *rate of return* is a measure of income divided by a measure of investment. Calculate the WWF's rate of return on total assets by dividing its net income for 1999 by its average total assets during 1999. Does this number seem big, small, or average to you?

s. Another important rate of return is the rate of return on stockholders' equity. Calculate the WWF's rate of return on shareholders' equity by dividing its net income for 1999 by its average shareholders' equity during 1999. Does this number seem big, small, or average to you?

t. Are income taxes an expense?

u. What does the WWF call its expense related to income taxes?

v. Satisfy yourself that the income tax expense reported in the WWF's income statements is very small. Why is it so small?

w. What is the purpose of the "Unaudited Pro Forma Information" given beneath the calculation of net income?

x. Who audited the WWF's financial statements?

y. What does the auditors' report tell you?

z. Would your view of the WWF's financial statements change if none of them were audited? If so, how? If not, why not?

aa. If Nicole Bass wins all her claims against the company and receives the total amounts she asks for, how much would the company have to pay her?

bb. Is this amount reflected in the company's balance sheet?

cc. How many lawsuits that might have a material adverse effect on the company can you find in Note 9, "Commitments and Contingencies"? What amounts related to these lawsuits are reflected on the company's balance sheet?

dd. Are the financial statements an important part of the company's IPO disclosures? That is, suppose you are a potential buyer of the company's stock in its IPO. Is the fact that the company presented financial statements something you would consider important? Why?

ee. As a potential investor, would you look to the financial statements as a stand-alone source of information about the company?

ff. Do the financial statements contain important information, *assessed in the light of the other information* about the WWF that you have or might acquire?

Chapter two

Balance Sheet Concepts: Assets, Liabilities and Equities

Questions . . . .

1. Give three examples of entities that issue financial statements.
2. From whose point of view are financial statements of corporations prepared?
3. What is a "Statement of Financial Position?"
4. What identity (equation) is the basis of a balance sheet?
5. Define assets.
6. Give five examples of assets, and explain why each of the five examples is an asset.
7. What is the difference between current assets and long-term assets?
8. What is valuation?
9. What is "market valuation"?
10. What is "accounting, or balance sheet, valuation"?
11. What is the difference between the "market value" and the "book value" of an asset or liability?
12. Give three different valuation bases used in balance sheets.
13. Define liabilities.
14. Give five examples of liabilities, and explain why each of the five examples is a liability.
15. What is the difference between current liabilities and long-term liabilities?
16. Define equity.
17. Give three examples of equities.
18. Suppose a company has only one asset, marketable securities. Marketable securities are carried on the balance sheet at their market values on the balance sheet date. Further suppose that the company has no liabilities. How would you expect the equity shown on the company's balance sheet to relate to the price at which the entire company could be purchased? Explain your answer.
19. Suppose that a company has only one asset, land. Land is carried on the balance sheet at its historical cost. Further suppose that the company has no liabilities. How would you expect the equity shown on the company's balance sheet to relate to the price at which the entire company could be purchased? Would it matter to you when the company purchased the land? Explain your answer.
20. Do debits or credits increase assets? Why?
21. Why does the bank credit your account when you deposit money?
22. What is a trial balance and why may it be useful?

Exercises . . . .

E2–1   The following is the December 31, 2002 balance sheet for Holdstock Co.:

Holdstock Co.
Statement of Financial Position
December 31, 2002

ASSETS		LIABILITIES	
Current assets		None	
Cash	$ 2,000		
Marketable securities	8,000	**EQUITY**	
Total current assets	$10,000	Common stock	?
Noncurrent assets	0	Retained earnings	0
Total assets	$10,000	Total equity	?

Holdstock's marketable securities are reported on its December 31, 2002 balance sheet at their market values at December 31, 2002. In other words, if Holdstock were to sell its marketable securities on December 31, 2002, it would have received $8,000 cash.

a. Determine the dollar amount reported for common stock on Holdstock's December 31, 2002 balance sheet.

b. On January 1, 2003, one of Holdstock's owners offers to sell you a 50 percent stake in Holdstock (i.e., half of Holdstock's common stock). How much would you be willing to pay? Ignore taxes.

E2–2 The following is the December 31, 2002 balance sheet for Holdland Co.

Holdland Co.
Statement of Financial Position
December 31, 2002

ASSETS		LIABILITIES	
Current assets		None	
Cash	$2,000		
Total current assets	$2,000	**EQUITY**	
Noncurrent assets		Common stock	?
Land	?	Retained earnings	0
Total assets	$?	Total equity	?

Holdland Co. was started on January 1, 1993. On that date, equity holders contributed $10,000 cash, $8,000 of which was immediately used to purchase land. No other transactions have occurred since then. If Holdland were to sell its land on December 31, 2002, Holdland would receive $16,000 cash.

a. Determine the dollar amount reported for land on Holdland's December 31, 2002 balance sheet.

b. Determine the dollar amount reported for common stock on Holdland's December 31, 2002 balance sheet.

c. On January 1, 2003, one of Holdland's owners offers to sell you a 50 percent stake in Holdland (i.e., half of Holdland's common stock). How much would you be willing to pay? Ignore taxes.

E2–3 Capcom, Inc. wishes to obtain additional cash. Its management is considering issuing a contract to interested investors. Investors purchasing the contract would have the right, but not the obligation, to purchase, for $15 per share, one share of common stock any time during the 12 months following the purchase of the contract. Investors electing not to convert their contracts into stock during the 12 months following purchase would receive no shares of stock.

a. What type of balance sheet account (asset, liability, or equity) do these contracts represent?

b. Assume that Capcom issues 10,000 of these contracts to investors, receiving $8 cash for each contract. List the Capcom balance sheet accounts that would change as a result, indicating whether they would increase or decrease and by how much. Create an account name for the contracts.

c. Prepare for Capcom the debits and credits to record the issuance of 10,000 of these contracts to investors. Assume that Capcom receives $8 cash for each contract. Create an account name for the contracts.

E2–4   Levcom, Inc. wishes to obtain additional cash. Its management is considering issuing a contract to interested investors. Each contract would require Levcom to pay $1,000 cash to the contract holder 10 years from the date the contract was issued.

a. What type of balance sheet account (asset, liability, or equity) do these contracts represent?

b. Assume that Levcom issues 200 of these contracts to investors, receiving $400 cash for each contract. List the Levcom balance sheet accounts that would change as a result, indicating whether those accounts would increase or decrease and by how much. Create an account name for the contracts.

c. Prepare for Levcom the debits and credits to record the issuance of 200 of these contracts to investors. Assume that Levcom receives $400 cash for each contract. Create an account name for the contracts.

E2–5   Coldwater Creek operates a direct mail catalog business primarily in the U.S. The company distributes four distinct catalogs entitled "Northcountry," "Spirit of the West," "Milepost," and "Bed and Bath." Items marketed through these catalogs include women's and men's apparel, jewelry, and household items. The company's executive offices are located in Sandpoint, Idaho, and its common stock is traded via the NASDAQ exchange.

Coldwater Creek produces catalogs that are mailed to potential customers. Coldwater estimates that new catalogs generate sales for about three months. After about three months, the items in a catalog start to become out of style, and /or customers lose interest in and forget about the catalog.

a. What type of balance sheet account (asset, liability, or equity) do the costs of producing the catalogs represent for Coldwater Creek?

b. Assume that Coldwater Creek pays $100,000 cash to a printing company at the time the catalogs are produced. List the Coldwater Creek balance sheet accounts that would change as a result, indicating whether those accounts would increase or decrease and by how much.

c. Prepare for Coldwater Creek the debits and credits to record the payment of $100,000 cash to a printing company for the production of new catalogs.

E2–6   The December 27, 1997 and December 28, 1996 balance sheets from Cache, Inc. are shown below. Cache, Inc. owns and operates a chain of women's apparel stores. The company's common stock is traded on the NASDAQ exchange under the symbol CACH.

Assume that the additional transactions listed below (not reflected in the balance sheet below) for Cache, Inc. occur on December 27, 1997.

a. Obtained $200,000 cash by borrowing from a bank. The loan is to be repaid on June 30, 1998.

b. Obtained $300,000 cash by issuing 100,000 shares of common stock to investors.

c. Acquired new store furnishings by paying $150,000 cash.

d. Acquired new inventory by paying $400,000 cash.

e. Received $300,000 cash from customers owing Cache for previous unpaid purchases.

CACHE, INC. AND SUBSIDIARIES
CONSOLIDATED BALANCE SHEETS
DECEMBER 27, 1997 AND DECEMBER 28, 1996

ASSETS

	December 27, 1997	December 28, 1996
CURRENT ASSETS		
Cash equivalents	$ 5,892,000	$ 2,160,000
Accounts receivable	1,573,000	1,378,000
Notes receivable from related parties	250,000	250,000
Inventories	18,219,000	18,010,000
Deferred income taxes and other assets	220,000	770,000
Prepaid expenses	528,000	542,000
Total current assets	26,682,000	23,110,000
PROPERTY AND EQUIPMENT	15,869,000	16,385,000
OTHER ASSETS	211,000	198,000
DEFERRED INCOME TAXES	746,000	917,000
	$43,508,000	$40,610,000

LIABILITIES AND STOCKHOLDERS' EQUITY

	December 27, 1997	December 28, 1996
CURRENT LIABILITIES		
Accounts payable	$10,737,000	$ 10,875,000
Income taxes payable	359,000	—
Accrued compensation	742,000	721,000
Accrued liabilities	3,862,000	3,310,000
Total current liabilities	15,700,000	14,906,000
SUBORDINATED INDEBTEDNESS		
TO RELATED PARTY	2,000,000	2,000,000
OTHER LIABILITIES	1,847,000	2,108,000
STOCKHOLDERS' EQUITY		
Common stock, par value $.01; authorized, 20,000,000 shares; issued and outstanding, 9,091,338 shares at December 27, 1997 and December 28, 1996	91,000	91,000
Additional paid-in capital	19,564,000	19,564,000
Retained earnings	4,306,000	1,941,000
Total stockholders' equity	23,961,000	21,596,000
	$43,508,000	$40,610,000

f. Paid $250,000 cash to suppliers of inventory items for amounts owed to the supplier due to earlier unpaid inventory purchases.

g. Paid $40,000 cash for store rent for the upcoming year.

h. Paid $30,000 cash to employees for salaries the employees earned during December of 1997.

i. Received a request from a major customer currently owing Cache $10,000, which is currently classified as an account receivable, that the customer would like an additional three months to pay. Cache granted the request, informing the customer that the account would be classified as a "note," with interest equal to 4.5 percent of the balance due at the end of the three-month term.

Prepare a new balance sheet for Cache, Inc. that reflects the additional transactions.

E2–7 Newman Properties, Inc. is a real estate management company. Newman signed management contracts on January 1, 1996, to manage three large shopping malls. A number of costs for preparing documents, travel, and other activities associated with securing tenants for the centers must be incurred before the malls are opened for business. These "up-front" costs for the three projects are as follows:

Project 1	Project 2	Project 3
$450,000	$600,000	$500,000

a. Classify the "up-front" costs as either an asset, liability, or equity on Newman's balance sheet. Briefly justify your answer.

b. Assume that the $1,550,000 total up-front costs are incurred and paid on March 1, 1996. Indicate the balance sheet accounts that would change as a result of the payment of the up-front costs and indicate the direction of the change in each account impacted.

c. Prepare the debits and credits to record the payment of the up-front costs on March 1, 1996.

E2–8 On December 31, 2000, Sellit, Inc.:

(1) Obtains $20,000 cash by selling common stock. Assume that the stock is sold at par value.

(2) Obtains $40,000 cash from Loanit Bank. The loan is due on December 31, 2003, and interest of 10 percent annually on the balance is due on January 1 of each year, excluding January 1, 2001.

(3) Buys land, paying $5,000 cash.

(4) Hires manager to begin work on January 1, 2001. The salary is $1,000 per month, payable on the first of each month, beginning February 1, 2001.

(5) Prepays six-months' rent on a portable building, paying $3,000 cash.

a. Prepare a balance sheet for Sellit as of the close of business on December 31, 2000 (i.e., reflecting the transactions above).

b. If Sellit were liquidated (i.e., all liabilities were paid and all remaining assets were sold with the proceeds distributed to common stock shareholders) at the opening of business on January 1, 2001, how much money would the shareholders receive?

c. Could Sellit pay a cash dividend to common stock shareholders on January 1, 2001? How large could that dividend be? Would anyone likely be upset if Sellit paid a large cash dividend on January 1, 2001? Who?

Problems . . . .

P2–1   You are trying to compare OshKosh B'Gosh's financial position at January 2, 1999, to its position at December 31, 1997. Your first observation is that there are a lot of numbers and details on OshKosh B'Gosh's balance sheets that are obscuring the big picture. Simplify OshKosh B'Gosh's balance sheets in Exhibit 2.1 by doing two things: (a) aggregating (i.e., adding together) various accounts into one account, and (b) stating all amounts in millions of dollars and rounding all dollar amounts to the nearest hundred thousand dollars.

a.   Aggregate the following and label the total "Liquid assets":
   • Cash and cash equivalents
   • Short-term investments
   • Accounts receivable, less allowances

b.   Aggregate the following and label the total "Other current assets":
   • Prepaid expenses and other current assets
   • Deferred income taxes (current)

c.   Aggregate the following and label the total "Long-term assets":
   • Property, plant, and equipment, net
   • Deferred income taxes (long-term)
   • Other assets

d.   Aggregate the following and label the total "Current liabilities":
   • Accounts payable
   • Accrued liabilities

e.   Aggregate the following and label the total "Shareholders' equity":
   • Preferred stock
   • Common stock, Class A
   • Common stock, Class B
   • Retained earnings

Does this help you compare the two balance sheets? In particular, do the aggregations help? Does the rounding help? Do you notice anything after simplifying that you had not noticed before? If so, briefly explain.

P2–2   Simplify the asset side of the following DaimlerChrysler balance sheets by aggregating and rounding. (You might first want to note that the convention in Germany is to show accounts in a different order than in the United States.) Aggregate, using these categories: fixed assets, inventories, receivables, cash and securities, and other assets. Round monetary amounts to the nearest billion.

P2–3   Frank's Balance Sheet, Part 1

Indicate the impact on assets, liabilities, and equity of each of the following transactions by placing the dollar amounts of the impact (and a + or – sign to indicate its direction) in the appropriate box.

Example:

Issued 10,000 shares of stock for $2 per share.

Assets	–	Liabilities	=	Equities
+20,000				+20,000

DaimlerChrysler AG
Balance Sheets
(in millions)

	Consolidated At December 31,	
	1998	1997
Assets	[EURO]	[EURO]
Intangible assets	2,561	2,422
Property, plant and equipment, net	29,532	28,558
Investments and long-term financial assets	2,851	2,397
Equipment on operating leases, net	14,662	11,092
Fixed assets	49,606	44,469
Inventories	11,796	10,897
Trade receivables	7,605	7,265
Receivables from financial services	26,468	21,717
Other receivables	10,775	11,376
Securities	12,160	10,180
Cash and cash equivalents	6,589	6,809
Current assets	75,393	68,244
Deferred taxes	5,016	5,688
Prepaid expenses	6,134	6,430
Total assets (thereof short-term 1998:		
[EURO] 57,953; 1997: [EURO] 54,370)	136,149	124,831
Liabilities and stockholders' equity		
Capital stock	2,561	2,391
Additional paid-in capital	7,274	2,958
Retained earnings	20,533	21,892
Accumulated other comprehensive income	(1)	1,143
Treasury stock	—	(424)
Preferred stock	—	—
Stockholders' equity	30,367	27,960
Minority interests	691	782
Accrued liabilities	34,629	35,787
Financial liabilities	40,430	34,375
Trade liabilities	12,848	12,026
Other liabilities	9,249	7,912
Deferred taxes	4,165	2,502
Deferred income	3,770	3,487
Total liabilities (thereof short-term 1998:		
[EURO] 58,181; 1997: [EURO] 50,918)	105,782	96,871
Total liabilities and stockholders' equity	136,149	124,831

a.   Borrowed $5,000 from State Bank

b.   Purchased equipment, paying $3,000 cash

c.   Purchased $8,000 of inventory on credit. Payment is due in 30 days.

d.   Sold inventory for $6,000 to customers, from whom payment is due in 30 days. The inventory cost Frank $4,000.

e. Paid $7,000 cash to suppliers of inventory in partial fulfillment of amounts owed.

f. Received $6,000 cash from customers for amounts owed by them.

g. Declared and paid a cash dividend of $2,000 to shareholders.

P2–4 Frank's Balance Sheet, Part 2

Record each transaction in the previous problem (a through g) in terms of debits and credits.

P2–5 Antler Corp., Part 1

Antler Corp. began operations on January 1, 2000. For each of the following transactions, events, or facts, indicate the impact on assets, liabilities, and equity by placing the dollar amounts of the item(s), and a + or – sign to indicate direction, in the appropriate box. Part (a) has been completed as an example.

a. Issued 15,000 shares of common stock for $3 per share.

Assets	–	Liabilities	=	Equities
+45,000				+45,000

b. January 15. Purchased $9,000 of inventory. Rather than pay cash, Antler bought the inventory on account.

c. January 16. Signed a note at State Bank. The note specifies that Antler receives $6,000 cash from State Bank on January 2, interest is to be paid on the last day of each month, and the loan is to be repaid on June 30.

d. January 16. Paid $500 cash for canvas sheets to keep inventory dry.

e. January 22. Paid $8,000 cash to inventory supplier in partial fulfillment of amounts owed.

f. January 31. Purchased equipment, paying $2,000 cash for a press and $1,000 cash for a computer.

g. January 31. Sold canvas sheets purchased earlier, receiving $500 in the form of a note receivable. The buyer promises to pay in 90 days.

h. January 31. Obtained a letter from State Bank, indicating that the due date on the note payable signed earlier can be extended to June 30, 2001.

i. January 31. Distributed $3,000 cash to owners.

j. January 31. Paid $30 interest to State Bank.

P2–6 Antler Corp., Part 2

a. Record each transaction (a. through j.) in Problem 2–5 (Antler Corp., Part 1) in terms of debits and credits.

b. Refer to the information presented in Problem 2–5 (Antler Corp., Part 1). Prepare a balance sheet for Antler Corp. as of the close of business, January 16, 2000.

c. Refer to the information presented in Problem 2–5 (Antler Corp., Part 1). Prepare a balance sheet for Antler Corp. as of the close of business, January 31, 2000.

d. Are the owners of Antler Corp. better or worse off at January 31, 2000, than at January 15, 2000? Justify your answer.

Cases and Projects ·

C2-1   Microsoft's Balance Sheet

Microsoft's balance sheets as of June 30, 1998, and June 30, 1999, are shown below.

Answer the following questions:

a.   What is the largest asset on Microsoft's balance sheet?

Microsoft Corp. Balance Sheets (In millions)	June 30 1998	June 30 1999
ASSETS		
Current assets:		
Cash and short-term investments	$13,927	$17,236
Accounts receivable	1,460	2,245
Other	502	752
Total current assets	15,889	20,233
Property and equipment	1,505	1,611
Equity and other investments	4,703	14,372
Other assets	260	940
Total assets	$22,357	$37,156
LIABILITIES AND STOCKHOLDERS' EQUITY		
Current liabilities:		
Accounts payable	$ 759	$ 874
Accrued compensation	359	396
Income taxes payable	915	1,607
Unearned revenue	2,888	4,239
Other	809	1,602
Total current liabilities	$ 5,730	$ 8,718
COMMITMENTS AND CONTINGENCIES		
Stockholders' equity:		
Convertible preferred stock—shares authorized, 100; shares issued and outstanding, 13	980	980
Common stock and paid-in capital—shares authorized, 12,000; shares issued and outstanding, 4,940 and 5,109	8,025	13,844
Retained earnings, including other comprehensive income of $666 and $1,787	7,622	13,614
Total stockholders' equity	$16,627	$28,438
Total liabilities and stockholders' equity	$22,357	$37,156

b. What is Microsoft's largest asset from an economic point of view, if you were asked to name the most important thing that will contribute to the future cash inflows of Microsoft?

c. Are your answers to (a) and (b) the same? (They should not be!) Why do they differ? (Here you should be thinking about the difference between Microsoft's economics and its accounting.)

d. What is the total amount of Microsoft's long-term liabilities?

e. What is the largest liability shown on Microsoft's balance sheet? What does it represent?

f. The current ratio is equal to current assets divided by current liabilities. Calculate Microsoft's current ratio as of June 30, 1998, and June 30, 1999.

g. If you were a supplier to Microsoft and Bill Gates asked you to allow Microsoft to purchase from you on credit, would you do it? Justify your answer in terms of your calculation of the current ratio.

h. Suppose that you are thinking about buying Microsoft common stock. Would Microsoft's current ratio be a consideration in your decision? How about Microsoft's ability to earn profits by continuing to sell its software? Is Microsoft's ability to earn profits by continuing to sell its software reflected on its balance sheets? If so, where is this ability shown?

C2–2 TJX, Inc., and OshKosh B'Gosh, Inc.

Refer to the TJX Companies, Inc., balance sheets, presented on page 63, and the OshKosh B'Gosh, Inc., financial statements presented in Exhibit 2.1. TJX Companies operates the TJ Maxx chain of clothing stores and other retail operations. OshKosh B'Gosh distributes clothing and operates retail outlets.

a. The current ratio is equal to current assets divided by current liabilities. Compute TJX's current ratio as of January 30, 1999.

b. Compute OshKosh B'Gosh's current ratio and compare it to TJX's. Based on this, which company is "safer," in the short run, from a creditor's perspective?

c. Consider the individual assets in OshKosh B'Gosh's current asset section. Are there any items listed that you think might be difficult to turn into cash quickly? If so, list them and provide a brief explanation.

d. Recompute both OshKosh B'Gosh's and TJX's current ratios, including in the numerator only those current assets that you think could be turned into cash quickly and easily.

e. Provide a brief discussion of how TJX has obtained financing, commenting specifically on the mix of debt and equity financing.

f. Which company, TJX or OshKosh B'Gosh, would be considered "riskier" from a long-term creditor's perspective?

g. TJX lists the asset "cash and cash equivalents." What is the difference between "cash" and "cash equivalents"?

h. Could TJX immediately pay off its long-term debt? How do we know? Describe what impact such a transaction would have on TJX's balance sheet. What impact would this action have on TJX's current ratio?

i. Assume that TJX issues common stock for $300,000 cash, then takes the cash and buys new stores costing $275,000. Show which balance sheet accounts would change and provide their new balances.

j. Instead of the transaction in i, assume that TJX obtains $300,000 cash from a group of banks in the form of a note payable due in five years, then takes the cash and buys new stores costing $275,000. The note matures in five equal portions over the five years. Provide the balance sheet accounts that would change and their new balances.

k. Refer to questions (i) and (j). Briefly discuss the impact the two methods of financing will have on measure(s) of TJX's credit risk.

The TJX Companies, Inc.—Consolidated Balance Sheets
In Thousands

	January 30, 1999	January 31, 1998
ASSETS		
Current assets:		
Cash and cash equivalents	$ 461,244	$ 404,369
Accounts receivable	67,345	60,735
Merchandise inventories	1,186,068	1,190,170
Prepaid expenses	28,448	27,357
Total current assets	$1,743,105	$1,682,631
Property at cost:		
Land and buildings	115,485	108,729
Leasehold costs and improvements	547,099	480,964
Furniture, fixtures and equipment	711,320	611,470
	$1,373,904	$1,201,163
Less: accumulated depreciation and amortization	617,302	515,027
	$ 756,602	$ 686,136
Other assets	27,436	36,645
Deferred income taxes	22,386	—
Goodwill and tradename, net of amortization	198,317	204,220
Total Assets	$2,747,846	$2,609,632
LIABILITIES		
Current liabilities:		
Current installments of long-term debt	$ 694	$ 23,360
Accounts payable	617,159	582,791
Accrued expenses and other current liabilities	688,993	611,506
Total current liabilities	$1,306,846	$1,217,657
Long-term debt, exclusive of current installments	220,344	221,024
Deferred income taxes	—	6,859
SHAREHOLDERS' EQUITY		
Preferred stock at face value, authorized 5,000,000 shares, par value $1, issued and outstanding cumulative convertible stock of 727,300 shares of 7% Series E at January 31, 1998	—	72,730
Common stock, authorized 600,000,000 shares, par value $1, issued and outstanding 322,140,770 and 159,901,247shares	322,141	159,901
Additional paid-in capital	—	198,736
Accumulated other comprehensive income (loss)	(1,529)	3,317
Retained earnings	900,044	729,408
Total shareholders' equity	$1,220,656	$1,164,092
Total Liabilities and Shareholders' Equity	$2,747,846	$2,609,632

Chapter three

Income Statement Concepts: Income, Revenues, and Expenses

Questions ....

1. Define income and describe its three important characteristics.
2. What are net assets?
3. Define revenues and give three examples of revenues.
4. Define expenses and give four examples of expenses.
5. Are the expenses in a period the cash outflows in that period? Explain.
6. Are expenses always outflows of cash? Explain.
7. Are the revenues in a period the cash inflows in that period? Explain.
8. Are revenues always inflows of cash? Explain.
9. Are dividends to shareholders an expense? Explain.
10. Is interest on outstanding debt an expense for the debtor? Explain.
11. Give three criteria that must be met for revenue to be recognized.
12. Give three examples of revenue recognition points.
13. What is accrual accounting?
14. What is matching?
15. Are increases in expenses debits or are they credits? Explain.
16. Are increases in revenues debits or are they credits? Explain.
17. What is a temporary account and what purpose do temporary accounts serve?
18. What are adjustments?
19. How does the process of adjusting the accounts relate to the accrual basis of accounting?
20. What is closing?
21. Do accounts that are not closed appear on the balance sheet? Are their final totals reflected somewhere on the balance sheet? Explain.
22. Do accounts that are closed appear on the balance sheet? Are their pre-closing totals reflected somewhere on the balance sheet? Explain.
23. Cash-basis accounting keeps account only of cash flows. Cash is the only asset that is recognized, and there is no adjustment process. When would cash-basis accounting recognize revenues? When would it recognize expenses?
24. Briefly assess the strengths and weaknesses of cash-basis accounting relative to accrual accounting.
25. "An advantage of cash-basis accounting is that it is totally objective." Comment.
26. "An advantage of cash-basis accounting is that management cannot manipulate cash income." Comment.

Exercises . . . .

E3–1   SLH, Inc. is a retailer, buying goods at one price and selling them at a higher price.

  a.   Why would SLH be able to sell goods at a higher price than it pays for them?

  b.   Assume that SLH had 100 inventory items on hand at December 31, 2001. Also, assume that the balance in SLH's inventory account was $100,000. Assume, on January 1, 2002, that SLH buys 500 inventory items that cost $500,000, paying cash. Indicate the impact of this transaction on the accounting equation. Indicate the specific accounts that would be impacted, the direction of the impact, and the amount.

  c.   Prepare a journal entry to record the transaction in (a).

  d.   What would the balance in SLH's inventory account be at the end of the day on January 1, 2002?

  e.   Assume that SLH sells 400 inventory items at various times from January 2, 2002, through January 31, 2002, for $1,500 cash each. What is the balance in SLH's inventory account at the end of the day, January 31, 2002?

  f.   How much did the inventory items that SLH sold during January 2002 cost? How much did the inventory items that SLH bought during January 2002 cost? Which one of these two should appear on SLH's January 2002 income statement as an expense?

E3–2   RetailBiz, Inc., is incorporated on December 1, 2000. During December, RetailBiz:

  a.   Issues common stock to various investors, raising $60,000 cash.

  b.   Buys a parcel of land, paying $5,000 cash.

Here is RetailBiz, Inc.'s balance sheet as of December 31, 2000.

RetailBiz, Inc.
Statement of Financial Position as of December 31, 2000

Assets		*Liabilities*	
Cash	$55,000	Total liabilities	0
Total current assets	$55,000	Stockholders' equity:	
		Common Stock	60,000
Land	5,000	Total liabilities & stockholders'	
Total assets	$60,000	equity	$60,000

During 2001:

  c.   RetailBiz receives delivery of 490,000 cans of product, paying $49,000 cash.

  d.   RetailBiz sells all 490,000 cans during 2001. The selling price is 15 cents per can, generating $73,500 (490,000 × $0.15) cash.

Required
Construct a December 31, 2001 balance sheet and an income statement for the year ended December 31, 2001, for RetailBiz, Inc.

E3–3   Information regarding LDH, Inc. is as follows:

LDH, Inc.
Statement of Financial Position as of December 31, 2000

Assets		Liabilities	
Cash	$52,000	Total current liabilities	None
Prepaid rent	$3,000	Note payable	40,000
Total current assets	$55,000	Equity:	
Land	5,000	Common stock	20,000
Total assets	$60,000	Total liabilities & equity	$60,000

a. During 2001, LDH purchases with cash, for 10 cents per can, and sells, for 15 cents per can, 490,000 cans of Drinkit, receiving cash for all sales.

b. The prepaid rent on December 31, 2000, gives LDH the contractual right to use a building for the first six months of 2001. On July 1, 2001, LDH prepays an additional eight months rent at $500 per month.

c. The loan is due on December 31, 2003, and interest of 10 percent annually on the balance is due on January 1 of each year, excluding January 1, 2001.

d. LDH's manager's salary is $1,000 per month, payable on the first of each month. Since the manager's first day was January 1, 2001, the manager's first paycheck is written on February 1, 2001, the second on March 1, the third on April 1, etc.

Construct a December 31, 2001 balance sheet and an income statement for the year ended December 31, 2001, for LDH, Inc.

E3–4 Refer to the information regarding LDH, Inc. in E3-3. How would LDH's 2001 income statement and December 31, 2001 balance sheet change if LDH declared and paid a $2,000 cash dividend on December 31, 2001?

E3–5 In 2001, Aamodt Construction Company began work on a construction project. Aamodt will be paid $2,200,000 when construction is completed. Sometimes Aamodt's customers are unable to pay the full contracted price. However, the vast majority of customers do pay, and the amount that Aamodt is unable to collect is very stable over time. On average, Aamodt is able to collect 95% of its contract amounts. Aamodt's progress on the project is as follows:

	2001	2002	2003
Percent completed as of December 31	10	40	90

What amounts of revenue should Aamodt recognize in 2001 and 2002?

E3–6 During 2003, Lizant Corp. paid an advertising agency $1,500,000 cash for various costs (television and radio air time, print ads, billboard space, ad and script writers, artwork, etc.) related to an advertising campaign during 2003. The purpose of the campaign was to raise consumer awareness of the Lizant brand name. The ads ran during 2003, and the campaign ended at the end of 2003.

a. Why do firms spend money on advertising?

b. Assume that we can be certain that Lizant's advertising campaign will generate additional sales for 2003 and 2004 in approximately equal amounts each year. Conceptually, should Lizant show anything on its 2003 year-end balance sheet? If so, how much? Assume that the $1,500,000 cash expenditure occurred at the beginning of 2003.

c. Assume that we can be certain that Lizant's advertising campaign will generate additional sales for 2003 only. Conceptually, should Lizant show anything on its 2003 year-end balance sheet? If so, how much? Assume that the $1,500,000 cash expenditure occurred at the beginning of 2003.

E3–7 Refer to the Coldwater Creek, Inc. financial statements provided for C3-3 on pages 37–39.

a. What was the balance in Coldwater's inventory account at the start of business on March 2, 1997?

b. What was the balance in Coldwater's inventory account at the close of business on February 28, 1998?

c. What kind of transaction makes Coldwater's inventory account balance increase? What kind of transaction makes Coldwater's inventory account balance decrease?

d. Coldwater sold many inventory items (i.e., goods) during the year ended February 28, 1998. How much (total) did all the inventory items Coldwater sold cost? Why does this number appear on Coldwater's income statement?

e. Given how much inventory Coldwater began the year with (part a) and how much they sold during the year (part d), why isn't the balance at the end of the year (February 28, 1998) negative? How much is the dollar amount of Coldwater's purchases of inventory during the year ended February 28, 1998?

Problems ....

P3–1 Newman Properties, Inc., is a real estate management company. Newman signed management contracts on January 1, 2001, to manage three large shopping malls. A number of costs for document preparation, travel, and other activities associated with securing tenants for the centers must be incurred before the malls are opened for business. These up-front costs for the three projects are as follows:

	Project 1	Project 2	Project 3
Up-front costs	$450,000	$600,000	$500,000

a. Tenants for Project 1 have not yet been secured. However, Newman expects to be able to rent all stores for 2001, 2002, 2003, and 2004 and estimates rental revenue will be $840,000 per year. Newman's management contract for Project 1 ends at the end of 2004. What amount should be shown on Newman's December 31, 2001 balance sheet for "Up-front costs: Project 1"?

b. Tenants for Project 2 have been secured and all stores have been rented for 2001, 2002, 2003, and 2004. The rental revenue for each year for Project 2 is as follows:

	2001	2002	2003	2004
Rental revenue	$200,000	$400,000	$400,000	$500,000

Newman's management contract on Project 2 ends at the end of 2004. What amount should be shown on Newman's December 31, 2001 balance sheet for "Up-front costs: Project 2"?

c. Newman was unable to secure tenants for Project 3 and, during 2001, decided to abandon the project. What amount should be shown on Newman's December 31, 2001 balance sheet for "Up-front costs: Project 3"?

P3–2 Miloslav began a magazine delivery service, which he named Miloslav's Magazines, on January 1, 2001. The following transactions occurred during 2001:

a.   Sold stock for $3,000 cash on January 1.

b.   Borrowed $20,000 cash on April 1. The interest rate on the loan is 12% annually, and the interest is due each December 31, until the note is repaid.

c.   Bought a bicycle for $1,000 cash on January 1. The bicycle has an estimated life of five years, and no salvage value.

d.   Bought 10,000 magazines for $2.00 cash each on April 5.

e.   Sold magazines at various times for a total of $22,500. All sales were on account.

f.   Collected $20,500 from customers.

g.   Paid himself a salary of $3,000 cash.

h.   Paid the stockholders a dividend of $50 on the $3,000 in stock.

i.   Paid the interest on the loan in b.

j.   On December 31, Miloslav determined by a physical count that there were 1,000 magazines left in the storage bin at the warehouse.

Required

Prepare journal entries for the above transactions. Post the journal entries to appropriate T-accounts. Prepare any necessary adjusting and closing entries needed at December 31, 2001. Prepare a December 31, 2001 balance sheet and an income statement for the year ended December 31, 2001.

P3–3 Ofer's Office Designs began operations on January 1, 2001. Listed below is a summary of events experienced by Ofer's Office Designs during 2001.

a.   The company issued 2,000 shares of common stock for cash at their par value of $50 per share.

b.   On April 1, 2001, the company purchased eight sets of office furniture that it will sell to customers. Each set cost $20,000. Ofer's paid $10,000 in cash and signed a two-year note with an 8% interest rate for the remainder of the purchase price. Interest on the note is due on January 1 of each year the note remains unpaid.

c.   The company performed consulting services for a total fee of $200,000, receiving $50,000 in cash up front.

d.   A potential customer communicated its intent to have Ofer's perform $80,000 of consulting services.

e.   The company paid $100,000 cash for wages.

f.   The company paid $20,000 cash for rent on July 1, 2001. The company is charged rent at the rate of $1,083.33 dollars per month. Prior to July 1, 2001, rent for January through June had not been paid. The remainder of the $20,000 payment was applied to future months' rent as it became due.

g.   On December 31, 2001, the company paid the holder of the note $15,000.

h.   The company declared and paid cash dividends of $19,000.

i.   The company received $30,000 in cash as payments for outstanding receivables.

j.   The company sold three sets of office furniture for $28,000 cash each.

Required

Prepare the journal entry(ies), if necessary, for each event. Also, prepare any closing entries as needed and prepare a December 31, 2001 balance sheet and an income statement for 2001. Ignore taxes.

P3–4   Ralphy started a business on April 1, 2001, and had the following transactions on April 1:

   a.   Issued 20,000 shares of $5 par value common stock for $100,000 cash.

   b.   Bought equipment to be used for making products, for $60,000. The equipment has a six-year life and is to be depreciated on a straight-line basis, with no salvage value.

   c.   Paid $4,000 for one year's rent on a building.

   d.   Bought $30,000 of inventory on credit.

   e.   Bought $25,000 of Yahoo common stock as a short-term investment.

   f.   Issued a bond with a face value of $20,000 and an interest rate of 10%. Interest is to be paid annually.

Between April 1 and December 31, the following transactions occurred:

   g.   Sold inventory that cost $25,000 for $40,000. All sales were on credit.

   h.   Paid $15,000 to suppliers of inventory for the credit purchase in (d) above.

   i.   Collected $30,000 from customers on their accounts.

   j.   A customer owing $200 declared bankruptcy, and notice was received that the customer would pay only $50 of this debt. The $50 payment was enclosed.

   k.   Salaries and wages of $6,000 were paid.

On December 31:

   l.   Salaries and wages of $1,000 had been earned but not paid.

   m.   The market value of Ralphy's inventory was $12,500.

Required

   1.   Enter the above transactions in T-accounts. Use appropriate account titles.

   2.   Enter all adjusting and closing entries required at December 31.

   3.   Prepare a balance sheet for December 31.

   4.   Prepare an income statement for the period April 1 to December 31.

P3–5   Rick and Stan started a business on October 1, 2002, and had the following transactions on October 1:

   a.   Issued 10,000 shares of $5 par value common stock for $110,000 cash.

   b.   Bought equipment to be used for making products for $60,000 cash. The equipment has a five-year life and is to be depreciated on a straight-line basis, with no salvage value.

   c.   Paid $3,000 for one year's rent on a building.

   d.   Bought $35,000 of inventory on credit.

   e.   Took out a $20,000 bank loan at an interest rate of 12%. Interest is to be paid annually.

Between October 1 and December 31, 2002, the following transactions occurred:

   f.   Sold inventory costing $25,000 for $45,000. All sales were on credit.

   g.   Paid $31,000 to suppliers of inventory for the credit purchase in (d).

h. Collected $36,000 from customers.

i. Salaries and wages of $16,000 were paid.

On December 31:

j. Salaries and wages of $2,000 had been earned but not paid.

k. The market value of Rick and Stan's inventory was $27,500.

Required

1. Enter the above transactions in T-accounts. Use appropriate account titles.

2. Enter all adjusting and closing entries required at December 31.

3. Prepare a balance sheet for December 31, 2002.

4. Prepare an income statement for the period October 1 to December 31, 2002.

Cases and Projects . . . .

C3–1 The 1995 Rubbermaid financial statements follow. Dollar amounts are in millions.

Rubbermaid
Consolidated Statement of Earnings (dollars in millions)

Year ended December 31	1995	1994
Net sales	$2,344	$2,169
Cost of sales	1,673	1,466
Selling, general, and administrative expenses	403	348
Restructuring costs	158	0
Other charges (credits), net:		
Interest expense	14	7
Interest income	(3)	(5)
Miscellaneous, net	4	(13)
Earnings before income taxes	95	366
Income taxes	35	139
Net earnings	$ 60	$ 227

Rubbermaid
Consolidated Balance Sheet (dollars in millions)

At December 31	1995	1994
Current assets		
Cash	$ 51	$ 92
Marketable securities	0	59
Receivables	499	471
Inventories	252	295
Other current assets	49	9
Total current assets	$ 851	$ 926
Property, plant, and equipment	1,262	1,163
Accumulated depreciation	(636)	(556)
Intangible assets, net	214	175
Total assets	$1,691	$1,708

Current liabilities		
Notes payable	$ 123	$ 22
Accounts payable	102	103
Accrued liabilities	190	171
Total current liabilities	$ 415	$ 296
Long-term debt	6	12
Other long-term liabilities	135	116
Shareholders' equity		
Common stock	234	233
Retained earnings	1,099	1,120
Foreign currency translation adj.	(20)	(18)
Treasury shares (at cost)	(178)	(51)
Total shareholders' equity	$1,135	$1,284

The following hypothetical transactions and events occurred during 1996. (These selected transactions are all the items that are relevant to answering the required questions.)

a. Purchased $1,800 of inventory on account.

b. Payments to suppliers of inventory totaled $1,850.

c. Inventory items costing $1,500 were sold in 1996 for $2,500. All sales were credit sales.

d. On December 31, 1996, Rubbermaid purchased property, plant, and equipment by paying $40 cash. No property, plant, and equipment was sold or discarded during the year.

e. 10 million shares of common stock were issued for $60 per share.

f. Accrued liabilities consist solely of salaries payable. $400 of salaries were paid with cash.

g. Employees earned $300 in salaries.

h. Property, plant, and equipment has a useful life of 10 years, with no salvage value. Rubbermaid uses straight-line depreciation for all depreciable assets.

i. Intangible assets (except for the prepaid insurance in j.) have a useful life of 15 years and no salvage value and originally cost $600. Assume straight-line amortization. No intangible assets were sold or acquired in 1996.

j. On September 30, 1996, Rubbermaid purchased a two-year insurance policy by paying $16 cash. Rubbermaid recorded the current portion of prepaid insurance in "Other current assets" and the long-term portion in "Intangible assets."

Required

Determine the amount that would be reported in the December 31, 1996 balance sheet or the 1996 income statement for the following items. If an item would not appear on either the income statement or the balance sheet, write '0' next to the item.

1. Accounts payable
2. Inventory
3. Property, plant, and equipment
4. Accumulated depreciation
5. Intangible assets, net
6. Other current assets
7. Insurance expense
8. Common stock

C3-1 Use the following hypothetical information and the Apple Computer, Inc., financial statements that follow to prepare a pro forma September 24, 1994 balance sheet and a pro forma fiscal 1994 income statement. (A pro forma statement is a statement compiled to show the effects of assumptions. Note that Apple's fiscal 1994 begins on September 25, 1993, and ends on September 24, 1994.) All dollar amounts given below, except per-share amounts, are in thousands.

Apple Computer Inc.
Consolidated Balance Sheet
as of September 24, 1993
(Dollars in thousands)

ASSETS

Current assets:	
Cash and cash equivalents	$676,413
Short-term investments	215,890
Accounts receivable, net of allowance	
for doubtful accounts of $83,776	1,381,946
Inventories	1,506,638
Deferred tax assets	268,085
Other current assets	289,383
Total current assets	$4,338,355
Property, plant, and equipment:	
Land and buildings	404,688
Machinery and equipment	578,272
Office furniture and equipment	167,905
Leasehold improvements	261,792
	$1,412,657
Accumulated depreciation and amortization	(753,111)
Net property, plant, and equipment	$659,546
Other assets	173,511
Total assets	$5,171,412

LIABILITIES AND SHAREHOLDERS' EQUITY:

Current liabilities:	
Short-term borrowings	$823,182
Accounts payable	742,622
Accrued compensation and employee benefits	144,779
Accrued marketing and distribution	174,547
Accrued restructuring costs	307,932
Other current liabilities	315,023
Total current liabilities	$2,508,085
Long-term debt	7,117
Deferred tax liabilities	629,832
Total liabilities	$3,145,036
Shareholders' equity:	
Common stock, no par value;	
320,000,000 shares authorized;	
116,147,035 shares issued and	
outstanding	203,613
Retained earnings	1,842,600
Accumulated translation adjustment	(19,835)
Total shareholders' equity	$2,026,378
Total liabilities and shareholders' equity	$5,171,412

a. Net sales increased from 1993 to 1994 by the same percentage that net sales increased from 1992 to 1993. All sales are credit sales.

b. Collections on sales totaled $6,500,000 during 1994.

c. Purchases of inventory during fiscal 1994 totaled $5,800,000, all on account.

d. A count of inventories on September 24, 1994, revealed inventory costing $1,520,000 is in various warehouses.

e. Payments to suppliers of inventory totaled $4,800,000.

f. Salaries earned by sales staff and corporate officers totaled $1,500,000.

g. Payments for salaries for sales staff and corporate officers totaled $1,400,000.

h. Research and development costs totaled $600,000, all paid in cash.

i. On March 25, 1994, Apple borrowed $500,000 from a bank. The loan is due March 24, 2000.

j. On September 24, 1994, Apple purchased machinery and equipment by paying $400,000 cash.

k. Depreciation expense totaled $170,000 for fiscal 1994.

l. Restructuring costs were $0 in 1994.

m. Interest and other income in 1994 was $75,000, all received in cash.

n. Deferred income taxes are the same at September 24, 1994, as at September 24, 1993.

o. Ignore the allowance for doubtful accounts; i.e., assume that the balance in accounts receivable at September 24, 1993, is $1,381,946.

p. All accrued restructuring costs at September 24, 1993, were paid during fiscal 1994.

q. Marketing and distribution expenses totaled $150,000 during 1994. $140,000 of marketing and distribution costs were paid in cash in 1994.

r. Assume no change in the accumulated translation adjustment during fiscal 1994.

s. Ten million shares of common stock were issued for $60 cash per share during 1994. (Remember, dollar amounts in the financial statements are in thousands. Numbers of shares and per share amounts are not in thousands.)

t. Apple incurred $49,800 in interest expense in fiscal 1994. Interest payments in fiscal 1994 totaled $49,000. Interest payable is included in "Other current liabilities."

u. The provision for income taxes in 1994 was $300,000, none of which was paid in cash. All of the deferred tax assets were used, and the remainder increased deferred tax liabilities.

v. Other current assets at September 24, 1993, consisted of office supplies and small, short-lived repair tools. $100,000 of these items were purchased in 1994 with cash. The balance in other current assets at September 24, 1994, was $250,000.

w. The other current liabilities at September 24, 1993, were paid during fiscal 1994.

x. On September 15, 1994, Apple declared cash dividends of $50,000. The dividends were paid on September 22, 1994.

y. During fiscal 1994, creditors agreed to extend the maturity date of Apple's short-term borrowings to October 10, 1994.

Apple Computer Inc.
Consolidated Statements of Income
(In thousands, except per-share amounts)

| | Fiscal years ended September 24 | |
	1993	1992
Net sales	$7,976,954	$7,086,542
Costs and expenses:		
Cost of sales	5,248,834	3,991,337
Research and development	664,564	602,135
Selling, general and administrative	1,632,362	1,687,262
Restructuring costs	320,856	0
	7,866,616	6,280,734
Net operating income	110,338	805,808
Interest and other income (expense), net	29,321	49,634
Income before income taxes	139,659	855,442
Provision for income taxes	53,070	325,069
Net income	$ 86,589	$ 530,373

C3–3 Coldwater Creek[1]

Coldwater Creek operates a direct mail catalog business, primarily in the U.S. The company distributes four distinct catalogs entitled "Northcountry," "Spirit of the West," "Milepost," and "Bed and Bath." Items marketed through these catalogs include women's and men's apparel, jewelry, and household items. The company's executive offices are located in Sandpoint, Idaho, and its web site is at www.coldwatercreek.com.

The major objective of this project is to gain insight into the major entries that resulted in Coldwater Creek's 1997 income statement and February 28, 1998 balance sheet. The entries will then tell us about major transactions and events that affected Coldwater Creek in fiscal 1997.

Required

Use the beginning and ending 1998 balance sheets, the 1998 income statement, and selected information from the footnotes to the financial statements to complete the attached set of T-accounts. Working through the T-accounts should do two things for you:

1. Help you make sure your view of the entries and events is not self-contradictory.

2. Enable you to get far more information out of the financial statements than you could by simply inspecting them.

Hints and Useful Assumptions

As we will see throughout this book, there is often more than one way to record a set of events and transactions. When trying to analyze financial statements, this means that a given set of financial statements can be consistent with different possible sets of entries. There is not one absolutely correct answer to this problem.

1. Accounts Payable relate only to purchases of Inventories.

2. Prepaid Expenses are related to Selling, General, and Administrative Expenses.

3. All depreciation is reflected in Selling, General, and Administrative Expenses.

[1] This case was developed for educational purposes only. Assumptions are adopted to simplify the required analysis and are not necessarily realistic or representative of the company's actual actions, nor are they to be construed as conveying any information or opinion. The company's full set of financial statements is available at www.sec.gov.

4. We combine Prepaid Catalog Costs and Deferred Catalog Costs into one account, which we call Catalog Costs. Amortization of catalog costs is reflected in Selling, General, and Administrative Expenses and is credited to Catalog Costs.

5. Income Taxes Payable and Deferred Income Taxes accounts both represent income taxes that have not yet been paid, but will be paid in a future period. For our purposes, these accounts can be treated like the liability associated with the Provision for Income Taxes. (Provision for Income Taxes is Coldwater Creek's name for the expense account related to income taxes.) Also, it is sufficient for our purposes to combine both Deferred Income Taxes accounts with Income Taxes Payable so that we analyze only the total of these three accounts and not the breakdown among them.

6. Accrued liabilities are associated with Selling, General, and Administrative Expenses. Catalog costs are first incurred as Accrued Liabilities, analogous to the way purchases of merchandise are first incurred as Accounts Payable.

7. There were no sales of property, plant, and equipment during the year ended February 28, 1998.

Coldwater Creek Inc. and Subsidiary—Consolidated Balance Sheets (In thousands, except share data)		
Assets	Feb. 28, 1998	Mar. 1, 1997
Current assets:		
Cash and cash equivalents	$ 331	$ 9,095
Receivables	4,019	2,342
Inventories	53,051	25,279
Prepaid expenses	2,729	456
Prepaid catalog costs	2,794	1,375
Total current assets	$62,924	$38,547
Deferred catalog costs	7,020	3,347
Property and equipment, net	26,661	20,080
Executive loans	1,620	—
Total assets	$98,225	$61,974
Liabilities and stockholders' equity		
Current liabilities:		
Revolving line of credit	$10,264	$ —
Accounts payable	27,275	18,061
Accrued liabilities	10,517	5,969
Income taxes payable	—	451
Deferred income taxes	919	76
Total current liabilities:	$48,975	$24,557
Deferred income taxes	375	230
Total Liabilities:	$49,350	$24,787
Stockholders' equity:		
Common stock, $.01 par value, 15,000,000 shares authorized, 10,120,118 issued and outstanding	$ 101	$ 101
Additional paid-in capital	38,748	38,748
Retained earnings (accumulated deficit)	10,026	(1,662)
Total stockholders' equity	48,875	37,187
Total liabilities and stockholders' equity	$98,225	$61,974

The accompanying notes are an integral part of these financial statements

Coldwater Creek Inc. and Subsidiary—Consolidated Statements of Operations
(In thousands, except per share data)

	Fiscal Year Ended		
	Feburary 28, 1998	March 1, 1997	March 2, 1996
Net sales	$246,697	$143,059	$75,905
Cost of sales	120,126	66,430	32,786
Gross profit	$126,571	$ 76,629	$43,119
Selling, general, and administrative expenses	107,083	64,463	37,356
Income from operations	$ 19,488	$ 12,166	$ 5,763
Interest, net, and other	57	(153)	(149)
Income before provision for income taxes	$ 19,545	$ 12,013	$ 5,614
Provision for income taxes	7,857	1,197	—
Net income	$ 11,688	$ 10,816	$ 5,614
Net income per share—basic	$1.15	$1.46	$0.77
Net income per share—diluted	$1.10	$1.41	$0.77

The accompanying notes are an integral part of these financial statements.

Coldwater Creek Inc. and Subsidiary
Notes to the Consolidated Financial Statements

1.   SIGNIFICANT ACCOUNTING POLICIES
Organizational Structure and Nature of Operations

Coldwater Creek Inc. (the "Company"), a Delaware corporation headquartered in Sandpoint, Idaho, is a specialty direct-mail retailer of apparel, gifts, jewelry, and home furnishings, marketing its merchandise through regular catalog mailings. The principal markets for the Company's merchandise are individuals within the United States. Net sales realized from other geographic markets, principally Canada and Japan, have been less than five percent of net sales in each reported period.

The Company also operates retail stores in Sandpoint, Idaho, and Jackson Hole, Wyoming, where it sells catalog items and unique store merchandise. Additionally, the Company operates four outlet stores through its wholly-owned subsidiary, Coldwater Creek Outlet Stores, Inc., which is consolidated in these financial statements. All material intercompany balances and transactions have been eliminated.

Revenue Recognition
The Company recognizes sales and the related cost of sales at the time merchandise is shipped to customers. . . .

Catalog Costs
Catalog costs include all direct costs associated with the production and mailing of the Company's direct-mail catalogs and are classified as prepaid catalog costs until they are mailed.

When the Company's catalogs are mailed, these costs are reclassified as deferred catalog costs and amortized over the periods in which the related revenues are expected to be realized. Substantially all revenues are generated within the first three months after a catalog is mailed. Amortization of deferred catalog costs was $66.6 million in fiscal 1997, $38.7 million in fiscal 1996, and $24.8 million in fiscal 1995.

3. PROPERTY AND EQUIPMENT
    Property and equipment, net, consists of:

	February 28, 1998	March 1, 1997
		(in thousands)
Land	$ 1,899	$ 150
Building and land improvements	14,383	12,028
Furniture and fixtures	2,434	1,751
Machinery and equipment	16,018	10,486
	34,734	24,415
Less accumulated depreciation	8,073	4,335
	$26,661	$20,080

5. EXECUTIVE LOAN PROGRAM

Effective June 30, 1997, the Company established an Executive Loan Program under which the Company may make, at its sole discretion and with prior approvals from the Chief Executive Officer and the Board of Directors' Compensation Committee, secured long-term loans to key executives. Each loan is secured by the executive's personal net assets, inclusive of all vested stock options in the Company, bears interest at three percent per annum, and becomes due and payable on the earlier of (i) the date 10 days before the date on which the vested stock options serving as partial security expire, or (ii) 90 days from the date on which the executive's employment with the Company terminates for any reason. If material, compensation expense is recognized by the Company for the difference between the stated interest rate and the prevailing prime rate.

Cash			**Accounts Receivable**			**Prepaid Expenses**		
	Dr.	Cr.		Dr.	Cr.		Dr.	Cr.
BB	9.1		BB	2.3		BB	0.5	
						EB	2.7	
			EB	4.0				

			Inventory			**Catalog Costs**		
				Dr.	Cr.		Dr.	Cr.
			BB	25.3		BB	4.7	
			EB	53.1		EB	9.8	
EB	0.3							

Executive Loans			**PP&E**			**Acc. Depreciation**		
	Dr.	Cr.		Dr.	Cr.		Dr.	Cr.
BB	0.0		BB	24.4				4.3	BB
EB	1.6		EB	34.7				8.1	EB

Accrued Liabilities

Dr.	Cr.
	6.0
	10.5

Revolving Line of Credit

Dr.	Cr.	
	0.0	BB
	10.3	EB

Accounts Payable

Dr.	Cr.	
	18.1	BB
	27.3	EB

Retained Earnings

	Dr.	Cr.	
BB	1.7		
		10.0	EB

Deferred & Payable Taxes

Dr.	Cr.	
	0.8	BB
	1.3	EB

Common Stock & APIC

Dr.	Cr.	
	38.8	BB
	38.8	EB

Cost of Goods Sold

Dr.	Cr.
0.0	

Sales

Dr.	Cr.
	0.0

Interest Revenue

Dr.	Cr.
	0.0

SG&A

Dr.	Cr.
	0.0

Prov. for Inc Tax

Dr.	Cr.
0.0	

Income Summary

Dr.	Cr.
0.0	

Chapter four

Cash Flow Statements

> **Questions** . . . .

1. Define cash and give three examples of different kinds of cash.
2. What is "restricted currency"? Is it cash? Justify your answer.
3. Define cash flow.
4. Define investing cash flows and give three examples of investing cash flows, at least one of which could result in a positive cash flow from investing.
5. Define financing cash flows and give three examples of financing cash flows, at least one of which could result in a negative cash flow from financing.
6. Define operating cash flows and give three examples of operating cash flows, at least one of which could result in a positive cash flow from operations, and one of which could result in a negative cash flow from operations.
7. "Cash flow from operations is just what is left over after considering cash flows from financing and investing." Comment.
8. Give two examples of noncash transactions.
9. Must noncash transactions be disclosed in the statement of cash flows? If so, where?
10. Compare and contrast the two methods of presenting cash flow statements. Address each section of the cash flow statement in your answer.
11. In a growing business, are cash flows from operations usually less than, equal to, or greater than net income? Explain your answer.
12. In a growing business, should cash flows from financing be positive or negative? Explain your answer.
13. In a growing business, should cash flows from investing be positive or negative? Explain your answer.
14. In a steady business that is neither in a state of growth or decline, are cash flows from operations usually less than, equal to, or greater than net income? Explain your answer.
15. In a steady business, should cash flows from financing be positive or negative? Explain your answer.
16. In a steady business, should cash flows from investing be positive or negative? Explain your answer.
17. In a steady business, how should cash flows from investing compare to depreciation expense? Explain your answer.
18. In a shrinking business, are cash flows from operations usually less than, equal to, or greater than net income? Explain your answer.
19. In a shrinking business, should cash flows from financing be positive or negative? Explain your answer.
20. In a shrinking business, are cash flows from investing usually positive or negative? Explain your answer.
21. What is the difference, if any, between cash paid to suppliers and the cost of goods sold?
22. What is the difference, if any, between sales and cash collected from customers?

23. Is cash collected from customers reflected in a cash flow statement that uses the indirect method? If so, how?

24. Refer to Exhibit 4.15, the indirect method statement of cash flows for Websell. Comment on the following statement: "Websell received $30,000 in cash from depreciation."

25. Where do dividends paid appear on the statement of cash flows? Where does interest paid appear on the statement of cash flows? Comment.

Exercises . . . .

E4–1   Miloslav began a magazine delivery service, which he named Miloslav's Magazines, on January 1, 2001. The following transactions occurred during 2001:

a.   Sold stock for $3,000 cash on January 1.

b.   Borrowed $20,000 cash on April 1. The interest rate on the loan is 12% annually, and the interest is due each December 31, until the note is repaid.

c.   Bought a bicycle for $1,000 cash on January 1. The bicycle has an estimated life of five years and no salvage value.

d.   Bought 10,000 magazines for $2.00 cash each on April 5.

e.   Sold magazines at various times for a total of $22,500. All sales were on account.

f.   Collected $20,500 from customers.

g.   Paid himself a salary of $3,000 cash.

h.   Paid the stockholders a dividend of $50 on the $3,000 in stock.

i.   Paid the interest on the loan in b.

j.   On December 31, Miloslav determined by a physical count that there were 1,000 magazines left in the storage bin at the warehouse.

Use the direct method to prepare a statement of cash flows for Miloslav's Magazines for the year ended December 31, 2001.

E4–2   Ofer's Office Designs began operations on January 1, 2001. Listed below is a summary of events experienced by Ofer's Office Designs during 2001.

a.   The company issued 2,000 shares of common stock for cash at their par value of $50 per share.

b.   On April 1, 2001, the company purchased eight sets of office furniture that it will sell to customers. Each set cost $20,000. Ofer's paid $10,000 in cash and signed a two-year note with an 8% interest rate for the remainder of the purchase price. Interest on the note is due on January 1 of each year the note remains unpaid.

c.   The company performed consulting services for a total fee of $200,000, receiving $50,000 in cash up front.

d.   A potential customer communicated its intent to have Ofer's perform $80,000 of consulting services.

e.   The company paid $100,000 cash for wages.

f.   The company paid $20,000 cash for rent on July 1, 2001. The company is charged rent at the rate of $1,083.33 dollars per month. Prior to July 1, 2001, rent for January through June had not been paid. The remainder of the $20,000 payment was applied to future month's rent as it became due.

g. On December 31, 2001, the company paid the holder of the note $15,000.

h. The company declared and paid cash dividends of $19,000.

i. The company received $30,000 in cash as payments for outstanding receivables.

j. The company sold three sets of office furniture for $28,000 cash each.

Use the direct method to prepare a statement of cash flows for Ofer's Office Designs for the year ended December 31, 2001.

E4–3 Ralphy started a business on April 1, 2001, and had the following transactions on April 1:

a. Issued 20,000 shares of $5 par value common stock for $100,000 cash.

b. Bought equipment to be used for making products, for $60,000. The equipment has a six-year life and is to be depreciated on a straight-line basis, with no salvage value.

c. Paid $4,000 for one year's rent on a building.

d. Bought $30,000 of inventory on credit.

e. Bought $25,000 of Yahoo common stock as a short-term investment.

f. Issued a bond with a face value of $20,000 and an interest rate of 10%. Interest is to be paid annually.

Between April 1 and December 31, the following transactions occurred:

g. Sold inventory that cost $25,000 for $40,000. All sales were on credit.

h. Paid $15,000 to suppliers of inventory for the credit purchase in (d) above.

i. Collected $30,000 from customers.

j. A customer owing $200 declared bankruptcy, and notice was received that the customer would pay only $50 of this debt. The $50 payment was enclosed.

k. Salaries and wages of $6,000 were paid.

On December:

l. Salaries and wages of $1,000 had been earned but not paid.

m. The market value of Ralphy's inventory was $12,500.

Use the direct method to prepare a statement of cash flows for Ralphy's business for the nine months ended December 31, 2001.

E4–4 Rick and Stan started a business on October 1, 2002, and had the following transactions on October 1:

a. Issued 10,000 shares of $5 par value common stock for $110,000 cash.

b. Bought equipment to be used for making products for $60,000 cash. The equipment has a five-year life and is to be depreciated on a straight-line basis, with no salvage value.

c. Paid $3,000 for one year's rent on a building.

d. Bought $35,000 of inventory on credit.

e. Took out a $20,000 bank loan at an interest rate of 12%. Interest is to be paid annually.

Between October 1 and December 31, 2002, the following transactions occurred:

f. Sold inventory costing $25,000 for $45,000. All sales were on credit.

g. Paid $31,000 to suppliers of inventory for the credit purchase in (d).

h. Collected $36,000 from customers.

i. Salaries and wages of $16,000 were paid.

On December 31:

j. Salaries and wages of $2,000 had been earned but not paid.

k. The market value of Rick and Stan's inventory was $27,500.

Use the direct method to prepare a statement of cash flows for Rick and Stan's business for the year ended December 31, 2002.

Problems . . . .

P4–1   On December 31, 2000, Sampson, Inc.:

a. Obtains $20,000 cash by selling common stock.

b. Obtains $40,000 cash from Loanit Bank. The loan is due on December 31, 2003, and interest of 10% on the balance is due on January 1 of each year, excluding January 1, 2001.

c. Buys land, paying $5,000 cash.

d. Hires a manager to begin work on January 1, 2001. The salary is $1,000 per month, payable on the first of each month, beginning February 1, 2001.

e. Prepays six months' rent on a portable building, paying $3,000 cash.

Sampson, Inc.'s balance sheet at the end of 2000 is shown below.

Statement of Financial Position as of December 31, 2000

Cash	$52,000	Total current liabilities	None
Prepaid rent	3,000		
Total current assets	$55,000	Note payable	$40,000
		Stockholders' equity:	
Land	5,000	Common stock	20,000
		Total liabilities &	
Total assets	$60,000	stockholders' equity	$60,000

During the year 2001:

a. Sampson purchases, for 10 cents cash per can, and sells, for 15 cents cash per can, 490,000 cans of Drinkit.

b. On July 1, 2001, Sampson prepays an additional eight months' rent, paying $4,000 cash.

c. Sampson pays a $2,000 cash dividend on December 31, 2001.

Required

Construct a statement of cash flows for the year ended December 31, 2001, for Sampson, Inc.

P4–2   Review Co.

Below is a balance sheet for Review Co. as of December 31, 2002.

Review Co.
Balance Sheet
December 31, 2002 (in thousands)

Assets			Liabilities and Equities		
Cash	$ 68.0		Accounts payable	$ 63.0	
Accounts receivable	340.0		Wages payable	13.0	
Inventories	75.0		Interest payable	3.0	
Prepaid rent	32.0		Taxes payable	6.0	
Total current assets		$515.0	Other accrued liabilities	5.0	
			Total current liabilities		$ 90.0
Buildings & machinery	$100.0		Senior debt	$100.0	
Accumulated depreciation	(25.0)		Subordinated debt	30.0	
Buildings & machinery, net		$ 75.0	Total noncurrent liabilities		130.0
Land		25.0	Common stock	$ 15.0	
Total noncurrent assets		$100.0	APIC	115.0	
Total assets		$615.0	Retained earnings	265.0	
			Shareholders' equity		395.0
			Total liabilities &		
			shareholders' equity		$615.0

The following information pertains to 2003 (all amounts are in thousands):

a. Sales were $3,000, all on account.

b. Collections on accounts receivable were $3,100.

c. A physical count of inventory found $95 on hand at December 31, 2003.

d. On January 1, 2003, Review bought a building for $50 cash.

e. On January 1, 2003, Review sold machinery for $1.5 that cost $10 and had accumulated depreciation as of January 1, 2003, of $8.

f. Review calculates depreciation expense using the straight-line method and an asset life of 10 years for buildings and machinery.

g. The senior debt has an interest rate of 6%.

h. The subordinated debt has an interest rate of 8%.

i. Dividends paid totaled $14.

j. Wages payable at the end of the year were $17.

k. Wages expense was $57.

l. Cash payments for miscellaneous expenses totaled $50. These payments are in addition to any miscellaneous expenses derived from prepaids or liability accounts.

m. Interest paid was $7.

n. Purchases were $2,820, all on account.

o. Payments on accounts payable were $2,700.

p. The balance of prepaid rent at December 31, 2003, was $30.

q. Additions to prepaid rent totaled $25.

r. The beginning balance of Other Accrued Liabilities was paid off in cash.

s.   Other accrued liabilities at the end of the year, all relating to miscellaneous expenses, amounted to $9.

t.   Review's tax expense for 2003 was $12.

u.   Unpaid taxes at December 31, 2003, were $7.

Required

1.   In a set of T-accounts, make all entries required under U.S. GAAP.

2.   Prepare a balance sheet for December 31, 2003.

3.   Prepare an income statement for the year ended December 31, 2003.

4.   Prepare a statement of cash flows, using the indirect method, for the year ended December 31, 2003.

P4–3   Grow Company

Below is a balance sheet for Grow Co. as of December 31, 2001:

Grow Co.
Balance Sheet
December 31, 2001 (in millions)

Assets		*Liabilities and Equities*	
Cash	$ 13.5	Accounts payable	$ 38.3
Accounts receivable	70.7	Wages payable	7.7
Inventories	84.3	Interest payable	3.8
Prepaid expenses	9.3	Other accrued expenses	24.0
Total current assets	$177.8	Taxes payable	1.5
		Total current liabilities	$ 75.3
Land	$ 3.7	Other liabilities:	
Buildings	49.8	Senior debt	$ 31.0
Machinery	57.6	Subordinated debt	49.4
Accumulated depreciation	(30.2)	Other long-term liabilities	41.6
	$ 80.9		$122.0
Other assets	18.6	Preferred stock	$ 11.3
Total assets	$277.3	Common stock	1.1
		APIC	50.4
		Retained earnings	17.2
		Shareholders' equity	$ 80.00
		Total liabilities &	
		shareholders' equity	$277.3

The following information pertains to 2002 (all amounts are in millions):

a.   Sales were $501.7, all on account.

b.   Collections on accounts receivable were $489.8.

c.   The cost of goods sold was $337.2.

d.   Depreciation expense was $10.5.

e.   Cash spent on research and development was $5.7.

f.   Tax expense was $7.

g.   Taxes payable at year-end were $5.7.

h.   Interest expense was $15.9.

i.   Other cash expenses were $21.7. The other expenses are classified as selling, general, and administrative (SG&A) expenses on the income statement.

j.   A senior debt issue raised $47.3.

k.   Dividends paid totaled $16.7.

l.   Wages expense (all SG&A) was $92.

m.   Unpaid wages at the end of the year were $6.9.

n.   Interest paid was $13.9.

o.   Other assets purchased for cash totaled $9.3.

p.   Land purchased for cash cost $0.5.

q.   A building was sold for $1.9 in cash. The building cost Grow $6.0 and had accumulated depreciation of $4.1.

r.   Purchases were $348.1, all on account.

s.   Payments on accounts payable were $336.7.

t.   Purchased a building for $10.5.

u.   Purchased machinery for $11.7.

v.   Expirations of prepaid items totaled $6. Prepaids are related to selling, general, and administrative expense accounts.

w.   Additions to prepaids totaled $8.1.

x.   Other accrued expenses at the end of the year, all relating to selling, general, and administrative expenses, totaled $29.3.

Required

1.   In a set of T-accounts, make all entries required under U.S. GAAP.

2.   Prepare a balance sheet for Grow as of December 31, 2002.

3.   Prepare an income statement for Grow for the year ended December 31, 2002.

4.   Prepare a statement of cash flows for Grow, using the direct method, for the year ended December 31, 2002.

5.   Prepare a statement of cash flows for Grow, using the indirect method, for the year ended December 31, 2002.

P4–4   ABC Widget Company

The post-closing trial balance on December 31, 2001, and the statement of cash flows for the year ended December 31, 2001, for the ABC Widget Company are presented below.

ABC Widget Company
Post-Closing Trial Balance
December 31, 2001

Debit balances:

Cash	$ 50,000
Accounts receivable	440,000
Inventory	640,000
Land	80,000
Buildings and equipment	1,000,000
Other long-term assets	200,000
	$2,410,000

Credit balances:

Accumulated depreciation	$ 400,000
Accounts payable	560,000
Other current liabilities	170,000
Bonds payable	200,000
Common stock	400,000
Retained earnings	680,000
	$2,410,000

ABC Widget Company
Statement of Cash Flows
For the Year Ended December 31, 2001

Operations:	
Net income	$ 400,000
Additions:	
Depreciation expense	120,000
Increase in accounts payable	50,000
Subtractions:	
Increase in accounts receivable	(60,000)
Increase in inventory	(80,000)
Decrease in other current liabilities	(90,000)
Cash from operations	$ 340,000
Investing:	
Sale of other long-term assets	$ 80,000
Sale of buildings and equipment	30,000
Sale of land	20,000
Acquisition of buildings and equipment	(260,000)
Cash from investing	$(130,000)
Financing:	
Common stock issued	$ 120,000
Bonds issued	80,000
Dividends paid	(400,000)
Cash from financing	$ (200,000)
Net change in cash	$ 10,000

The firm sold other long-term assets, buildings, equipment, and land for cash at their net book value. The accumulated depreciation of the equipment sold was $40,000.

Required

Prepare a balance sheet as of December 31, 2000.

P4–5   Active Company

The balance sheets for Active Company for 2000 and 2001 and the income statement 2001 are shown below.

Active Company
Balance Sheet
December 31, 2000

Assets		*Liabilities and Stockholders' Equity*	
Cash	$ 52,000	Accounts payable for inventory	$136,000
Accounts receivable	93,000	Interest payable	10,000
Inventory	151,000	Mortgage payable	120,000
Land	30,000	Common stock	250,000
Equipment	690,000	Retained earnings	140,000
Accumulated depreciation	(460,000)	Total liabilities & stockholders'	
Patents	100,000	equity	$656,000
Total assets	$656,000		

Active Company
Balance Sheet
December 31, 2001

Assets		*Liabilities and Stockholders' Equity*	
Cash	$109,000	Accounts payable for inventory	$136,000
Accounts receivable	93,000	Interest payable	10,000
Inventory	151,000	Mortgage payable	110,000
Land	25,000	Common stock	270,000
Equipment	730,000	Retained earnings	166,000
Accumulated depreciation	(506,000)	Total liabilities & stockholders'	
Patents	90,000	equity	$692,000
Total assets	$692,000		

Active Company
Income Statement
For the Year Ended December 31, 2001

Revenues		$1,200,000
Expenses:		
Cost of goods sold	$788,000	
Wages and salaries	280,000	
Depreciation	54,000	
Interest	12,000	
Income taxes	22,000	
Amortization of patent	10,000	$1,166,000
Net income before gains and losses		34,000
Loss on disposal of equipment		(2,000)
Gain on sale of land		3,000
Gain on early payment of mortgage		1,000
Net income		$ 36,000
Dividends on common stock		10,000
Additions to retained earnings for the year		$ 26,000
Retained earnings, January 1		140,000
Retained earnings, December 31		$ 166,000

Notes:

a. During the year, the firm sold equipment for $4,000 that had cost $14,000 and had $8,000 of accumulated depreciation.

b. During the year, the company acquired equipment in exchange for $10,000 of its common stock.

c. During the year, land with an acquisition cost of $5,000 was sold for $8,000 cash.

d. Wages and salaries expense includes $10,000 of compensation paid to employees in the form of common stock.

e. Mortgage principal of $10,000 was paid off during the year. The bank agreed to accept $9,000 cash as payment.

Required

Prepare a statement of cash flows for Active Company for the 2001 fiscal year, supporting the statement with a worksheet.

Cases and Projects ....

C4–1 EDGAR

The Securities and Exchange Commission (SEC) is an agency of the United States government. Its primary responsibility is the regulation of the markets for stocks and bonds. The SEC requires that companies whose shares are publicly traded file a variety of reports in electronic format. These reports are available to the public through the SEC's EDGAR (Electronic Data Gathering And Reporting) system, which is fully accessible through the World Wide Web.[2]

There are many types of required filings, but the ones of most interest to us are the 10-K and 10-Q reports. The 10-K is the primary form that carries the company's annual financial statements prepared in accordance with generally accepted accounting principles (GAAP). The 10-Q contains the company's quarterly GAAP-based financial statements.

Required:

1. Choose three publicly traded companies whose financial reports are available through the EDGAR web site. For each company, find its most recent 10-K from the EDGAR web site. (Do not print out the entire document.) Locate each company's statement of cash flows. Does each company use the direct or the indirect method in its cash flow statement?

2. For one of the three companies:

   a. Compare the company's cash flow from operations with its net income. Identify, if you can, any major sources of the difference between cash flow from operations and net income.

   b. Were the company's cash flows from investing positive or negative?

   c. How does the company's cash flow from investing compare to its depreciation expense?

   d. Were the company's cash flows from financing positive or negative?

   e. Did the company disclose any noncash transactions?

   f. How much did the company pay in income taxes? Where did you find this number?

   g. How much did the company pay in interest? Where did you find this number?

---

[2] The reports are stored as text files (*.txt) on the EDGAR web site. You can either download the files or view them straight from your browser, if you have configured your browser properly.

C4-2 Coldwater Creek's Cash Flows

Use the financial statements for Coldwater Creek, shown on pages 37–38, and the cash flow statements below to answer the following:

a. Assume that Coldwater Creek has no allowance for doubtful accounts or bad debt expense, and assume that all sales are credit sales. What was the amount of cash collections for the year ended February 28, 1998?

b. What was the amount of total purchases for the year ended February 28, 1998?

c. What amount of cash was paid on account for the year ended February 28, 1998?

d. The company generated positive income for the year ended February 28, 1998, but cash flow from operations was negative. What was the primary cause of the difference between the two?

Coldwater Creek, Inc., and Subsidiary
Consolidated Statements of Cash Flows—(in thousands)

	February 28, 1998	March 1, 1997	March 2, 1996
Operating Activities:			
Net income	$ 11,688	$ 10,816	$ 5,614
Noncash items:			
Depreciation	3,738	2,176	995
Deferred income tax provision	988	746	—
Net change in current assets and liabilities:			
Receivables	(1,677)	(769)	(1,299)
Inventories	(27,772)	(17,027)	(2,441)
Prepaid expenses	(2,273)	(308)	(5)
Prepaid catalog costs	(1,419)	(797)	(189)
Accounts payable	9,924	10,715	2,685
Accrued liabilities	4,968	3,019	2,112
Income taxes payable	(451)	451	—
Increase in deferred catalog costs	(3,673)	(1,265)	(1,271)
Net Cash (used in) Provided by Operating Activities:	$ (5,959)	$ 7,757	$ 6,201
Investing Activities:			
Purchase of property and equipment	(10,319)	(11,883)	(2,590)
Proceeds on sale of equipment	—	—	1,105
Loans to executives	(1,620)	—	—
Net Cash Used in Investing Activities	$(11,939)	$(11,883)	$(1,485)
Financing Activities:			
Payments on capital leases	—	(173)	(136)
Net advances (repayments) under revolving line of credit	10,264	—	(3,700)
Net proceeds from initial public offering of common shares	38,776	—	—
Distributions to stockholders	(1,130)	(25,800)	(2,157)
Net Cash Provided by (used in) Financing Activities	$ 9,134	$ 12,803	$(5,993)
Net (Decrease) Increase in Cash and Cash Equivalents	(8,764)	8,677	(1,277)
Cash and Cash Equivalents, Beginning	9,095	418	1,695
Cash and Cash Equivalents, Ending	$ 331	$ 9,095	$ 418
Supplemental Cash Flow Data:			
Cash paid for interest	99	243	339
Cash paid for income taxes	8,170	—	—

C4–3   Med-Design Corporation

The Med-Design annual report is given below.

THE MED-DESIGN CORPORATION AND SUBSIDIARIES
(Excerpts)

Med-Design designs and develops safety medical devices intended to reduce the incidence of accidental needle sticks. Med-Design has three core products. Each of these products incorporates Med-Design's novel proprietary retraction technology that enables a health care professional, with no substantial change in operating technique and using one hand, to permanently retract the needle into the body of the device which can then be safely discarded. Med-Design has several U.S. and foreign patents and many patent applications pending.

RESEARCH AND DEVELOPMENT

Med-Design has devoted substantially all of its research and development efforts since its formation to safety needles and equipment necessary to assemble the safety needle devices. Research and development expenses amounted to $1,106,501 in 1998 and $1,605,668 in 1997.

MANAGEMENT'S DISCUSSION AND ANALYSIS

The following discussion and analysis should be read in conjunction with the consolidated financial statements and notes thereto of Med-Design, which appear elsewhere herein.

To date, Med-Design has earned no revenues from product sales; however, Med-Design generated revenues in 1998 from licensing activities and anticipates that revenues will be recorded during the next twelve months from licensing of additional products to Becton Dickinson and/or other strategic partners.

The Med-Design Corporation and Subsidiaries
Consolidated Balance Sheet

	December 31, 1998	December 31, 1997
Assets		
Current assets:		
Cash and cash equivalents	$ 32,883	$ 114,079
Short-term investments	—	546,591
Available-for-sale securities	6,111,620	5,617,284
Prepaid expenses and other current assets	173,006	152,547
Total current assets	$6,317,509	$6,430,501
Property, plant, and equipment, net	$865,267	$1,181,481
Patents, net of accumulated amortization of $80,766 in 1998 and $44,164 in 1997	788,629	681,048
Debt issue costs, net of accumulated amortization of $53,720 at December 31, 1998	511,480	—
Total assets	$8,482,885	$8,293,030
Liabilities and Stockholders' Equity		
Current liabilities:		
Short-term borrowings	$ 250,000	$4,630,500
Current maturities of long-term debt and capital lease obligations	10,492	199,821
Accounts payable	215,426	205,625
Accrued expenses	$ 176,697	$ 213,042
Total current liabilities	$ 652,615	$ 5,248,988

Long-term debt and capital lease obligations, less current maturities	1,579,824	154,674
Total liabilities	$2,232,439	$5,403,662
Stockholders' equity		
Preferred stock, $.01 par value, 5,000,000 shares authorized; 300,000 shares issued and outstanding	$ 3,000	$ —
Common stock, $.01 par value, 20,000,000 shares authorized; 7,951,570 shares issued and outstanding	79,516	79,516
Additional paid-in capital	24,244,554	21,764,194
Accumulated deficit	(18,084,352)	(18,967,241)
Accumulated other comprehensive income	7,728	12,899
Total stockholders' equity	$6,250,446	$2,889,368
Total liabilities and stockholders equity	$8,482,885	$8,293,030

The accompanying notes are an integral part of these financial statements.

The Med-Design Corporation and Subsidiaries
Consolidated Statement of Operations

	Year ended December 31,	
	1998	1997
Revenue:		
Licensing revenue	$4,500,000	$ —
Total revenue	$4,500,000	—
Operating expense:		
Marketing	$ 82,335	$ 192,201
General and administrative	2,447,866	3,410,569
Research and development	1,106,501	1,605,668
Total operating expenses	$3,636,702	$ 5,208,438
Income (loss) from operations	$ 863,298	$(5,208,438)
Interest expense	(242,521)	(421,967)
Investment income	262,112	410,572
Net income (loss)	$ 882,889	$(5,219,833)
Basic and diluted earnings (loss) per common share	$ 0.11	$ (0.66)

The accompanying notes are an integral part of these financial statements.

The Med-Design Corporation and Subsidiaries
Statement of Cash Flows

	Year ended December 31,	
	1998	1997
Cash flows from operating activities:		
Net income (loss)	$ 882,889	$(5,219,833)
Adjustments to reconcile net income (loss) to operating cash flows:		
Depreciation and amortization	289,022	233,111
Issuance of warrants for services	380,802	821,000
Repricing of stock options	85,200	62,080
Amortization of debt issue costs	53,720	—
Debt issue costs in connection with private-investor loan	28,158	—

Loss on sale of available-for-sale securities	—	7,046
Changes in operating assets and liabilities:		
Prepaid expenses and other current assets	6,545	(55,086)
Accounts payable	9,801	32,714
Accrued expenses	(36,346)	84,896
Net cash provided by (used in) operating activities	$1,699,791	$(4,034,072)
Cash flows from investing activities:		
Purchases of property and equipment	$	$ (115,195)
Sale of property and equipment	36,791	—
Additions to patents	(144,183)	(215,432)
Investments in available-for-sale securities, net	(499,507)	3,572
Sale (purchase) of short-term investment	546,591	(11,343)
Net cash used in investing activities	$ (60,308)	$ (338,398)
Cash flows from financing activities:		
Capital lease payments	$ (17,633)	$ (11,508)
Proceeds from long-term borrowings	—	14,410
Repayment of long-term borrowings	(296,546)	(235,425)
Proceeds from issuance of common stock in connection with exercise of warrants	—	254,800
Proceeds from short-term borrowing	250,000	184,000
Repayment of short-term borrowing	(4,630,500)	(2,000,000)
Other	—	14,136
Proceeds of private placement, debenture bonds	1,550,000	—
Debt issue costs	(76,000)	—
Proceeds of private placement, net of offering costs	—	4,617,497
Proceeds from issuance of Series A preferred stock	1,500,000	—
Net cash provided by (used in) financing activities	$(1,720,679)	$ 2,837,910
Decrease in cash	$ (81,196)	$(1,534,560)
Cash and cash equivalents, beginning of period	114,079	1,648,639
Cash and cash equivalents, end of period	$32,883	$ 114,079
Cash paid during the period:		
Interest	$ 219,176	$ 396,144
Noncash investing and financing activities:		
Issuance of warrants in partial payment of patents	—	$ 300,833
Capital lease obligation incurred	—	$ 49,000
Change in unrealized gain (loss) on available-for-sale securities	$ (5,171)	$ (10,596)
Debt issue costs	$ 489,200	—

The accompanying notes are an integral part of these financial statements.

NOTES TO CONSOLIDATED FINANCIAL STATEMENTS (Excerpts)

Patents:

Patents, patent applications, and rights are stated at acquisition costs. Amortization of patents is recorded by using the straight-line method over the legal lives of the patents. Amortization expense from the years ended December 31, 1998 and 1997, was $36,602 and $9,840, respectively.

Debt Issue Cost:

Debt issue costs consist of fees and other costs incurred in obtaining debt and are amortized on a straight-line basis over the life of the debt.

Revenue Recognition:
License fee revenues from proprietary products are recognized upon the signing of a contract when Med-Design has no further obligation under the contract and when collectibility of the license fee is probable.

Stock Option Repricing:
On October 10, 1997, Med-Design repriced previously issued stock options on 32,000 shares of Common Stock for two directors. The options were issued on June 3, 1996, at an exercise price of $20.50 a share and were repriced to $4.50 a share. In connection with the repricing of these stock options, Med-Design recorded compensation expense of $62,080.

Warrants
In connection with the initial public offering, Med-Design issued warrants to the Underwriter to purchase 300,000 shares of common stock, of which warrants to purchase 111,000 were exercised in 1996 and 52,000 were exercised in 1997. In addition, on August 15, 1995, Med-Design issued warrants to purchase from Med-Design 100,000 shares of common stock at $7.50 per share, in consideration for the execution of an agreement for consulting services. The warrants were exercisable upon issuance and expired on August 15, 1998.

On January 23, 1997, Med-Design completed the sale of 1,000,000 shares of common stock. In connection with the sale, Med-Design also sold to the placement agent, for nominal consideration, warrants to purchase 100,000 shares of common stock. These warrants are exercisable at a price of $5.50 per share of common stock for a period of four years commencing January 22, 1998.

On March 19, 1997, Med-Design issued warrants to purchase 100,000 shares of common stock at an exercise price of $7.50 per share to a director of Med-Design, who was engaged to perform certain consulting services on behalf of Med-Design. The warrants are exercisable upon issuance and expire on March 19, 2000. In connection with the issuance of these warrants, Med-Design recorded consulting expense in the amount of $436,000 for the year ended December 31, 1997.

On October 10, 1997, Med-Design issued warrants to purchase 100,000 shares of common stock at an exercise price of $5.44 to a director of Med-Design who was engaged to perform certain consulting services on behalf of Med-Design. These warrants are exercisable upon issuance and expire on October 10, 2000. In connection with the issuance of these warrants, Med-Design recorded consulting expense in the amount of $385,000 for the year ended December 31, 1997.

On January 14, 1998, Med-Design issued warrants to purchase 100,000 shares of common stock at an exercise price of $2.88 per share to a director of Med-Design who was engaged to perform certain consulting services. The warrants are exercisable upon issuance and expire on January 14, 2003. Med-Design recorded consulting expense of $194,000 in relation to these warrants.

Med-Design also repriced 200,000 previously issued warrants to a director on January 14, 1998. The warrants were issued on March 19, 1997, and October 10, 1997, at an exercise price of $7.50 per share and $5.44 per share respectively and were repriced to $2.88. In connection with the repricing of these warrants, Med-Design recorded consulting expense of $85,200.

On September 9, 1998, Med-Design issued warrants to purchase 200,000 shares of common stock at a price of $1.25 per share to a director of Med-Design who was engaged to perform certain consulting services. The warrants vested upon completion of performance, which took place on December 23, 1998. The warrants expire on September 9, 2003. Med-Design recorded consulting expense of $186,802.

A **warrant** is the right to buy stock at a specified price, called the **exercise price**. "Warrant" is another name for "option."

Required

Answer the following questions related to Med-Design's annual report. Explain and justify all answers.

1. Where is the $1,106,501 expenditure on research and development included in Med-Design's 1998 balance sheet?

2. What was the total cash dividend paid to shareholders of Med-Design stock during the year ended December 31, 1998? Be sure to justify your answer.

3. How much depreciation expense is there in Med-Design's 1998 income statement?

4. Why is Depreciation and Amortization added back to net income in order to obtain cash flow from operations in the statement of cash flows? Be precise.

5. Why is the $380,802 for Issuance of Warrants for Service added back to net income in the statement of cash flows in order to obtain cash flow from operations?

6. On January 14, 1998, Med-Design issued warrants to purchase 100,000 shares of common stock at an exercise price of $2.88 per share to a director of Med-Design who was engaged to perform consulting services. Med-Design recorded consulting expense of $194,000 in relation to these warrants. Give a plausible journal entry to record this transaction.

7. All increases to the Prepaid Expenses and Other Current Assets account in 1998 involved an offsetting credit to cash, with one exception. One of the prepayments was "paid for" by issuing warrants. What was the value of the warrants issued in this transaction?

8. Was there a gain or loss on the sale of property and equipment during 1998? Explain.

9. Marketing expenses are either paid immediately with cash when incurred or are credited to the Accrued Expenses account. No other items are included in the Accrued Expenses account. What was the cash outflow to pay marketing costs in 1998?

C4–4 Dick Clark Productions*

Dick Clark Productions is a publicly traded company (over the counter) whose principal shareholder is Dick Clark (radio and television personality). The company produces and markets television programming to the major broadcast networks, syndicators, and cable systems. The company also operates a chain of restaurants under the name "Dick Clark's American Bandstand Grill." Excerpts from Dick Clark Production's annual report are shown below.

Consolidated Balance Sheets
Year Ended June 30,

	1995	1994
Assets		
Cash and cash equivalents	$ 3,297,000	$ 4,336,000
Marketable securities	25,769,000	24,348,000
Accounts receivable	2,303,000	3,944,000
Program costs, net	4,306,000	1,474,000
Prepaid royalty	3,128,000	—
Leasehold improvements and equipment	7,152,000	7,162,000
Current and deferred income taxes	—	83,000
Goodwill and other assets	2,353,000	2,970,000
Total assets	$48,308,000	$44,317,000

* This case was inspired by one appearing in R. Beatty and J. R. M. Hand, *Business Applications for Corporate Accounting*, South-Western College Publishing (Cincinnati, 1995).

	1995	1994
Liabilities & Stockholders' Equity		
Accounts payable	$ 4,109,000	$ 5,492,000
Accrued residuals and participations	1,438,000	1,881,000
Production advances and deferred revenue	4,097,000	2,286,000
Current and deferred income taxes	348,000	—
Total liabilities	9,992,000	9,659,000
Commitments and contingencies		
Minority interest	524,000	965,000
Stockholders' equity:		
Class A common stock, $.01 par value,		
2,000,000 shares authorized		
750,000 shares outstanding	7,000	7,000
Common stock, $.01 par value,		
20,000,000 shares authorized		
7,528,500 shares outstanding at June 30, 1995 and		
7,527,000 shares outstanding at June 30, 1994	76,000	76,000
Additional paid-in capital	7,790,000	7,783,000
Retained earnings	29,919,000	25,827,000
Total stockholders' equity	37,792,000	33,693,000
Total liabilities & stockholders' equity	$48,308,000	$44,317,000

The accompanying notes are an integral part of these consolidated financial statements.

Consolidated Statements of Operations

		Year ended June 30,	
	1995	1994	1993
Gross revenues	$46,645,000	$58,296,000	$43,428,000
Costs related to revenue	37,551,000	47,615,000	38,350,000
Gross profit	9,094,000	10,681,000	5,078,000
General and administrative expenses	4,145,000	4,113,000	3,529,000
Minority interest expense	107,000	507,000	305,000
Interest and other income	(1,711,000)	(1,455,000)	(1,444,000)
Income before provision (credit) for income taxes	6,553,000	7,516,000	2,688,000
Provision (credit) for income taxes	2,461,000	2,640,000	(510,000)
Income before cumulative effect of accounting change	4,092,000	4,876,000	3,198,000
Cumulative effect of accounting change		(262,000)	
Net income	$ 4,092,000	$ 5,138,000	$ 3,198,000
Income per share before cumulative effect of accounting change	$ 0.49	$0.59	$0.39
Cumulative effect of accounting change	—	0.03	—
Net income	$ 0.49	$0.62	$0.39
Weighted average number of shares outstanding	8,278,000	8,266,000	8,265,000

The accompanying notes are an integral part of these consolidated financial statements.

Consolidated Statements of Cash Flows

	Year ended June 30,		
	1995	1994	1993
Cash flows from operating activities			
Net income	$4,092,000	$5,138,000	$3,198,000
Adjustments to reconcile net income to net cash provided by operations			
Amortization expense	20,858,000	37,111,000	28,702,000
Depreciation expense	981,000	567,000	507,000
Minority interest, net	(441,000)	375,000	(533,000)
Disposals of leasehold improvements & equipment	177,000	—	1,148,000
Changes in assets and liabilities			
Accounts receivable	1,641,000	410,000	(1,604,000)
Prepaid royalty	(3,128,000)	—	—
Goodwill and other assets	(27,000)	(1,494,000)	(755,000)
Accounts payable, accrued residuals and participations	(1,826,000)	2,583,000	(414,000)
Production advances and deferred revenue	1,811,000	(5,097,000)	5,831,000
Current and deferred income taxes	431,000	(1,280,000)	(1,654,000)
Net cash provided by operations	24,569,000	38,313,000	34,426,000
Cash flows from investing activities			
Investment in program costs	(23,046,000)	(32,426,000)	(31,163,000)
Purchases of marketable securities	(14,224,000)	(16,920,000)	(16,040,000)
Sales of marketable securities	12,803,000	17,375,000	15,774,000
Capital expenditures	(1,148,000)	(4,836,000)	(2,118,000)
Net cash used for investing activities	(25,615,000)	(36,807,000)	(33,547,000)
Cash flows from financing activities			
Exercise of stock options	7,000	54,000	—
Net cash provided by financing activities	7,000	54,000	—
Net increase (decrease) in cash and cash equivalents	(1,039,000)	1,560,000	879,000
Cash and cash equivalents at beginning of the year	4,336,000	2,776,000	1,897,000
Cash and cash equivalents at end of the year	$3,297,000	$4,336,000	$2,776,000

The accompanying notes are an integral part of these consolidated financial statements.

NOTES TO CONSOLIDATED FINANCIAL STATEMENTS

2) Summary of Significant Accounting Policies

Revenues:

A majority of the Company's revenues are derived from the development and production of television programming. Revenues from television program licensing agreements are recognized when each program becomes contractually available for broadcast or when a program is delivered to the buyer. Revenues earned currently which are to be received in future periods are discounted to their present value using the effective interest method.

Depending on the type of contract, revenues for Dick Clark Corporate Productions, Inc. are recognized when services are completed for a live event or when a tape or film is delivered to a customer or when services are completed pursuant to a phase of a contract which provides for periodic payment. Revenues for the Company's skin care business are recognized as the products are shipped.

Program Cost:

Program costs, which include acquired film rights, residual costs, third-party participations and indirect production costs (production overhead) are charged to operations on an individual program basis in the ratio that the current year's gross revenues for each program bears to management's estimate of total ultimate gross revenue (for the current and future years) for that program from all sources. This method of accounting is commonly referred to as the individual-film-forecast method. For the fiscal years ended June 30, 1995, 1994 and 1993 there are $3,576,000, $3,171,000 and $2,555,000, respectively, of production overhead included within program costs.

Program costs are stated at the lower of unamortized cost or estimated net realizable value on an individual program basis. Ultimate revenue forecasts for programs are periodically reviewed by management and revised if warranted by changing conditions. When estimates of total revenue indicate that a program will result in an ultimate loss, the entire loss is recognized. There were no significant write-downs of program costs in the fiscal years ended June 30, 1995, 1994 and 1993.

The Company periodically reviews the status of projects in development. If, in the opinion of the Company's management, any such projects are not planned for production, the costs and any reimbursements and earned advances related thereto are charged to the appropriate profit and loss accounts. Substantially all production and distribution costs are amortized in the initial year of availability, except with respect to successful television series and television movies. During fiscal 1995, 100% of production costs for shows delivered during the year were amortized.

3) Program Costs

The Company is engaged, as one of its principal activities, in the development and production of a wide range of television and corporate programming. Program costs consist of the following:

| | Year ended June 30, | |
	1995	1994
Released, net of amortization		
Movies for television	$ 257,000	$ 284,000
Television programs	—	12,000
	257,000	296,000
In process		
Movies for television	—	8,000
Television programs	1,832,000	278,000
Corporate programs	1,345,000	82,000
	3,177,000	368,000
Project development costs		
Movies for television	772,000	673,000
Television programs	77,000	33,000
Corporate programs	23,000	104,000
	872,000	810,000
Program costs, net	$4,306,000	$1,474,000

The increase in program costs in process from June 30, 1994 to June 30, 1995 is primarily the result of costs incurred toward the end of fiscal year 1995 with respect to The Tempestt Bledsoe Show and a project for a corporate client.

Management's estimate of forecasted revenues related to released programs exceeds the unamortized costs on an individual program basis. Such forecasted revenue is subject to revision in future periods if warranted by changing conditions such as market appeal and availability of new markets. The Company currently anticipates that all of such revenue and related amortization will be recognized under the individual-film-forecast method where programs are available for broadcast in certain secondary markets in years ranging from 1996 through 2001. While management can forecast ultimate revenue based on experience and current market conditions, specific annual amortization charges to operations are not predictable because revenue recognition is dependent upon various external factors including expiration of network license agreements and availability for broadcasting in certain secondary markets. Program costs associated with corporate productions are amortized as projects or identifiable elements pursuant to a contract are delivered.

Based on management's estimates of gross revenues as of June 30, 1995, approximately 66% of the $257,000 in unamortized program costs applicable to released programs will be amortized during the three years ending June 30, 1998.

Required

1. In your own words, what are program costs?
2. On which financial statement do you see the account 'program costs, net'?
3. Explain the rationale for why program costs net appear on this financial statement.
4. Describe the flow of dollars through the account program costs net, explaining the transactions and or events that increase the account and those that decrease it.
5. List the amount of cash generated in 1995 from each of operating, investing, and financing activities.
6. Suggest an explanation for why cash flow from operations is so dramatically different from net income in 1995, 1994, and 1993. Does this mean that the income statement is useless in this situation?
7. Given the amount of cash generated by operations, why isn't the cash balance changing more rapidly?
8. Describe how Dick Clark's 1995 cash flow statement would change if dollars spent developing programming were classified as an operating cash flow.
9. What was the balance in the program costs net account at the end of fiscal 1995?
10. If Dick Clark Productions had decided to expense all remaining program costs on June 30, 1995, what would income before taxes have been for the year ended June 30, 1995?
11. Assume that Dick Clark Productions expensed all remaining program costs on June 30, 1995. Assume that income tax expense is unaffected and remains $2,461,000. What would cash flow from operations have been for the year ended June 30, 1995?

Chapter_{five}

Using the Accounting Framework: America Online, Inc.

> *Questions* . . . .

1. Indicate two possible reasons why a company's total assets would decrease from the beginning of the year to the end of the year.
2. Explain why an increase in an equity account could reflect an increase in assets, but not a decrease.
3. If a company has an account called "accumulated deficit," what logical conclusions can you make?
4. If you encounter an unfamiliar account in a company's financial statements, where should you go for further information?
5. What is a deferred cost? Where would it be found in the financial statements?
6. What is the general test for recording a cost as an asset?
7. If it is determined that an asset on the balance sheet has no future benefit, what does proper accounting tell us to do?
8. What does the expression "taking a charge" mean when referring to financial statements?
9. Give an expression that would have the same meaning as "taking a charge" when referring to a company's financial statements.
10. A company's statement of cash flows begins with "Net income." Is the company using the direct or indirect method? Explain.
11. Why are depreciation and amortization expense added back to net income in the statement of cash flows (indirect method)?
12. Why would an increase in prepaid expenses be deducted from net income in the statement of cash flows (indirect method)?
13. Indicate the impact on a company's income statement, balance sheet and cash flow statement of overestimating the useful lives of plant assets.
14. Many airlines have an account on their balance sheets named "air traffic liability." What does this account represent, and what types of transactions or events would cause this account to increase? When would it decrease?
15. What events will normally increase a company's Retained Earnings account? What events will decrease this account?
16. Give three ways an entity's total assets could increase.
17. Give three ways an entity's total assets could decrease.
18. Suppose an entity's total assets increase because it issues debt. How will this affect the entity's income statement, balance sheet and statement of cash flows?
19. Suppose an entity's total assets increase because it earns a profit. How will this affect the entity's income statement, balance sheet and statement of cash flows?
20. Suppose an entity's total assets increase in a year. How should this affect the entity's net income in the following year?
21. Everything else constant, will AOL's reported income for 1998 be higher or lower because it wrote off its Deferred subscriber acquisition costs in 1997?

22. Suppose AOL's Deferred subscriber acquisition costs actually do generate benefits for AOL in 1998. Will AOL's net income for 1998 be understated, overstated or properly stated? Justify your answer.
23. Give an example of an asset that you probably would find on the balance sheet of a manufacturing company that you probably would not find on the balance sheet of a consulting firm.
24. Explain how the usage of the asset you named in Question 23 above impacts the income statement of the manufacturing firm.
25. Explain how the acquisition and usage of the asset you named in Question 23 above affects the cash flow statement of the manufacturing firm.
26. For which type of firm is it more likely that inventories and cost of goods sold would be major components of its assets and expenses: large retail grocer or fast food chain? Justify your answer.
27. Everything else equal, would you expect a firm with a lot of competitors or with no competitors to report higher accounting net income? Justify your answer.
28. Comment on the following statement: "The nature of a firm's business and its environment are big factors in determining what the firm's financial statements look like."
29. Give two reasons shareholders' equity could increase.
30. Give two reasons shareholders' equity could decrease.
31. McDonald's Corp. reported net income of about $1.9 billion for its 1999 fiscal year. Do we know whether McDonald's total assets increased from the end of 1998 to the end of 1999? Justify your answer.

Exercises

E5-1 In December, 2000, the Financial Accounting Standards Board announced a proposal to change the way companies account for goodwill, an intangible asset. The board is proposing that purchased goodwill, related to acquisitions that have already taken place, would not have to be amortized in future periods. Previously, companies were required to amortize goodwill over a period not to exceed 40 years. Companies would be required to write down purchased goodwill if it was determined that the goodwill had become impaired in value. How will such an accounting change affect a company's income statement and balance sheet compared to the previous regulations?

E5-2 On February 7, 2001, Cisco Systems announced its second quarter results. Financial analysts were concerned by several aspects of this report: inventories grew by $600 million for the second consecutive quarter, nearly doubling their level from six months before and accounts receivable grew faster than sales during the quarter.

a. What would be some possible explanations for the changes?

b. Why would they concern financial analysts?

E5-3 The notes to the consolidated financial statements of TJX Companies for the fiscal year ended January 31, 2000, contained the following:

"Effective January 31, 1999, the Company changed its method of accounting for layaway sales in compliance with Staff Accounting Bulletin No. 101 'Revenue Recognition in Financial Statements,' issued by the Securities and Exchange Commission during the fourth quarter of fiscal 2000. Under the new accounting method, the Company will defer recognition of a layaway sale and its related profit to the accounting period when the customer picks up the layaway merchandise. The cumulative effect of this change for periods prior to January 31, 1999 of $5.2 million . . . is shown as the cumulative effect of accounting change in the Consolidated Statements of Income."

a. Explain how the Staff Accounting Bulletin's regulation better conforms to the revenue recognition criteria of Generally Accepted Accounting Principles.

b. How would this accounting change affect TJX's income statement and balance sheet for the current reporting period?

c. Assuming that customers had made deposits on merchandise previously recognized as layaway sales, name the specific accounts on the income statement and balance sheet that would be affected by this accounting change, indicating whether they would increase or decrease as a result of the change. Ignore income tax considerations.

E5-4 An excerpt from the Wall Street Journal on February 15, 2001 stated:

Viacom Inc. posted a 77% decline in fourth-quarter net income, but the media company, whose holdings include CBS, MTV and Paramount Pictures, made strong gains in its closely watched cash flow. . . . Cash flow . . . leapt in the quarter to $1.36 billion, from $595 million a year ago. . . . Viacom said it anticipates cash-flow growth of 20% this year, to more than $6.2 billion.

Explain how it is possible for a company's income to decline 77 percent while cash flow increases significantly.

E5-5 For each of the following transactions, events, or facts, indicate the impact on revenues, expenses, income, assets, liabilities, and equity by placing a + or − sign to indicate direction, in the appropriate box. Write NE for no effect. Be sure to place an answer in every box. Part (a) has been completed as an example.

a. Provided services on account.

Revenues	Expenses	Income	Assets	Liabilities	Equities
+	NE	+	+	NE	+

b. Received an advance to provide services in the future.

c. Paid a two-year insurance policy in advance.

d. Paid (in cash) the salaries of employees for current work performed.

e. Amortized intangible assets.

f. Purchased inventory on credit.

g. Sold inventory for cash at a profit.

h. Recognized the expiration of one year of insurance policy purchased in c.

i. Performed a portion of the services that had been provided for in b.

j. Recorded depreciation on plant assets.

k. Accrued wages earned by employees but not yet paid at year-end.

m. Recognized interest expense on a bank loan. ▾

n. Accrued commissions owed to salespeople at year-end.

Transaction	Revenues	Expenses	Income	Assets	Liabilities	Equities
b.						
c.						
d.						
e.						
f.						
g.						
h.						
i.						
j.						
k.						
l.						
m.						

E5-6   Indicate the impact that each of the following errors or omissions would have on a a company's revenues, expenses, income, assets, liabilities and equities. Place the symbols U = Understate, O = Overstate or NE = No effect in the appropriate box. Part (a) has been completed as an example. Be sure to place an answer in every box.

a.   Failed to accrue salaries earned by employees but unpaid at year-end.

Revenues	Expenses	Income	Assets	Liabilities	Equities
NE	U	O	NE	U	O

b.   Understated depreciation expense at year-end.

c.   Overestimated the period used to amortize a patent.

d.   Failed to accrue revenue earned but not yet recorded.

e.   Failed to adjust unearned revenue for services that had been performed.

f.   Recorded rent expense in the prepaid rent account.

g.   Omitted an invoice for new computers purchased and received at year-end.

h.   Omitted an invoice received for electricity at year-end.

i.   Failed to make an adjusting entry for insurance expired.

j.   Overbilled customers for services provided at year-end.

Transaction	Revenues	Expenses	Income	Assets	Liabilities	Equities
b.						
c.						
d.						
e.						
f.						
g.						
h.						
i.						
j.						

Problems* ·

P5-1   AOL's Deferred subscriber acquisition costs prior to 1996

The "Other assets" section of AOL's balance sheets at June 30, 1996 and June 30, 1995 show Deferred subscriber acquisition costs of $314,181,000 and $77,229,000, respectively. The following is excerpted from the "Cash flow from operating activities" section of AOL's Statements of Cash Flows:

	Year ended June 30,		
($ in thousands)	1996	1995	1994
Adjustments to reconcile net income to net cash (used in) provided by operating activities			
Amortization of deferred subscriber acquisition costs	126,072	60,924	17,922
Changes in assets and liabilities			
Deferred subscriber acquisition costs	(363,024)	(111,761)	(37,424)

a.   Show all the activity in the Deferred subscriber acquisition costs from June 30, 1995 to June 30, 1996 in a T-account analogous to the one in Exhibit 5.8.

b.   Extend your description of Deferred subscriber acquisition costs to include all activity from June 30, 1994 to June 30, 1995 in a T-account analogous to the one in Exhibit 5.8. (You need to work backwards to calculate the balance of Deferred subscriber acquisition costs at June 30, 1994.)

c.   Extend your description of Deferred subscriber acquisition costs to include all activity from June 30, 1993 to June 30, 1994 in a T-account analogous to the one in Exhibit 5.8. (You need to work backwards to calculate the balance of Deferred subscriber acquisition costs at June 30, 1993.)

P5-2   Microsoft's unearned revenue

The largest liability listed on Microsoft's June 30, 1998 and 1999 balance sheets is Unearned revenue of $2.9 billion and $4.2 billion, respectively. This amount represents cash received from customers that Microsoft will recognize as revenue in future periods. As of June 30, 1998 and 1999, however, Microsoft has declared these amounts as not yet earned, and therefore not yet recognizable as revenue.

a.   Suppose Microsoft decides that all amounts in Unearned revenue are earned in fiscal 2000. (That is, the balance in the unearned revenue account is zero at the end of the year.) What effect will this decision have on Microsoft's 2000 income statement, its June 30, 2000 balance sheet, and its 2000 cash flow statement?

b.   Suppose Microsoft receives $3.0 billion in fiscal 2000 that it decides is unearned revenue. Also suppose that Microsoft decides that $2.0 billion of the $4.2 billion balance in Unearned revenue at June 30, 1999 has been earned. What effects will these decisions have on Microsoft's June 30, 2000 balance sheet, its income statement for fiscal 2000 and its cash flow statement for fiscal 2000?

*Unless otherwise noted, ignore income taxes in all problems.

P5-3   An *asset impairment* occurs when the future cash flows that are expected to be generated by the asset fall short of its book value. An asset that has been impaired must be written down (i.e., its book value must be reduced) to bring its book value into line with the future benefits it will generate. Suppose an asset that has a book value of $10 million is found to be impaired and must be written down to $8 million. The asset has 10 years of life left, and is depreciated on a straight-line basis.

   a.   What effect will the write down have on the income statement, cash flow statement, and ending balance sheet in the year the write down occurs?

   b.   What effect will the write down have on the income statements, cash flow statements, and ending balance sheets in the years after the write down, but before the asset is retired?

   c.   What effect will the write down have on the income statements, cash flow statements, and ending balance sheets in the years after the asset has been retired?

P5-4   In the United States, research and development (R&D) costs generally are not recognized as assets; that is, they are expensed as incurred. Suppose a corporation incurs $50 million of R&D costs in its first year of operation. These expenditures will generate cash flows over the next 10 years.

   a.   In comparison to capitalization of the costs of R&D, how does the requirement that R&D costs be expensed as incurred affect the income statement, balance sheet, and cash flow statement of the company in the first year of the company's life?

   b.   How does the requirement that R&D costs be expensed as incurred affect the income statement, balance sheet, and cash flow statement of the company in the next 10 years of the company's life? Assume that no further R&D expenditures are made after the first year.

P5-5   When one company buys another, GAAP require that the identifiable assets of the acquired company be written up to their fair market value, as long as the written up total book value of the company does not exceed the price paid for it. In the "new economy" companies are often acquired for their intellectual property, which often includes projects at various stages of development. A common practice in the 1990's was to write off large amounts of the purchase price of acquired companies as being related to "in-process R&D." That is, the acquiring company would take a write off in the amount of this R&D in the year the company was acquired.

   a.   What is the effect of the write off of in-process R&D on the acquiring firm's income statement, ending balance sheet and cash flow statement in the year of the write off?

   b.   What is the effect of the write off of in-process R&D on the acquiring firm's income statement, ending balance sheet and cash flow statement in the year after the write off?

   c.   Why would an acquiring firm want to write off in-process R&D?

   d.   Why would the United States SEC require more than 50 companies to reduce their write offs of in-process R&D?

P5-6   A company planning to restructure its operations that meets certain formal requirements is allowed to accrue expected costs in the year the restructuring plan is adopted. That is, the company is allowed recognize expected restructuring costs by setting up a liability. Suppose restructuring costs are estimated to be $100 million.

   a.   Give the entry required to recognize the expected restructuring costs.

   b.   How would recognition of these costs affect the income statement, ending balance sheet, and cash flow statement in the period in which this recognition occurs?

c.   How would recognition of these costs affect the income statement, ending balance sheet, and cash flow statement in the periods in which this restructuring actually takes place? Assume that actual restructuring costs are exactly as expected.

d.   Why might a company intentionally overestimate restructuring costs?

P5-7   Leslie Fay once had a problem with failure to recognize returns of merchandise from stores. When the merchandise was shipped to distributors, it was recorded as a sale on account. When it was returned, the item was placed back in inventory (no journal entry was made), but the sale and the receivable remained on the books. Further, inventory was taken periodically, so the merchandise was counted as being in ending inventory (i.e., Leslie Fay computed the cost of goods sold by taking the beginning-of-the-year inventory value, adding purchases made throughout the year, and subtracting the value of the ending inventory obtained through a physical count at year-end).

a.   Assume all these problems occurred in one fiscal year. What effects did the failure to account properly for returns have on Leslie Fay's ending balance sheet, income statement and cash flow statement in the year of the fraud?

b.   A common method of committing financial reporting fraud is to continue to recognize sales for a few days after the end of the reporting period. Mechanically, this is accomplished by holding open the sales and cost of goods sold accounts when they should have been closed. What effects does this technique have on the income statement and ending balance sheet in the first year it is done?

c.   What effects does this technique have on the income statement and ending balance sheet in the year *following* the year in which it is done?

P5-8   The New York Times reported on February 3, 2001 that the high tech company Critical Path had suspended two executives and began a investigation into its own financial practices. Critical Path supplies systems that support corporate e-mail, and had recently reported disappointing earnings. The company had blamed its disappointing results in part on its auditors, PricewaterhouseCoopers, who insisted that Critical Path change its accounting for $7 million of licensing fees. The licensing fee entitles the purchaser of the license to the use of the software and to support over several accounting periods. Critical Path had counted the $7 million as Revenue. PricewaterhouseCoopers thought the $7 million was Unearned revenue that should be recognized as revenues over several subsequent periods. Before the disallowed revenues, Critical Path had reported revenues of $52 million.

a.   Relative to Critical Path's original treatment of recognizing the $7 million of revenue immediately, what effect does the change in treatment have on Critical Path's assets?

b.   Relative to Critical Path's original treatment of recognizing the $7 million of revenue immediately, what effect does the change in treatment have on Critical Path's liabilities?

c.   Relative to Critical Path's original treatment of recognizing the $7 million of revenue immediately, what effect does the change in treatment have on Critical Path's equities?

P5-9   **Garden Life Plan (Revenue Recognition)**

The Company is a sales organization that sells pre-need mortuary services. Approximately 25% of each sales contract is paid in cash and the remainder is paid under an installment contract over varying terms which are generally 60 months. The first 30% of each contract is earned and recorded as revenue by the Company. This amount is used to cover the Company's initial "acquisition costs" (i.e., sales commissions and administrative costs) and is not refundable to customers under the terms of the contract. The remaining 70% is collected by the

Company and paid to Garden Life Funeral Plan Trust (Trust), a trust administered by Pacific Century Trust. The Trust assets are invested primarily in available-for-sale securities.

The Company has an agreement with Hosoi Garden Mortuary, Inc. (Hosoi) which gives the Company the exclusive right to solicit pre-need funeral service arrangements for service by Hosoi. The agreement also commits Hosoi to perform the funeral services provided for in the Prepaid Funeral Service Contracts for the Funeral Reserve. The agreement expires in September 2001 but Hosoi's responsibility to service the pre-need arrangements sold prior to such expiration continues indefinitely.

If a contract owner dies before the contract is fully paid, his or her estate must pay the balance of the contract. When a contract owner dies, the Trust pays the mortuary service provider (primarily Hosoi) for the contracted services at prices stipulated in the original contract (70% of the contract price). Such payments are made from Trust principal. The service provider absorbs any difference between the actual costs to perform the contracted services and the amounts received from the Trust under the terms of the contract.

To ensure that funds will be available when the funeral services are performed, the market value of the Trust assets must be equal to or greater than the prospective obligation of the Trust.

TRUST FUND INCOME—Trust assets in excess of the required Trust principal are redeemable by the Company. Realized gains and losses on available-for-sale securities held by the Trust are recognized as Trust fund income or loss in the statement of income. Unrealized gains and losses on available-for-sale securities held by the Trust are included, net of deferred income taxes, in other comprehensive income.

In the audit of GLP's financial statements for its year ended May 31, 1999 the following disagreement on accounting principles and practice and disclosure remains unresolved (Deloitte & Touche's letter, dated February 17, 2000, is attached):

> Revenue recognition—GLP's former auditors takes the position that 30% of each Prepaid Funeral Service Contract, ie. the non-refundable portion, should be deferred until such time as the funeral services have been performed. Previously, GLP recognized the non-refundable portion in the year of sale of the Prepaid Funeral Service Contract.
>
>> Disclosure of contingent liability—GLP's former auditors believe that GLP is contingently liable for any costs in excess of the Funeral Reserve, in Trust, in providing alternate funeral services if Hosoi Garden Mortuary, Inc. (the registrant) is unable to perform its contractual obligation as the principal servicing mortuary.
>>
>> The former auditors believe that GLP should provide a reserve for the excess of current and expected service cost over the Funeral Reserve (in Trust).
>>
>> The management of GLP does not believe that a Funeral Reserve is necessary at this time as there is no indication that Hosoi Garden Mortuary, Inc. will not be able to perform its contractual obligation.

February 17, 2000

Mr. John Farias, Jr.
Garden Life Plan, Ltd.
P.O. Box 1246
Kaneohe, Hawaii 96744

Dear John:

In the conference call on Friday, February 11, a request was made that we summarize our position with regard to Garden Life Plan's revenue recognition policy. For convenience, I have also summarized our position with regard to the deferral of direct incremental selling costs and the consolidation of Garden Life Plan (GLP) with Garden Life Funeral Plan Trust (GLFPT).

Revenue Recognition

We believe it is clear that GLP is primarily responsible for providing the funeral services under the Prepaid Funeral Service Contract. Paragraph 14 under General Covenants in the contract indicates "Seller will secure performance of the specified Funeral Services at no further cost to the Contract Buyer". The contract holder is not a party to the agreement between GLP and Hosoi. We believe the contract holder would look to GLP for performance in the event Hosoi was unable to fulfill its obligations.

Generally Accepted Accounting Principles have long held that revenue is to be recognized when realized, and that realization occurs when the following conditions are met:

The earnings process is complete.

An exchange has taken place.

More recently, the Securities and Exchange Commission issued Staff Accounting Bulletin 101, Revenue Recognition in Financial Statements. The staff believes that revenue generally is realized or realizable and earned when all of the following criteria are met:

Persuasive evidence of an arrangement exists,

delivery has occurred or services have been rendered,

The seller's price to the buyer is fixed or determinable, and

Collectibility is reasonably assured.

We do not believe that services have been rendered until such time as the funeral services have been performed. It is only at that time that GLP has no further obligation to the contract holder. Accordingly, we believe that revenue should only be recognized when the funeral services have taken place.

Deferral of Direct Selling Cost

Because we believe revenues should only be recognized when the funeral services have taken place, we also believe that the direct selling costs incurred in the production of such revenues can be deferred. The costs to be deferred should, however, be directly related to the sale of the Prepaid Funeral Service Contracts and should be incremental to costs that would otherwise be incurred by GLP. In addition, the costs should not be for expenditures that require expense recognition, such as advertising. General and administrative costs should not be deferred. Any deferred selling costs should be recognized as expense at the same time as the related revenue is recognized.

Consolidated Financial Statements for GLP and GLFPT

Although we recognize that GLFPT is set up for the individual contract holders (and required by State law), paragraph 3 of the Prepaid Funeral Service Contract gives GLP the "absolute authority to direct and redirect the investment of all funds held by the Trustee". In addition, GLP is the beneficiary of all earnings on assets in the GLFPT. GLP is also ultimately responsible to the contract holders for the fulfillment of the services under the contract if the GLFPT assets are insufficient to meet that need.

We believe GLFPT is a special purpose entity (SPE) requiring consolidation as discussed in Appendix D-14 of the Emerging Issues Task Force, which states, in part:

"Certain characteristics of those transactions raise questions about whether SPEs should be consolidated (notwithstanding the lack of majority ownership) and. . . . Generally, the SEC staff believes that for nonconsolidation and . . . to be appropriate, the majority owner (or owners) of the SPE must be an independent third party who has made a substantive capital investment in the SPE, has control of the SPE, and has substantive risks and rewards of ownership of the assets of the SPE (including residuals). Conversely, the SEC staff believes that nonconsolidation and . . . (is) not appropriate by the sponsor or transferor when the majority owner of the SPE makes only a nominal capital investment, the activities of the SPE are virtually all on the sponsor's or transferor's behalf, and the substantive risks and rewards of the assets or the debt of the SPE rest directly or indirectly with the sponsor or transferor."

We believe that GLFPT does not qualify for non-consolidation under the criteria in the preceding paragraph and, accordingly, believe consolidation to be appropriate.

Conclusion

Our judgment on the appropriate application of Generally Accepted Accounting Principles as stated herein is based upon the facts provided to us by the Company as summarized above. The, ultimate responsibility for the decision on the appropriate application of Generally Accepted Accounting Principles rests with management of the Company.

We trust this is responsive to your request.

Very truly yours,

/s/ I. Patrick Griggs
I. Patrick Griggs

Required

Deloitte & Touche resigned from future audits and the Board of Garden Life Plans refused to reappoint the firm to perform the audit of the company. Pick either management's or the auditor's position in this revenue recognition dispute and present arguments why that position is the correct one. Be sure your answer includes an analysis of how the income statements, balance sheets and cash flow statements would differ between the two alternatives.

Cases and Projects . . . .

C5-1 Amazon.com

The following pages contain the financial statements for Amazon.com for the fiscal years ended 12/31/99 and 12/31/98. The business is described in its annual report as follows: Amazon.com. Inc., an Internet retailer, was incorporated in July, 1994, and opened its virtual doors on the Web in July, 1995. Amazon.com offers book, music CD, video, DVD, computer game, and other titles on its Web sites.

Amazon.com Inc
Income Statements
For the years ended:

	12/31/99	12/31/98
Net sales	$1,639,839,000	$609,819,000
Cost of sales	1,349,194,000	476,155,000
Gross profit	290,645,000	133,664,000
Operating expenses:		
Marketing and sales	413,150,000	132,654,000
Technology and content	159,722,000	46,424,000
General and administrative	70,144,000	15,618,000
Stock-based compensation	30,618,000	1,889,000
Amortization of goodwill and other intangibles	214,694,000	42,599,000
Merger, acquisition and investment-related costs	8,072,000	3,535,000
Total operating expenses	896,400,000	242,719,000
Loss from operations	(605,755,000)	(109,055,000)
Interest income	45,451,000	14,053,000
Interest expense	(84,566,000)	(26,639,000)
Other income, net	1,671,000	—
Net interest income (expense) and other	(37,444,000)	(12,586,000)
Loss before equity in losses of equity-method investees	(643,199,000)	(121,641,000)
Equity in losses of equity-method investees	(76,769,000)	(2,905,000)
Net loss	($719,968,000)	($124,546,000)
Basic and diluted loss per share	($2,200)	($420)
Shares used in computation of basic and diluted loss per share	326,753,000	296,344,000

Amazon.com Inc
Balance Sheets As of:

	12/31/99	12/31/98
Current assets:		
Cash and cash equivalents	$133,309,000	$71,583,000
Marketable securities	572,879,000	301,862,000
Inventories	220,646,000	29,501,000
Prepaid expenses and other current assets	85,344,000	21,308,000
Total current assets	1,012,178,000	424,254,000
Fixed assets, net	317,613,000	29,791,000
Goodwill, net	534,699,000	174,052,000
Other purchased intangibles, net	195,445,000	4,586,000
Investments in equity-method investees	226,727,000	7,740,000
Other investments	144,735,000	0
Deferred charges and other	40,154,000	8,037,000
Total assets	$2,471,551,000	$648,460,000
LIABILITIES AND STOCKHOLDERS' EQUITY		
Current liabilities:		
Accounts payable	$463,026,000	$113,273,000
Accrued expenses and other current liabilities	126,017,000	34,413,000
Accrued advertising	55,892,000	13,071,000
Deferred revenue	54,790,000	0
Interest payable	24,888,000	10,000
Current portion of long-term debt and other	14,322,000	808,000
Total current liabilities	738,935,000	161,575,000
Long-term debt and other	1,466,338,000	348,140,000

Stockholders' equity:
  Preferred stock, $0.01 par value:
    Authorized shares — 150,000
    Issued and outstanding shares — none

Issued and outstanding shares — none	$0	$0
Common stock, $0.01 par value:		
Authorized shares — 1,500,000		
Issued and outstanding shares — 345,155 and		
318,534 shares at December 31, 1999 and 1998,		
respectively	3,452,000	3,186,000
Additional paid-in capital	1,195,540,000	298,537,000
Note receivable for common stock	(1,171,000)	(1,099,000)
Stock-based compensation	(47,806,000)	(1,625,000)
Accumulated other comprehensive income (loss)	(1,709,000)	1,806,000
Accumulated deficit	(882,028,000)	(162,060,000)
Total stockholders' equity	266,278,000	138,745,000
Total liabilities and stockholders' equity	$2,471,551,000	$648,460,000

Amazon.com Inc
Cash Flow Statements
For the years ended:

	12/31/99	12/31/98
OPERATING ACTIVITIES:		
Net loss	($719,968,000)	($124,546,000)
Adjustments to reconcile net loss to net cash provided (used) in operating activities:		
Depreciation and amortization of fixed assets	36,806,000	9,421,000
Amortization of deferred stock-based compensation	30,618,000	2,386,000
Equity in losses of equity-method investees	76,769,000	2,905,000
Amortization of goodwill and other intangibles	214,694,000	42,599,000
Non-cash merger, acquisition, and investment related costs	8,072,000	1,561,000
Non-cash revenue for advertising and promotional services	(5,837,000)	0
Loss on sale of marketable securities	8,688,000	271,000
Non-cash interest expense	29,171,000	23,970,000
Net cash used in operating activities before changes in operating assets and liabilities	($320,987,000)	($41,433,000)
Changes in operating assets and liabilities, net of effects from acquisitions:		
Inventories	(172,069,000)	(20,513,000)
Prepaid expenses and other current assets	(60,628,000)	(16,758,000)
Accounts payable	330,166,000	78,674,000
Accrued expenses and other current liabilities	65,121,000	21,615,000
Accrued advertising	42,382,000	9,617,000
Deferred revenue	262,000	0
Interest payable	24,878,000	(167,000)
Net cash provided by changes in operating assets and liabilities, net of effects from acquisitions	230,112,000	72,468,000
Net cash provided (used) in operating activities	($90,875,000)	$31,035,000
INVESTING ACTIVITIES:		
Sales and maturities of marketable securities	2,064,101,000	227,789,000
Purchases of marketable securities	(2,359,398,000)	(504,435,000)
Purchases of fixed assets	(287,055,000)	(28,333,000)
Acquisitions and investments in businesses, net of cash acquired	(369,607,000)	(19,019,000)
Net cash used in investing activities	($951,959,000)	($323,998,000)

FINANCING ACTIVITIES:

Proceeds from issuance of capital stock and exercise of stock options	64,469,000	14,366,000
Proceeds from long-term debt	1,263,639,000	325,987,000
Repayment of long-term debt	(188,886,000)	(78,108,000)
Financing costs	(35,151,000)	(7,783,000)
Net cash provided by financing activities	$1,104,071,000	$254,462,000
Effect of exchange rate changes	$489,000	($35,000)
Net increase (decrease) in cash and cash equivalents	61,726,000	(38,536,000)
Cash and cash equivalents at beginning of period	71,583,000	110,119,000
Cash and cash equivalents at end of period	133,309,000	71,583,000
Supplemental Cash Flow Information:		
Fixed assets acquired under capital leases	$25,850,000	—
Fixed assets acquired under financing agreements	$5,608,000	—
Stock issued in connection with business acquisitions	$774,409,000	$217,241,000
Equity securities of other companies received for non-cash revenue for advertising and promotional services	$54,402,000	—
Cash paid for interest, net of amounts capitalized	$59,688,000	$26,629,000

Required

a. Show the changes in the accounting equation from 1998 to 1999 (i.e., justify that the change in total assets equals the change in total liabilities plus the change in equity).

b. What specific account on Amazon.com's balance sheet reflects the net loss of $719,968.000? Explain the change in the account in the balance sheet. Would the T-account have a debit or credit balance? Explain.

c. Generally, we would expect assets to decrease when a company incurs a loss of $719,968,000. Amazon.com's assets increased by $1,823,091,000. Give three possible explanations for this increase using information found in the financial statements.

d. Using Amazon.com's financial statements, provide an account analysis of the interest payable account. Include the beginning balance, ending balance and all changes to the account. Assume that all interest is accrued before it is paid. Label each item.

e. Provide a plausible journal entry for the increases and decreases in the interest payable account.

f. Give an example of something that would be included in the Prepaid expenses account. Why is this account listed as an asset?

g. Why are depreciation and amortization of fixed assets added back to the net loss in the statement of cash flows?

h. Amazon.com's balance sheet has a fiscal year that corresponds with the calendar year. Most retailers fiscal years end in January or February. Why do most retailers end their fiscal years in January or February? What do you think would change in Amazon.com's financial statements if the company's fiscal year ended in February rather than December? How might this affect an investor's opinion of the company?

i. Give examples of items that might be included in the Deferred revenue account for Amazon.com. Why is this account classified as a liability?

j. Assume the marketable securities that were sold had an accounting book value of $1,000,000,000. What was their fair market value when they were sold?

k. Why was the loss on sale of marketable securities added back to the net loss in the statement of cash flows?

l.   What does the account gross profit represent? Did Amazon.com make more or less money on each sale in 1999 compared to 1998?

m. Give three examples of items that might be included in the accrued expenses and other current liabilities account.

n.   Analyze the inventory account to determine the total purchases of inventory by Amazon.com during 1999.

C5-2 Lucent Technologies

Excerpts from Lucent Technologies 2000 income statement and balance sheet for the year ended September 30, 2000 include the following items:

Revenues:	$33,813,000,000
Costs	19,539,000,000
Gross margin	14,274,000,000
Operating expenses	11,289,000,000
Net income	1,219,000,000
Assets:	$48,792,000,000
Liabilities	$22,620,000,000
Shareowners' Equity	$26,172,000,000

On December 21, 2000, the company announced that it would have to restate the results of operations for the fiscal 2000 financial statements. Included in this restatement was a decrease in revenues of $679 million. Among the adjustments were the following:

$199 million for credits or one time discounts offered to customers

$28 million for partial shipment of equipment

$452 million for sales on shipments to distributors on goods not sold to end customers

In addition, the company announced a "restructuring charge" for the first quarter of fiscal 2001 that could reach as high as $1.6 billion.

Required

a.   Briefly explain why the items listed previously should not have been included in Lucent's revenues based on Generally Accepted Accounting Principles.

b.   What balance sheet accounts would be affected by the adjustment in Lucent's revenues? Be specific. Provide the names of the accounts and whether they would increase or decrease.

c.   Would any other income statement accounts be affected by this revenue adjustment?

d.   Explain how the "restructuring charge" will affect Lucent's 2001 income statement, balance sheet, and statement of cash flows. The company uses the indirect method for the statement of cash flows.

e.   Lucent's accounting for revenue has been described by some as "aggressive." Explain.

f.   What effect would these announcements have had on Lucent's stock?

C5-3 Explore the Web

In our study of accounting, we have encountered the concept of unearned or "deferred" revenue. To further understand unearned revenue, obtain the most recent 10-K from the SEC's EDGAR Web site of three companies in different industries that report unearned revenue in their financial statements. Print out the income statement, balance sheet and statement of cash flows and accompanying footnotes from these companies. (Remember that the account may not be called unearned revenue; it has many names). One of those companies should be Microsoft.

Required

Answer the following questions about the three companies:

a.   What industry is the company in?

b.   What account name does the company use to describe unearned revenue?

c.   What types of transactions would result in unearned revenue for that company?

d.   How does unearned revenue affect the statement of cash flows?

e.   Are the dollar amounts of unearned revenue in the statement of cash flows and the balance sheet the same? Explain.

f.   Determine whether the individual company's financial statement footnotes, particularly "summary of significant accounting policies," describe the accounting method used for unearned revenue.

g.   Have there been any significant changes in the unearned revenue account in recent years? If so, to what would you attribute the change? Would you view this change as a positive or negative event for the company?

h.   Is there any correlation between the change in unearned revenue and the change in revenue in the company's income statement?

i.   Give several examples of companies that would have little or no unearned revenue. Explain why.

j.   Microsoft's footnotes describe a change in the company's accounting for unearned revenue. Describe how that change affected Microsoft's financial statements.

C5-4   Lands' End Special Charges and Subsequent Reversal

Lands' End describes its business in its 10K as follows:

> Item 1. Business
>
> Lands' End, Inc., is a leading direct marketer of traditionally styled, casual clothing for men, women and children, accessories, domestics, shoes and soft luggage. The company strives to provide products of exceptional quality at prices representing honest value, enhanced by a commitment to excellence in customer service and an unconditional guarantee. The company offers its products through multiple distribution channels consisting of regular mailings of its monthly primary catalogs, prospecting catalogs, specialty catalogs as well as through the Internet, its international businesses, and its inlet and outlet retail stores.

Like many businesses, Lands' End tries a number of strategies to leverage its expertise and know-how to further benefit its shareholders. Some of these strategies do not work out and have to be abandoned.

In its 1999 fiscal year, Lands' End abandoned two of its efforts, and recorded a "special charge" as a result. (That is, it debited a temporary account and credited a liability account.) From Note 9 to its financial statements:

> During fiscal year 1999, in connection with changes in executive management, the company announced a Plan designed to reduce administrative and operational costs stemming from duplicative responsibilities and certain non-profitable operations. This Plan included the reduction of staff positions, the closing of three outlet stores, the liquidation of the Willis & Geiger operations and the termination of a licensing agreement with MontBell Co. Ltd. A non-recurring charge of $12.6 million was recorded in fiscal 1999 related to these matters.

The following are excerpts from Lands' End's income statements, balance sheets and cash flow statements.

Consolidated Statement of Operations
Lands' End, Inc. & Subsidiaries
(In thousands)

| | For the period ended | | |
	January 28, 2000	January 29, 1999	January 30, 1988
Net sales	$1,319,823	$1,371,375	$1,263,629
Cost of sales	727,291	754,661	675,138
Gross profit	592,532	616,714	588,491
Selling, general and administrative expenses	515,375	544,446	489,923
Non-recurring charge (credit)	(1,774)	12,600	—
Income from operations	78,931	59,668	98,568
Other income (expense):			
Interest expense	(1,890)	(7,734)	(1,995)
Interest income	882	16	1,725
Gain on sale of subsidiary	—	—	7,805
Other	(1,679)	(2,450)	(4,278)
Total other income (expense), net	(2,687)	(10,168)	3,257
Income before income taxes	76,244	49,500	101,825
Income tax provision	28,210	18,315	37,675
Net income	$48,034	$31,185	$64,150

Consolidated Balance Sheets (Liabilities and Equities Only)
Lands' End, Inc. & Subsidiaries
(In thousands)

	January 28, 2000	January 29, 1999
Liabilities and shareholders' investment		
Current liabilities:		
Lines of credit	$11,724	$38,942
Accounts payable	74,510	87,922
Reserve for returns	7,869	7,193
Accrued liabilities	43,754	54,392
Accrued profit sharing	2,760	2,256
Income taxes payable	10,255	14,578
Total current liabilities	150,872	205,283
Deferred income taxes	9,117	8,133
Shareholders' investment:		
Common stock, 40,221 shares issued	402	402
Donated capital	8,400	8,400
Additional paid-in capital	29,709	26,994
Deferred compensation	(236)	(394)
Accumulated other comprehensive income	2,675	2,003
Retained earnings	454,430	406,396
Treasury stock, 10,071 and 10,317 shares at cost, respectively	(199,173)	(201,298)
Total shareholders' investment	296,207	242,503
Total liabilities and shareholders' investment	$456,196	$455,919

Consolidated Statements of Cash Flows
(Operating Activities Only)
Lands' End, Inc. & Subsidiaries
(In thousands)

	For the period ended		
	Jan. 28, 2000	Jan. 29, 1999	Jan. 30, 1988
Cash flows from (used for) operating activities:			
Net income	$48,034	$31,185	$64,150

Adjustments to reconcile net income to
   net cash flows from operating
   activities—			

Non-recurring charge (credit)	(1,774)	12,600	—
Depreciation and amortization	20,715	18,731	15,127
Deferred compensation expense	158	653	323
Deferred income taxes	8,270	(5,948)	(1,158)
Pre-tax gain on sale of subsidiary	—	—	(7,805)
Loss on disposal of fixed assets	926	586	1,127

Changes in assets and liabilities
    excluding the effects of
    divestitures:			

Receivables, net	3,330	(5,640)	(7,019)
Inventory	57,493	21,468	(104,545)
Prepaid advertising	4,785	(2,844)	(7,447)
Other prepaid expenses	1,773	(2,504)	(1,366)
Accounts payable	(13,412)	4,179	11,616
Reserve for returns	676	1,065	944
Accrued liabilities	(7,664)	6,993	8,755
Accrued profit sharing	504	(2,030)	1,349
Income taxes payable	(4,323)	(5,899)	(1,047)
Other	3,387	1,665	64
Net cash flows from (used for) operating activities	122,878	74,260	(26,932)

Additional excerpts from notes to Lands' End financial statements:

Below is a summary of related costs for the periods ended January 28, 2000:

(In thousands)

	Balance 1/29/99	Cost Incurred	Charges Reversed	Balance 1/28/00
Severance costs	$6,700	$(5,693)	$0	$1,007
Asset impairments	3,199	(2,057)	(1,111)	31
Facility exit costs and other	2,590	(1,820)	(663)	107
Total	$12,489	$(9,570)	$(1,774)	$1,145

For the year ended January 28, 2000, the company executed the Plan and incurred costs totaling $9.6 million. In addition, there was a reversal of $1.8 million of the reserves recorded in fiscal 1999. Those included $0.7 million for better than expected lease termination settlements related to fiscal 2000 store closings, and $1.1 million for better than anticipated sell-through of Willis & Geiger inventory liquidations. . . . The balance of $1.1 million, predominantly severance, will be paid in fiscal 2001.

Required

a.   What temporary account did Lands' End debit in fiscal 1999 to record the costs discussed in Note 9 to its financial statements?

b.   What is most likely the liability account that Lands' End credited in fiscal 1999 to record the costs discussed in Note 9 to its financial statements?

c.   What was the effect of the special charge on **1999** income from operations?

d.   What amounts related to the special charges appear on Lands' End's 1999 statement of cash flows? Why does this amount appear on the cash flow statement?

e.   How much cash did Lands' End spend in 1999 on the severance costs, asset impairments, and facility exit costs detailed in the table from Note 9? (Hint: You can't get this from the cash flow statement. Instead, analyze the liability amounts that were established when the Plan mentioned in Note 9 was adopted.)

f.   What was the effect of the reversal of the special charge on 2000 income from operations?

g.   How much cash did Lands' End spend in 2000 on the severance costs, asset impairments, and facility exit costs detailed in the table from Note 9? (Hint: You can't get this from the cash flow statement. Instead, analyze the liability amounts that were established when the Plan mentioned in Note 9 was adopted.)

h.   What amounts related to the reversal of the special charges appear on Lands' End's 2000 statement of cash flows? Why does this amount appear on the cash flow statement?

C5-5   The Med-Design Corporation and Subsidiaries.

Refer to C4-3 on page 52.

Required

Answer the following questions that relate to the Med-Design annual report excerpts. **Explain and justify all answers.**

a.   Give an example of what might be included in the "accrued expenses" account on Med-Design's 1998 balance sheet.

b.   Give an example of what might be included in the "prepaid expenses and other current assets" account on Med-Design's 1998 balance sheet.

c.   How much of the principal amount of long-term debt and capital lease obligations will Med-Design have to pay during *1999*?

d.   Explain the change (list all of the major transactions which account for the change) in the balance of the "short-term borrowings" account from December 31, 1997 to December 31, 1998.

e.   What is the amount of the transfer from "long-term debt and capital lease obligations" to "Current maturities of long-term debt and capital" during 1998?

f.   Explain the change (list all of the major transactions which account for the change) in the balance of the "long-term debt and capital lease obligations" account from December 31, 1997 to December 31, 1998.

g.   Give journal entries that explain the change in the "available-for-sale-securities" account from the beginning to the end of 1998.

Chapter six

Economic Concepts: Behind the Accounting Numbers

Questions

1. What is the purpose of accounting adjustments?
2. What two factors give rise to the need to make adjustments?
3. Give three examples of adjustments.
4. Discuss the two approaches to framing the making of adjustments. Give an example of each.
5. A company depreciates an asset over a useful life of five years. Is this an allocation adjustment or a "plug" adjustment?
6. What do we mean by the "balance sheet approach" of accounting?
7. What two properties of cash flow streams affect their value?
8. What is interest?
9. What is compound interest?
10. What is a future value?
11. What is a present value?
12. What role do present values play in accounting?
13. What is an expected value?
14. Can expected value and present value be combined? Why would we want to do this? Explain your answer.
15. What role does expected value play in accounting?
16. What do we mean by the normal economic earnings of an asset?
17. Explain the following statement: Normal economic earnings are always positive.
18. What do we mean by the abnormal economic earnings of an asset?
19. Explain the following statement: Abnormal economic earnings can be either positive or negative.

Exercises

E6-1 If you deposited $100 in the bank at 3% simple annual interest on January 1, 2002, how much would you have in the account on December 31, 2005 if you made no withdrawals?

E6-2 If you deposited $100 in the bank at 3% simple annual interest on *each* January 1 from January 1, 2002 through January 1, 2005, how much would you have in the account on December 31, 2005 if you made no withdrawals?

E6-3 If you deposited $100 in the bank at 3% simple annual interest on January 1, 2002, how much would you have in the account on December 31, 2005 if you withdrew $3 on each December 31 from December 31, 2002 through December 31, 2005? (Assume the December 31, 2005 withdrawal was made.)

E6-4 If you deposited $100 in the bank at 3% simple annual interest on January 1, 2002, how much would you have in the account on December 31, 2005 if you withdrew $20 on each December 31 from December 31, 2002 through December 31, 2005? (Assume the December 31, 2005 withdrawal was made.)

E6-5 If you deposited $100 in the bank on January 1, 2002, and it accumulated to $105.50 on December 31, 2002, what annual interest rate did you earn on the account?

E6-6 If you deposited $100 in the bank on January 1, 2002, and it accumulated to $112.55 on December 31, 2003, what annual interest rate did you earn on the account?

E6-7 If you borrowed $100 at 4% annual interest on January 1, 2002, how much would you have to repay at December 31, 2006?

E6-8 If you borrowed $100 at 4% annual interest on January 1, 2002 and if you paid your creditor $4 on each December 31 until your loan was repaid, how much would you owe on January 1, 2008?

E6-9 If you wanted to withdraw $108 on December 31, 2002, how much would you have to deposit on January 1, 2002 in an account that pays 8% interest? Justify your answer.

E6-10 What is the present value on January 1, 2002 of the opportunity to receive $100 on each December 31 from December 31, 2002 through December 31, 2005? Assume the appropriate interest rate is 5%.

E6-11 What is the present value on January 1, 2002 of the opportunity to receive $100 on December 31, 2002. Assume the interest rate is 6%.

E6-12 A borrower offers to pay you $4 on December 31, 2002 and $104 on December 31, 2003. What is the present value of this offer on January 1, 2002? Assume the interest rate is 4%.

E6-13 Repeat exercise 12 assuming the interest rate is 5%.

E6-14 Repeat exercise 12 assuming the interest rate is 3%.

E6-15 Suppose there is a 50% chance you will receive $1,000 and a 50% chance you will receive $2,000 one year from now. What is the expected amount you expect to receive?

E6-16 Repeat exercise 15 supposing there is a 60% chance you will receive $1,000 and a 40% chance you will receive $2,000.

E6-17 Repeat exercise 15 supposing there is a 40% chance you will receive $1,000 and a 60% chance you will receive $2,000.

E6-18 What is the present value of the expected cash flow from the opportunity in exercise 15? Assume an interest rate of 6%.

E6-19 What is the present value of the expected cash flow from the opportunity in exercise 16? Assume an interest rate of 6%.

E6-20 What is the present value of the expected cash flow from the opportunity in exercise 17? Assume an interest rate of 6%.

E6-21 Suppose you deposit $200 in a bank on January 1 of year-one. Assuming that you can earn 6% interest, compounded annually, how much will you have at the end of year 3?

E6-22   Assume that today you have $500 in your savings account. The account was established three years ago with one lump-sum investment, and there have been no withdrawals. Assuming an interest rate of 5%, what must have been the amount of the original investment?

E6-23   Assume that after initially depositing $700, after two years you have a total $801.43 in your savings account. Assuming that interest is compounded annually, and there were no withdrawals, what must have been the interest rate?

E6-24   Assume that you have a choice between two investments. Investment A initially will be worth $400 and will earn 4% interest, compounded annually for three years. Investment B initially will be worth $380 and will earn 8% interest, compounded annually for three years. Which investment should you choose? Show computations to support your answer.

Problems . . . .

P6-1   On December 31, 2000, Sierra Corporation reported inventory of $800,000, which represented 40,000 units with a historic cost of $20 per unit. During 2001, Sierra purchased 300,000 units at $20 per unit. According to its computerized sales records, Sierra sold 310,000 units during 2001 at $38 per unit.

Required

a.   Determine cost of goods sold and gross profit for 2001 based on the information provided.

b.   Use your answer from a. to determine the balance sheet value of inventory at December 31, 2001.

c.   Assume that Sierra performed a physical count of the inventory that remained on hand at December 31, 2001, which revealed that 28,000 units were on hand. Compute the balance sheet value of the inventory at December 31, 2001.

d.   Use the value of the inventory to record a plug adjustment for cost of goods sold for 2001.

e.   Compare your answers from b. and d. and speculate on the possible causes for the differences noted.

f.   Briefly explain which approach (allocation versus balance sheet) you would recommend for use in preparing GAAP financial statements.

P6-2   Many employers provide vacation benefits to their employees. When vacation benefits vest, an employer is obligated to pay employees for unused vacation days upon termination of employment. The Financial Accounting Standards Board requires that employers accrue a liability for unused vacation days and recognize an expense for vacation benefits in the period the employees earn the benefit, as opposed to the period the vacation is taken.

At December 31, 2001, New Corporation reported accrued vacation pay of $32,000. The liability represented 160 vacation days earned and vested by employees during the first year of operations (2001) that had not yet been taken. During 2002, employees earned a total of 1,000 days and used 970 days, which includes the 160 days accrued in 2001. The average daily pay rate during 2002 was $210.

Required

a.   Compute vacation pay expense for 2002. Use that estimate to determine the balance sheet value of accrued vacation pay at December 31, 2002.

b.   Estimate the amount of the liability for accrued vacation pay at December 31, 2002, based on the total accumulated unused days. Use that estimate to determine the vacation pay expense for 2002.

c.   Compare the results of the two different approaches. Identify the approach you would use in preparing the GAAP financial statements. Explain your rationale.

P6-3   RFS's Present Values

The following table gives the net cash inflows at each point in time associated with nine alternatives. For example, item 1 pays $83.96 immediately. Item 9 pays nothing immediately, $100 one year hence, $50 two years hence, and $200 three years hence.

Item	Time			
	0	1	2	3
1	$83.96			
2				$100.00
3		$50.00	$40.00	$1.42
4		$6.00	$6.00	$106.00
5				$119.10
6		$20.00	$25.00	$30.00
7		$35.00	$30.00	$25.00
8		$55.00	$55.00	$55.00
9		$100.00	$50.00	$200.00

We begin with a set of questions about items 1, 2, and 3. The interest rate applicable to all nine items, unless specified otherwise, is 6% annually. In providing your answers, answer to the nearest $0.01 and expect some minor rounding errors.

a.   What is the present value of item 1?

b.   What is the present value of item 2?

c.   What is the present value of item 3?

d.   Suppose you had item 1 and invested its balance in an investment that pays 6% per period.

Complete the following table:

Initial investment	Value at time 1	Value at time 2	Value at time 3
$83.96			

Suppose a bank is willing to lend money at 6%. That is, the bank is willing to extend credit so long as it earns 6% on its investment. If you owned only item 2, how much could you borrow from the bank at time 0? That is, how much would the bank loan you in exchange for a payment of $100 three years hence?

e.   Suppose you own item 1 and invest it immediately in a bank account that pays 6% annually. Also, suppose you want to create the cash flow pattern of item 3. Complete the following table:

Time 0		Time 1			Time 2			Time 3	
Value	Balance	Withdrawal	Balance Forward	Balance	Withdrawal	Balance Forward	Balance	Withdrawal
$83.96	89.00	50.00	39.00						

In two sentences or less, what do these calculations tell you about the concept of present values?

f.   The cash flows of item 4 are those of a $100 face value bond with a 6% coupon and a maturity of three periods. What is the present value of item 4?

g.   The cash flows of item 5 are those of a zero-coupon bond. What is the present value of item 5?

From what you know from earlier calculations, if you had item 5, could you replicate the cash flows of item 4 if you had access to a bank account that pays 6% interest?

h.   What is the present value of item 6?

i.   What is the present value of item 7?

j.   What is the present value of item 8?

k.   Notice that the present value of item 8 is equal to the present value of item 6 plus the present value of item 7. Why is this true?

l.   Complete the following table for item 9:

Time 0	Time 1		Time 2		Time 3
Value	Value before payment	Value after payment	Value before payment	Value after payment	Value before payment

m.   Now suppose the interest rate changes unexpectedly to 8% the instant before time 2. Complete the following table for item 9 (values at time 0 and 1 should be as in l.):

Time 0	Time 1		Time 2		Time 3
Value	Value before payment	Value after payment	Value before payment	Value after payment	Value before payment

P6-4   On January 1, 2001, Murphy Company acquired a patent from an investor at a cost of $120,000. Murphy expects to derive benefits from the patent by licensing it to others over a four-year period. Murphy determined its purchase price by discounting future cash flows at a rate of 6%.

Required

a.   Determine the amount of amortization expense that Murphy will recognize on December 31, 2001 assuming Murphy used an allocation approach to record the adjustment.

b.   Determine the balance sheet value of the patent on December 31, 2001.

P6-5   Refer to P6-4. Assume that, at December 31, 2001, Murphy is evaluating the economic value of the patent. Murphy estimates that cash flows from licensing over the next three years will vary from:

	Low	High
2002	$20,000	$32,000
2003	$25,000	$36,000
2004	$30,000	$40,000

Murphy estimates that there is a 75% probability that the cash flows will be in the high range.

Required

a. Determine the expected value of the future licensing cash flows by year.

b. Determine the economic value of the patent on December 31, 2001 based on the expected future licensing cash flows.

c. Determine the amount of amortization expense for 2002 based on the economic value of the patent.

P6-6   During 2001, Alana Corporation purchased a non-interest-bearing promissory note of a distressed customer of one of its subsidiaries. The note has a face value of $200,000, which is due in three years. Alana projected that there was a 60% chance that the maker would pay the $200,000 on maturity and a 40% chance that it would only pay only $40,000.

Required

a. Computed the expected value of the note at the time of purchase.

b. Compute the purchase price of the note assuming a 12% discount rate.

P6-7   Refer to P6-6. Assume that, one year after the note was acquired, Alana adjusted its probabilities based on information that indicated that the maker of the note had made significant strides that increased the likelihood that it would be able to pay the note at maturity. Alana estimated that the new probabilities were 80% that the note would be paid in full and 20% that only $150,000 would be paid.

Required

a. Compute the new expected value of the note.

b. Compute the new economic value of the note.

c. Determine the amount by which the economic value of the note increased from one year to the next. How much of that increase is normal economic earnings and how much is abnormal economic earnings?

P6-8   On 1/1/2000, A.J. Corporation issues a $10,000 bond paying 6% interest annually for five years.

Required

a. Determine the present value of the bond at an interest rate of 6%.

b. Determine the present value of the bond at an interest rate of 8%.

c. Determine the present value of the bond at an interest rate of 4%.

d. What do your answers in a, b, and c tell you about what investors would be willing to pay for the bond on 1/1/2000?

P6-9   Refer to P6-8.

a. What would be the present value of the bond using an interest rate at 6% on 1/1/2003, two years before its maturity?

b. What would happen to the bond's present value on 1/1/2003 if you discounted the cash flows at 8% instead of 6%?

c. What would happen to the bond's present value on 1/1/2003 if you discounted the cash flows at 4% instead of 6%?

d. What do your answers in a, b, and c tell you about the selling price of bonds prior to their maturity date?

Cases and Projects ....

C6-1   Create a Spreadsheet to Calculate Present Values

Suppose you have an asset that will pay $150 at the end of each of the next five years, and the interest rate is 10%. Create a spreadsheet that will efficiently calculate the present values of the remaining cash flows from the asset at the beginning of each of the next five years. Do not use any built-in present value functions.

C6-2   Create a Spreadsheet to Find an Interest Rate

Suppose you have an asset that will pay $150 at the end of each of the next five years. Create a spreadsheet that will efficiently calculate the interest rate that makes the present value of the asset's cash flows equal to $650. Round your answer to the nearest one-tenth of one percent, and do not use any built-in present value functions.

Chapter seven

Financial Statement Analysis: Connecting Economic Concepts to Accounting Reports

Questions . . . .

1. Give two examples of assets whose book values are very close to their economic values. Justify your answer.
2. Give two examples of liabilities whose book values are very close to their economic values. Justify your answer.
3. At what point in time is the book value of any recognized asset closest to its economic value?
4. Give two examples of assets whose book values are probably different from their known economic values. Justify your answer.
5. Give two examples of liabilities whose book values are probably different from their known economic values. Justify your answer.
6. Give an example of a recognized asset whose economic value is difficult to determine. Justify your answer.
7. Give two examples of assets that have economic values but are not recognized in GAAP balance sheets. Justify your answer.
8. Give an example of a liability that has economic value but is not recognized in U.S. GAAP balance sheets. Justify your answer.
9. Explain why it is more difficult to estimate the economic value of Amazon.com than that of Citicorp.
10. What is a market-to-book ratio?
11. What is an accounting return on equity?
12. What is an economic return on equity?
13. What, if any, is the difference between the economic investment of the owner of a firm and the book value of that owner's equity?
14. Explain why market-to-book ratios are typically greater than one.
15. Which company should have a higher accounting return on equity: one with a high market-to-book ratio or one with a low market-to-book ratio? Justify your answer.

Exercises . . . .

E7-1 XYZ Co. had ten million shares of common stock outstanding, the closing price of which was $15 per share on December 31, 2002. Total common shareholders' equity on the December 31, 2002 balance sheet was $50 million. Calculate the market-to-book ratio for XYZ Co. at December 31, 2002.

E7-2   QRS Co. had five million shares of common stock outstanding, the closing price of which was $7.50 per share on January 31, 2002. QRS Co.'s balance sheet as of January 31, 2002 showed that common stock was the only form of equity, and there was $12.5 million in Common stock and Additional paid-in capital, and Retained earnings of $20 million. These were the only shareholders' equity accounts. Calculate the market-to-book ratio for QRS Co. at January 31, 2002.

E7-3   LMN Co. had 25 million shares of $1 par value common stock outstanding on June 30, 2002, the closing price of which was $4 per share on that date. LMN Co.'s balance sheet as of June 30, 2002 showed that common stock was the only form of equity, and there were only three shareholders' equity accounts: Common stock, Additional paid-in capital, and Retained earnings. The balances in Additional paid-in capital and Retained earnings were $50 million and $25 million, respectively. Calculate the market-to-book ratio for LMN Co. at June 30, 2002.

E7-4   ABC Co. had 10 million shares of $1 par value common stock outstanding on December 31, 2002, the closing price of which was $76 per share on that date. ABC Co.'s balance sheet on December 31, 2002 showed that common stock was the only form of equity, and the shareholders' equity accounts consisted of Common stock and additional paid-in capital of $40 million and Retained earnings (deficit) of ($2 million). Calculate the market-to-book ratio for ABC Co. at December 31, 2002.

E7-5   XYZ Co. had net income in 2003 of $5 million. Its total common shareholders' equity on December 31, 2002 was $50 million. Calculate its accounting return on equity for 2003 using only the beginning amount of common shareholders' equity.

E7-6   Refer to E7-5. Suppose XYZ Co.'s common shares were selling at $15 per share on December 31, 2002 and $16.50 per share on December 31, 2003. XYZ Co. pays no dividends. Calculate its economic return on equity for 2003. Compare the economic return on equity you calculated here with the accounting return on equity you calculated in E7-5.

E7-7   Refer to E7-5. Suppose XYZ Co.'s common shares were selling at $15 per share on December 31, 2002 and $20.00 per share on December 31, 2003. XYZ Co. pays no dividends. Calculate its economic return on equity for 2003. Compare the economic return on equity you calculated here with the accounting return on equity you calculated in E7-5.

E7-8   Refer to E7-5. Suppose XYZ Co.'s common shares were selling at $15 per share on December 31, 2002 and $14.00 per share on December 31, 2003. XYZ Co. pays no dividends. Calculate its economic return on equity for 2003. Compare the economic return on equity you calculated here with the accounting return on equity you calculated in E7-5.

E7-9   A very controversial area of accounting is that of accounting for employee stock options. Many high-tech companies have attracted employees at lower than market salaries by offering options, allowing employees to purchase shares at prices substantially below market value. Although the Internal Revenue Service treats such options as compensation expense for tax purposes when they are exercised, companies are not required to expense the value of such options in their GAAP financial statements. Recently, the Financial Accounting Standards Board has required footnotes in annual reports disclosing the value of such options. In April of 1999, in a research report related to this issue, a research analyst named Andrew Smithers described the impact that expensing stock options would have had on the earnings of publicly held companies. According to Smithers, "If corporations had accounted properly and fully for the costs of options, published profits would have been reduced by a whopping 56% in 1997 and 50% in 1998." At the time of the study, the average S&P stock was selling at 34 times earnings (PE ratio) and 7 times book value. Source: Barron's: April 12, 1999 and February 26, 2001.

Required

If publicly held corporations were required to expense the value of stock options, what would be the likely impact on price-to-earnings ratios and market-to-book values? Explain your answer.

Problems . . . .

P7-1 McDonald's Corporation

According to its 10K, McDonald's Corporation (the Company)

> ... develops, operates, franchises and services a worldwide system of restaurants that prepare, assemble, package and sell a limited menu of value-priced foods. McDonald's operates primarily in the quick-service hamburger restaurant business. Beginning in 1999, the Company also operates other restaurant concepts: Aroma Cafe', Chipotle Mexican Grill and Donatos Pizza.
>
> All restaurants are operated by the Company or, under the terms of franchise arrangements, by franchisees who are independent third parties, or by affiliates operating under joint-venture agreements between the Company and local business people.

Required

a. Complete the accompanying worksheet, which is analogous to the asset parts of Exhibits 7.2 and 7.5.

McDonald's Corporation
Consolidated Balance Sheet
Asset Side Only
December 31, 1999
(In millions)

ASSETS	GAAP	Economic	Difference
Current assets			
Cash and equivalents	$419.5		
Accounts and notes receivable	708.1		
Inventories, at cost, not in excess of market	82.7		
Prepaid expenses and other current assets	362.0		
Total current assets	$1,572.3		
Other assets			
Investments in and advances to affiliates	$1,002.2		
Intangible assets-net	1,261.8		
Miscellaneous	822.4		
Total other assets	$3,086.4		
Property and equipment			
Property and equipment, at cost	$22,450.8		
Accumulated depreciation and amortization	(6,126.3)		
Net property and equipment	16,324.5		
Total assets	$20,983.2	$54,000.0	

b. Provide brief justifications for your entries in the economic value column.

c. Briefly discuss why the unexplained difference between the book value and the market value of McDonald's assets is as large as it is.

P7-2 Websell

Refer to the Websell example in Exhibit 3.7 on page 68. Make a worksheet analogous to Exhibits 7.2 and 7.5. To the best of your ability, fill in the economic values column for all the assets and liabilities.

If Websell were a publicly traded company, what do you think its market-to-book ratio would be? Justify your answer.

P7-3 Zions Bancorp

On December 28, 1999, the following appeared in the Wall Street Journal:

Shares of Zions Bancorp slipped 9.6% in the wake of its announcement that it would restate financial results back through 1996 and postpone a merger. The restated results and the delayed merger are the result of the Securities and Exchange Commission—in a regulatory development with broad potential impact on banks—disallowing Zions' accounting treatment of a series of recent acquisitions. Late Thursday, Zions announced the SEC determined that 12 acquisitions accounted for as "pooling of interests" should have been treated as purchases under the agency's accounting rules. That will require the company to record $500 million in "goodwill," representing the difference between the total paid for the banks, acquired since 1997, and their book value.

Required

a. What impact would the required change likely have had on Zions Bancorp's market-to-book ratio? Explain your answer.

b. Using Figure 7.1 as a guide, in what category would you place the "goodwill" that Zions Bancorp would be required to record as a result of this ruling? Explain.

c. How will this affect Zions Bancorp's assets, income, and cash flow?

d. Why do you think Zions Bancorp's stock fell nearly 10% in one day?

e. Why would banks be opposed to this regulatory development? Explain.

f. Is the Wall Street Journal definition of "goodwill" the correct accounting definition? Explain.

P7-4 CMS Energy Corporation

CMS Energy Corporation is an integrated energy company with businesses in oil and gas exploration and production, electricity and natural gas distribution, and energy marketing and trading. The following note appeared in the company's 2000 annual report:

In 2000, CMS Energy adopted the provisions of the SAB No. 101 summarizing the SEC staff's views on revenue recognition policies based upon existing generally accepted accounting principles. As a result, the oil and gas exploration and production industry's long-standing practice of recording inventories at their net realizable amount at the time of production was viewed as inappropriate. Rather, inventories should be presented at the lower of cost or market. Consequently, in conforming to the interpretations of SAB No. 101, EMS Energy implemented a change in the recording of these oil and gas exploration and production inventories as of January 1, 2000. . . . The cumulative effect of this one-time non-cash accounting change decreased 2000 income by $7 million, or $5 million, net of tax, or $.04 per basic and diluted share of CMS Energy

Common Stock. The pro forma effect on prior years' consolidated net income of retroactively recording inventories as if the new method of accounting had been in effect for all periods is not material.

Required

a. What would be the likely effect of this accounting change on CMS's assets, income, and cash flows? Explain.

b. What would be the likely effect of this accounting change on CMS Energy's market-to-book ratio? Explain.

P7-5 Figure 7.1 identifies differences between economic values and accounting valuations.

Required

Place each of the assets and liabilities listed below into one of the following valuation categories:

A1: Assets and liabilities with valuations very close to their true economic values.

A2: Assets and liabilities with known economic values that are different from the accounting values.

A3: Assets and liabilities for which it is difficult to obtain economic values.

A4: Assets and liabilities that have economic value but are not listed in the balance sheet.

a.	Cash	i.	Deferred federal income taxes
b.	Employee stock options	j.	Residual advertising
c.	Held-to-maturity securities	k.	Accounts receivable
d.	Purchased goodwill	l.	Intellectual property
e.	Internally developed patents	m.	Oil and gas reserves
f.	Available-for-sale securities	n.	Internal goodwill
g.	Buildings	o.	Corporate trademarks
h.	Operating leases		

Cases and Projects . . . .

C7-1 Harrington Financial Group is, according to its 10K,

... a savings and loan holding company incorporated on March 3, 1988 to acquire and hold all of the outstanding common stock of Harrington Bank, FSB (the "Bank"), a federally chartered savings bank with principal offices in Richmond, Indiana and seven full-service branch offices located in Carmel, Fishers, Noblesville and Indianapolis, Indiana, and Mission, Kansas. The Company also opened an additional branch in July of 1999 in Chapel Hill, North Carolina.

The Company is a growing community bank with a focus on the origination and management of mortgage loans and securities. The Bank also operates a commercial loan division for business customers and owns a 51% interest in Harrington Wealth Management Company (HWM), which provides trust, investment management, and custody services for individuals and institutions.

(Harrington, therefore, is a lot like the Harrodsburg example in the chapter.)

Required

a.   Complete the accompanying worksheet that is analogous to Exhibits 7.2 and 7.5.

b.   Provide brief justifications for your entries in the economic value column.

c.   Briefly discuss why the unexplained difference between the book value and the market value is as large (or small) as it is.

Harrington Financial Group Inc.
Consolidated Balance Sheets
June 30, 1999
(Dollars in thousands except share data)

ASSETS	GAAP	Economic	Difference
Cash	$1,414		
Interest-bearing deposits	8,087		
Total cash and cash equivalents	9,501	_____	_____
Securities held for trading—at fair value			
(amortized cost of $188,130 and $289,137)	183,200		
Securities available for sale—at fair value			
(amortized cost of $461 and $924)	502		
Loans receivable (net of allowance for loan			
losses of $868 and $360)	259,674		
Interest receivable, net	2,340		
Premises and equipment, net	6,499		
Federal Home Loan Bank of Indianapolis			
stock—at cost	4,878		
Deferred income taxes, net	596		
Income taxes receivable	569		
Other	3,580		
Assets not recognized by GAAP			
TOTAL ASSETS	$471,339	_____	_____

LIABILITIES AND STOCKHOLDERS' EQUITY

Deposits	$333,245		
Securities sold under agreements to repurchase	60,198		
Federal Home Loan Bank advances	40,000		
Note payable	13,995		
Interest payable on securities sold under			
agreements to repurchase	66		
Other interest payable	1,925		
Advance payments by borrowers for taxes			
and insurance	795		
Accrued expenses payable and other liabilities	1,039		
Liabilities not recognized by GAAP			
Total liabilities	451,263	_____	_____

(Continued)

MINORITY INTEREST	937	
STOCKHOLDERS' EQUITY:		
Preferred Stock ($1 par value) Authorized and unissued—5,000,000 shares		
Common Stock:		
Voting ($.125 par value) Authorized—10,000,000 shares, Issued 3,399,938 shares, Outstanding 3,205,382 and 3,275,886 shares	425	
Additional paid-in capital	16,946	
Treasury stock, 194,556 and 124,052 shares at cost	(2,162)	
Accumulated other comprehensive income (loss), net of deferred tax of $16 and $(1)	25	
Retained earnings	3,905	
Total stockholders' equity	19,139	23,239
TOTAL LIABILITIES AND STOCKHOLDERS' EQUITY	$471,339	

C7-2 Oshkosh B'Gosh

Refer to the Oshkosh B'Gosh's January 2, 1999 balance sheet in Exhibit 2.1 on page 25. On December 31, 1998, the last trading day before January 2, 1999, Oshkosh's Class A common stock closed at $20.1875 per share. Its Class B common stock was not traded, but is convertible into Class A shares on a share-for-share basis. Therefore, consider it as also being worth $20.1875 per share.

Required

a. Calculate the market-to-book ratio for Oshkosh B'Gosh at January 2, 1999.

b. Make a worksheet analogous to Exhibits 7.2 and 7.5. To the best of your ability, fill in the economic values column for all the assets and liabilities.

c. Provide justifications for your entries in the Economic value column.

d. Discuss why the difference between the book value and the economic value is as large (or small) as it is.

C7-3 Coldwater Creek

Refer to the Coldwater Creek February 26, 2000 balance sheet given in Exhibit 16.1 on page 329. The closing price of Coldwater's common stock on February 26, 2000 was $18.125 per share.

Required

a. Calculate the market-to-book ratio for Coldwater Creek at February 26, 2000.

b. Make a worksheet analogous to Exhibits 7.2 and 7.5. To the best of your ability, fill in the economic values column for all the assets and liabilities.

    c.   Provide justifications for your entries in the Economic value column.

    d.   Discuss why the difference between the book value and the economic value is as large (or small) as it is.

C7-4   Internet Research Project

Select two companies in different industries. Log on to Edgar to find their latest financial reports.

Required

    a.   Calculate the market-to-book ratio for each of the two companies as of the most recent balance sheet date. Use the average stock price information for the last quarter of the year provided in the company's annual report to determine each company's market value.

    b.   Make a worksheet analogous to Exhibits 7.2 and 7.5. To the best of your ability, fill in the economic values column for all the assets and liabilities for each of the two companies.

    c.   Provide justifications for your entries in the Economic value column.

    d.   Discuss why the difference between the book value and the economic value is as large (or small) as it is.

    e.   How do the relative market-to-book value ratios of the two companies compare to what you would have expected, using Figure 7.2 as a guide?

Chapter eight

Accounts Receivable

Questions . . . .

1. What is the balance sheet classification of accounts receivable?
2. Explain the difference between gross receivables and net receivables.
3. How is the percentage of gross receivables not expected to be collected computed?
4. What is the income statement classification of bad debt expense?
5. What are the three components of the economic value of accounts receivable?
6. What criteria must be present under Generally Accepted Accounting Principles for an account receivable and revenue to be recognized on a company's books?
7. Explain why GAAP for accounts receivable ignore interest.
8. Identify the type of account and the financial statement where each of the following would be found: bad debt expense, accounts receivable, allowance for doubtful accounts.
9. Explain the meaning of the expression "written-off."
10. Explain how the write-off of an account receivable affects the following: net income, net accounts receivable, total assets, current ratio, gross accounts receivable.
11. Explain the difference in philosophy between the aging method and the percentage of sales method of estimating bad debt expense.
12. Explain why the direct write-off method is not preferred GAAP.
13. When is the direct write-off method allowed under GAAP?
14. Explain why the market-to-book value ratio of accounts receivable is usually less than one.
15. Why does the percentage of sales method result in smoother income statements than the aging method?
16. Why does the aging method result in more accurate balance sheet valuation of accounts receivable than the percentage of sales method?
17. Under what circumstances will market and book values of accounts receivable differ significantly from one?
18. What is factoring?
19. What does factoring without recourse mean?
20. Explain why management may have incentives to overstate expected uncollectible accounts.
21. If a company's accounts receivable turnover is 4.6, how long did it take the company to collect an average account receivable?

Exercises . . . .

E8-1 Alerin Corporation was established on 1/1/2001. During 2001, the company experienced the following:

a. Credit sales: $100,000

b. Collections on credit sales: $60,000

c.   Write-offs of accounts deemed uncollectible: $4,000

d.   Aging analysis of accounts deemed uncollectible at 12/31/2001 shows $8,000 of potentially uncollectible accounts.

Required

a.   Prepare entries for a–d assuming Alerin uses the allowance method (aging approach).

b.   Compute the following at year end:

1.   Net accounts receivable

2.   Bad debt expense

E8-2   Refer to Exercise 8-1. Assume the company estimates bad debts using the percentage of sales approach. At year end, the company estimates that 8 percent of credit sales will become uncollectible.

Required

a.   Repeat requirements for a and b using the percentage of sales approach.

b.   If the direct write-off approach were used, how would your entries be different?

c.   Explain why the direct write-off approach does not usually conform to Generally Accepted Accounting Principles.

E8-3   Tara Co.'s December 31, 2000 allowance for uncollectible accounts was a $12,000 credit balance. During 2001, Tara wrote off $7,000 in receivables. There were no collections of previously written-off accounts. Following is an aging of Tara Co.'s accounts receivable at December 31, 2001:

Days Outstanding	Amount	Estimated % Uncollectible
0–60	$120,000	1%
61–120	90,000	2%
Over 120	120,000	6%
	$330,000	

Required

Use the aging method to calculate the net accounts receivable that would be listed on Tara Co., Inc's December 31, 2001 balance sheet and the bad debt expense that Tara Co. would record for 2001.

E8-4   The notes to McKesson HBOC's financial statements for the year ended March 31, 1999 include the following:

| | | March 31 | |
| Receivables: | 1999 | 1998 | 1997 |
		(in millions)	
Customer accounts	$2,322.0	$1,802.8	$1,477.4
Other	443.2	240.9	195.2
Total	2,765.2	2,043.7	1,672.6
Allowances	(181.5)	(83.7)	(60.4)
Net	$2,583.7	$1,960.0	$1,612.2
Sales:	$30,382.3	$22,419.3	$16,914.3

Required

a. Compute McKesson HBOC's receivables turnover, days receivables outstanding, and the percentage of accounts receivable not expected to be collected for 1998 and 1999.

b. Do McKesson's ratios indicate improved or deteriorating accounts receivable ratios?

E8-5 Erin Corporation had the following balance sheet information on January 16, 2001:

Accounts receivable	$300,000
Allowance for doubtful accounts	(15,282)
Accounts receivable, net	$284,718

On January 16, 2001, the company received notification from Alissa Corporation that it filed for bankruptcy. The controller of Erin Corporation decided to write off Alissa's account, which totaled $4,250.

Required

a. Prepare the entry necessary to write off Alissa Corporation's account.

b. What will be the net accounts receivable after the write-off?

c. What impact will the write-off have on Erin's 2001 net income?

E8-6 The following data were extracted from May Company's books at December 31, 2001, prior to the preparation of adjusting entries.

	Debit	*Credit*
Accounts receivable	$950,000	
Allowance for doubtful accounts		$3,500
Net credit sales		$6,000,000

Required

Prepare the year-end adjusting entry assuming that:

a. May estimates bad debts expense as 1.5% of net credit sales.

b. May estimates the provision for bad debts as 9% of accounts receivable.

c. Determine the net realizable value of accounts receivable after the adjustments in a and b have been made.

E8-7 Refer to the data in E8-6. Repeat requirements assuming that the allowance for doubtful accounts had a debit balance of $5,000 before adjustment.

Problems . . . .

P8-1 At December 31, 2000, before the adjusting entry for bad debt expense, Rogal Co. had a balance of $384,000 in its accounts receivable account and had a credit balance of $3,800 in the allowance for doubtful accouts account. Sales for 2000 were $1,200,000, all of which were on credit. The company has aged its accounts as follows:

Age in days	Amount	Percent Estimated Uncollectible
0–10	$296,000	1
11–60	42,000	5
61–180	34,000	15
Over 180	12,000	30
TOTAL	$384,000	

a. Using the aging method:

1. Determine Rogal's bad debt expense for 2000.

2. Assume that on January 1, 2001, $10,000 of specific receivables are identified as uncollectible and are written off. Does this write-off affect 2001's income before taxes?

3. Assume that on January 1, 2001, $10,000 of specific receivables are identified as uncollectible and are written off, and that no collections on accounts or sales on account were made on that day. Compute the balance of net accounts receivable on January 1, 2001 (after the write-off) and compare it to the balance of net accounts receivable as of December 31, 2000 (immediately before the write-off).

b. Suppose that instead of aging, Rogal uses the percent of sales method to estimate bad debt expense. Suppose Rogal estimates that one-half of one percent of credit sales are uncollectible. Determine the December 31, 2000 balance in the Allowance for doubtful accounts account.

c. Briefly explain why accountants don't just wait until specific accounts become uncollectible before recognizing any bad debt expense.

P8-2   On January 1, 2001, Boyce Corporation had a debit balance of $2,000,000 in accounts receivable and a credit balance of $140,000 in the allowance for doubtful accounts. The following events took place during 2001:

Credit sales	$2,600,000
Collections on credits sales	$2,400,000
Accounts written off as uncollectible	$150,000
Recovery of accounts written off in prior years (not included in above)	$1,200
Percentage of 2001 sales deemed uncollectible	6%

Required

a. Prepare journal entries for all transactions and adjustments to Boyce's books for 2001.

b. What will be the bad debt expense in Boyce's income statement for 2001?

c. What will be the net accounts receivable on Boyce's balance sheet at December 31, 2001?

d. Assume that in 2002, Boyce experiences only a 5% loss on sales made in 2001. How will this fact affect Boyce's 2002 financial statements?

P8-3   Refer to P8-2. Assume that, instead of estimating bad debts at 6% of credit sales, Boyce estimates that uncollectible accounts will be 5% of the balance in accounts receivable at year-end.

Required

Repeat the requirements in a–c from P8-2 under the new assumption.

P8-4   The 10Ks for Sears, Roebuck, and Company for 1998 and 1999 contained the following notes related to delinquent accounts receivable:

1998 10K

Under the Company's proprietary credit system, uncollectible accounts are generally charged off automatically when the customer's past due balance is 8 times the scheduled minimum monthly payment, except that accounts may be charged off sooner in the event of customer bankruptcy....

1999 10K

In the 4th Quarter of 1998, the Company converted 12% of its managed portfolio of credit card receivables to a new credit processing system. Under the new system, the uncollectible accounts will be charged off automatically when the customer fails to make a payment in each of the last 8 billing cycles.... The remaining 88% of accounts ...will be converted to the new system in 1999.

Under the old system, Sears accounts usually would be written off about 270 days after the first payment was missed. The new system will result in a charge when accounts are 240 days overdue.

Required

a.   Analyze the effect that the new system would likely have on Sears 1998 and 1999 financial statements.

b.   Sear's management is responsible for any estimates related to the change in the policy of accounting for uncollectible accounts. What would be the impact of overestimating the potential uncollectible accounts on 1998, 1999, and subsequent financial statements?

P8-5   Sears, Roebuck, and Co.'s 1998 annual report includes the following:

(in millions)

Cash flows from operating activities	1998	1997	1996
Net income	$1,048	$1,188	$1,271
Adjustments to reconcile net income to net cash provided by (used in) operating activities:			
Provision for uncollectible accounts	1,287	1,532	971

Required

a.   Provide the adjusting entry made by Sears to recognize uncollectible accounts in 1998.

b.   Sears wrote off $2.04 billion in bad accounts in 1998. Prepare the journal entry to write off the uncollectible accounts.

c.   Indicate the impact on Sear's income from the entries provided in a and b.

d.   Explain why the provision for uncollectible accounts is added back to net income to determine Sear's cash provided by operating activities.

P8-6   The balance sheet of Arnold Corporation reported the following at 12/31/2000:

Accounts receivable	$235,000,000
Allowance for doubtful accounts	23,000,000
Net accounts receivable	$212,000,000

Arnold has an accounts receivable turnover of 4.05.
Assume that the appropriate discount rate is 12%.

Required

a. Compute the economic value of Arnold's accounts receivable.

b. Explain why Generally Accepted Accounting Principles ignore interest in accounting for accounts receivable.

c. Compute the market-to-book value ratio for Arnold's accounts receivables.

d. What potential problems exist for financial analysts because of the differences between book and economic values of accounts receivables?

Cases and Projects . . . .

C8-1 The following appeared in the Wall Street Journal in January of 1997, related to Cascade Communication's fourth quarter 1996 results:

> On the surface, the fourth quarter results should delight any investor: Sales were up 139 percent from a year ago . . . and profits rose 157 percent to $23.4 million, or 24 cents a share. Analysts had expected Cascade to earn about 23 cents a share. . . . Some analysts were particularly alarmed that Cascade's "days sales outstanding," a measure of accounts receivable, rose to 70 at the end of the year from 47 at the end of September. . . .

Cascade's stock fell 23⅛ points to 41, wiping out $2.3 billion of the company's market value in a single day. Cascade is a provider of frame-relay switches and other switch products that help manage the flow of information across computer networks.

a. Explain how the days sales outstanding for Cascade would have been computed.

b. What concerns do you think analysts had that would result in such a loss in stock value, in spite of the company beating earnings expectations?

C8-2 Mentor Corporation
(excerpted from 10K, filed 6/28/2000)

Mentor Corporation was incorporated in April 1969. The Company develops, manufactures and markets a broad range of products for the medical specialties of plastic and general surgery and urology. The Company's products are sold to hospitals, physicians and through various health care dealers, wholesalers, and retail outlets.

The Company grants credit terms in the normal course of business to its customers, primarily hospitals, doctors and distributors. As part of its ongoing control procedures, the Company monitors the credit worthiness of its customers. Bad debts have been minimal. The Company does not normally require collateral or other security to support credit sales. No customer accounted for more than 10% of the Company's revenues or accounts receivable balance for all periods presented.

Revenue Recognition: Sales and related cost of sales are recognized primarily upon the shipment of products. The Company allows credit for products returned within its policy terms. Such returns are estimated and an allowance provided at the time of sale. The Company provides a warranty on certain of its implants and capital equipment products against defects in workmanship and material. Estimated warranty costs are provided at the time of sale and periodically adjusted to reflect actual experience.

Consolidated statements of financial position, income, and cash flows are shown on pages 100–102. Schedule II, valuation and qualifying accounts and reserves, is shown on page 103.

Required

a. Prepare journal entries for 1999 and 2000 to record the following:

    a.   Bad debt expense

    b.   Write-off of uncollectible accounts

b.   Compute the ratio of *bad debt expense* to *net sales revenue* for 1998, 1999 and 2000. Also compute the ratio of the *allowance for doubtful accounts* balance to the *gross accounts receivable* balance for each of the three years (gross accounts receivable were $33,274 at the end of 1998). What do these ratios tell you about the method used by Mentor to account for bad debts (i.e., did they likely use percentage-of-sales or age accounts to compute bad debt expense)?

c.   Compute the receivable turnover for 1999 and 2000. Use net sales in the numerator and the average balance of net receivables in the denominator. How many days worth of receivables are on average outstanding? Would it be more days if a significant amount of the sales were cash sales?

d.   Suppose Mentor's cost of capital is 10%. What is the economic value to mentor of doubling its receivable turns?

e.   What do you think the accrued sales returns and allowances account alluded to in Schedule II represents? What is your best estimate of the gross amount of sales made during fiscal year 2000?

f.   How did the write-off of specific accounts receivable that were deemed uncollectible in fiscal 2000 affect cash flow in 2000?

g.   Approximately how much cash was collected in fiscal 2000 from customers?

Mentor Corporation
Consolidated Statements of Financial Position
(in thousands)

	March 31,	
	2000	1999
Assets		
Current assets:		
Cash and cash equivalents	$ 24,313	$ 19,533
Marketable securities	52,563	2,088
Accounts receivable, net of allowance for doubtful		
accounts of $2,976 in 2000 and $2,072 in 1999	45,310	37,431
Inventories	34,441	30,552
Deferred income taxes	5,739	7,919
Net assets of discontinued operations		39,899
Prepaid expenses and other	6,096	4,340
Total current assets	168,462	141,762
Property and equipment, net	36,522	34,995
Intangibles, net	4,008	2,342
Goodwill, net	4,394	4,885
Long-term marketable securities and investments	12,848	8,356
Other assets	4,472	3,671
	$230,706	$196,011

(Continued)

Liabilities and shareholders' equity
Current liabilities:

Accounts payable and accrued liabilities	$ 39,845	$ 26,848
Income taxes payable	3,868	3,770
Dividends payable	608	612
Short-term bank borrowings		4,000
Total current liabilities	44,321	35,230
Deferred income taxes	2,743	2,163

Commitments and contingencies
Shareholders' equity:
Common Stock, $.10 par value:
Authorized-50,000,000 shares; Issued and
outstanding—24,208,834 shares in 2000;

24,548,537 shares in 1999;	2,421	2,455
Capital in excess of par value	9,876	21,502
Accumulated other comprehensive income (loss)	2,323	(261)
Retained earnings	169,022	134,922
	183,642	158,618
	$230,706	$196,011

Mentor Corporation
Consolidated Statements of Income
(in thousands, except per share data)
Year Ended March 31,

	2000	1999	1998
Net sales	$247,344	$202,783	$180,267
Costs and expenses:			
Cost of sales	92,657	76,174	59,122
Selling, general and administrative	98,555	81,648	69,180
Research and development	16,701	14,820	15,179
	207,913	172,642	143,481
Operating income from continuing operations	39,431	30,141	36,786
Interest expense	(34)	(272)	(27)
Interest income	2,982	926	1,338
Other income, net	10	93	307
Income from continuing operations before income taxes	42,389	30,888	38,404
Income taxes	13,563	10,447	13,575
Income from continuing operations	28,826	20,441	24,829
Income (loss) from discontinued operations, net of taxes	7,713	(6,479)	(932)
Net income	$ 36,539	$ 13,962	$ 23,897
Basic earnings (loss) per share:			
Continuing operations	$ 1.18	$ 0.83	$ 1.00
Discontinued operations	.32	(0.26)	(0.04)
Basic earnings per share	$ 1.50	$ 0.57	$ 0.96
Diluted earnings (loss) per share:			
Continuing operations	$ 1.16	$ 0.80	$ 0.94
Discontinued operations	.30	(0.25)	(0.03)
Diluted earnings per share	$ 1.46	$ 0.55	$ 0.91

See notes to consolidated financial statements.

Mentor Corporation
Consolidated Statements of Cash Flows
(in thousands)

	Year Ended March 31,		
	2000	1999	1998
Cash From Operating Activities:			
Income from continuing operations	$ 28,826	$ 20,441	$ 24,829
Adjustments to derive cash flows from continuing operating activities:			
Depreciation	7,760	7,537	6,187
Amortization	973	974	1,026
Deferred income taxes	529	(1,165)	216
Loss on sale of assets	401	107	261
Gains on long-term marketable securities and investments write-downs, net	(134)		
Changes in operating assets and liabilities:			
Accounts receivable	(7,879)	(5,764)	(1,066)
Inventories and other current assets	(5,645)	(1,522)	(3,681)
Accounts payable and accrued liabilities	11,631	1,918	2,088
Income taxes payable	(4,994)	(1,422)	2,952
Net cash provided by continuing operating activities	31,468	21,104	32,812
Net cash provided by (used for) discontinued operating activities	(8,557)	1,720	(4,832)
Net cash provided by operating activities	22,911	22,824	27,980
Cash From Investing Activities:			
Purchases of property and equipment	(9,195)	(10,850)	(11,081)
Purchases of intangibles and goodwill	(2,240)	(2,866)	(612)
Purchases of marketable securities	(50,715)		(9,073)
Sales of marketable securities	3,757	9,519	9,213
Investment in manufacturing partners			(7,006)
Other, net	(1,028)	(2,053)	(1,037)
Net cash used for continuing investing activities	(59,421)	(6,250)	(19,596)
Net cash provided by (used for) discontinued investing activities	59,392	(1,423)	(5,927)
Net cash used for investing activities	(29)	(7,673)	(25,523)
Cash From Financing Activities:			
Repurchase of common stock	(19,402)	(20,452)	(4,081)
Proceeds from exercise of stock options	7,742	6,718	4,726
Dividends paid	(2,442)	(2,460)	(2,489)
Borrowings under line of credit agreement		6,900	
Repayments under line of credit agreement	(4,000)	(2,900)	
Reduction in long-term debt		(50)	(8)
Net cash used for financing activities	(18,102)	(12,244)	(1,852)
Increase in cash and equivalents	4,780	2,907	605
Cash and cash equivalents at beginning of year	19,533	16,626	16,021
Cash and cash equivalents at end of year	$ 24,313	$ 19,533	$ 16,626

See notes to consolidated financial statements.

Mentor Corporation and Subsidiaries
Schedule II
Valuation and Qualifying Accounts and Reserves
(In thousands)

COL. A	COL. B	COL. C		COL. D	COL. E
		Additions			
Description	*Balance at Beginning of Period*	*Charged to Costs and Expenses*	*Charged to Other Accounts*	*Deductions*	*Balance at End of Period*
Year Ended March 31, 2000					
Deducted from asset accounts:					
Allowance for doubtful accounts	$2,072	$1,888		$ 984	$ 2,976
Liability Reserves:					
Warranty and related reserves	$4,248	$6,515	$ —	$4,200	$ 6,563
Accrued sales returns and allowances	5,126	1,275			6,401
	$9,374	$7,790	$ —	$4,200	$12,964
Year Ended March 31, 1999					
Deducted from asset accounts:					
Allowance for doubtful accounts	$1,606	$ 960	$ —	$ 494	$ 2,072
Liability Reserves:					
Warranty and related reserves	$3,580	$3,825	$ —	$3,157	$ 4,248
Accrued sales returns and allowances	5,503			377	5,126
	$9,083	$3,825	$ —	$3,534	$ 9,374
Year Ended March 31, 1998					
Deducted from asset accounts:					
Allowance for doubtful accounts	$1,497	$ 933	$ —	$ 824	$ 1,606
Liability Reserves:					
Warranty and related reserves	$3,400	$2,385	$ —	$2,205	$ 3,580
Accrued sales returns and allowances	5,398	105			5,503
	$8,798	$2,490	$ —	$2,205	$ 9,083

C8-3 Pete is examining the credit and collection policies of three identical firms. The three firms extend credit to customers by making sales on account. At the time of sale, it is not known whether any particular customer will pay his or her debt. DIRECT Company uses the direct write-off method of accounting for bad debts. %SALES Company sets up an allowance account as a percentage of sales, and AGING Company uses the aging method.

For simplicity, we suppose all three firms make a total of $100 in sales at Time 0. No further sales are made. All ultimately experience the same collections. Collections from customers will take one of four possible routes, as given in the table below:

Possible Collection Paths			
Path	Time 1	Time 2	Time 3
1	80	15	5
2	80	15	0
3	80	10	10
4	80	10	0

Each collection path is equally likely. Therefore, the probability of going down any one path is $1/4$.

Required

a. What are the expected collections for each firm as of Time 0, when the sales are made?

b. Give the journal entries to record the sales and any applicable accounting for bad debts at Time 0 for each of the three firms. For those firms that use an allowance account, assume they set it up at the expected value of uncollectible accounts.

c. Give the journal entries to record bad debt expense and write-offs for each of the three companies for each of the three periods for Path 1. Assume that AGING Co.'s entries are driven by the expected value of collections at the end of the period.

d. Give the journal entries to record bad debt expense and write-offs for each of the three companies for each of the three periods for Path 2. Assume that AGING Co.'s entries are driven by the expected value of collections at the end of the period.

e. Give the journal entries to record bad debt expense and write-offs for each of the three companies for each of the three periods for Path 3. Assume that AGING Co.'s entries are driven by the expected value of collections at the end of the period.

f. Give the journal entries to record bad debt expense and write-offs for each of the three companies for each of the three periods for Path 4. Assume that AGING Co.'s entries are driven by the expected value of collections at the end of the period.

g. Does the difference in the net accounts receivable for the three companies equal the difference in cumulative bad debt expense? Why or why not?

h. Which method of accounting for bad debts seems to give the best estimate of the accounts receivable that are likely to be collected?

i. Which method of accounting for bad debts seems the most like an accrual method. I.e., which method seems to best match expenses and revenues? Is this method different from the method you think gives the best estimates of likely collections? What does this say about the accrual process?

j. Do any of these methods take into account the time value of money?

k. What do you think "economic" accounting for bad debts would look like?

l. Does the allowance for uncollectible accounts become negative for any of the companies? If so, what does this mean?

m. Which method do you think is most informative? Why might the companies choose different methods? Do you think there is information in the fact that a particular company chooses a particular accounting method?

Chapter nine

Inventories

Questions . . . .

1. What factors can cause inventories to earn abnormal positive or negative rates of return?

2. What are the three categories of inventory that a manufacturing firm will hold?

3. Describe three factors that cause stock-out costs.

4. What is the fundamental inventory balance equation?

5. What formula is used to compute cost of goods sold?

6. What is the difference between a periodic inventory system and a perpetual inventory system?

7. Why is a physical count of inventory required if a company is using a perpetual inventory system?

8. What are three commonly used cost flow assumptions allowed by GAAP?

9. What types of companies are likely to use the Specific Item Identification method?

10. Wnat does the lower of cost or market rule state?

11. What is the LIFO conformity rule?

12. If a company is expecting prices to fall and its inventory levels to remain the same or increase, what inventory method might it prefer to use?

13. Give two journal entries that can be made to write down inventory.

14. In periods of rising prices, which inventory cost flow assumption will result in the highest net income? What are you assuming about the level of inventory?

15. In periods of rising prices and constant or increasing inventory levels, which inventory method will result in the highest income taxes?

16. In periods of falling prices, which inventory cost flow assumption will result in the highest inventory valuation on the balance sheet?

17. What effect does the liquidation of old inventory generally have on a company's profits when it is using the LIFO cost flow assumption?

18. How is gross profit percentage calculated?

19. Why are organizations that use LIFO required to disclose what their inventory would have been if they had used FIFO?

20. When prices are rising, will a company's inventory turnover be higher or lower if it uses the LIFO cost flow assumption?

21. How are days inventory held computed?

22. What is a LIFO reserve?

Exercises

E9-1 *Required*

For each of the following situations, fill in the blank with FIFO, LIFO, or Average Costing:

1. _____ would result in the highest amount of assets in periods of rising prices.

2. _____ would result in the highest net income in periods of rising prices.

3. _____ would result in the greatest inventory turnover in periods of rising prices.

4. _____ would produce the least amount of inventory value in periods of falling prices.

5. _____ would produce the lowest net income in a periods of falling prices.

6. _____ would produce the same unit cost for assets and cost of goods sold periods of rising prices.

7. _____ would be the preferred method to reduce income taxes in periods of rising prices and non-decreasing levels of inventory.

8. _____ would be the preferred method for "start–ups" and companies paying no income taxes in periods of rising prices.

9. _____ usually results in a balance sheet valuation of inventory farthest away from its economic value.

10. _____ would result in the highest after-tax cash flow in periods of rising prices and non-decreasing levels of inventory.

E9-2 The inventory records of Maypen Corporation indicated the following at December 31, 2000:

	Units	Cost per unit	Total cost
Beginning inventory: 1/1/00	1,000	$4.50	$4,500
Purchases:			
2/2/00	500	5.00	2,500
4/1/00	1,650	5.00	8,250
6/30/00	1,400	6.00	8,400
10/31/00	1,000	6.50	6,500
12/31/00	600	7.00	4,200
Available for sale	6,150		$34,350

An ending inventory revealed 1,200 units at 12/31/00. All units sold during the year were sold for $10 per unit.

Required

a. Compute the ending inventory value and cost of goods sold for 2000 under FIFO, LIFO, and average cost flow assumptions. Assume a periodic inventory system.

b. What would be the gross profit and gross profit percentage under each cost flow assumption?

c. What inventory cost flow assumption do you think Maypen would use if it were: 1) a recent start-up online retailer of children's toys; 2) a leading large "bricks and mortar" retailer. Give reasons for your answer.

E9-3 Selected data from the quarterly income statements for 2000 for Intel Corp. appear below.

(In millions)
For the Quarter Ended

	December 30, 2000	September 30, 2000	July 1, 2000	April 1, 2000
Net revenues	$8,702	$8,731	$8,300	$7,993
Cost of sales	3,230	3,148	3,283	2,989
Net income	$2,193	$2,509	$3,137	$2,696
Earnings per share	.33	.36	.45	.39

On March 9, 2001, Intel announced that it expected sales for the first quarter of 2001 to fall about 25% from the $8.7 billion reported for the fourth quarter of 2000. The company also expected gross profits to fall to 51% of sales, and expenses to fall 15% from the fourth quarter.

Required

a. Compute Intel's expected income before taxes for the first quarter of 2001 if these predictions are accurate.

b. Compute Intel's gross profit percentage of sales for each quarter of 2000.

E9-4 Comparative income statement data for fiscal years 1998 through 2000 for Dell Computer follow:

(In millions)

	January 28, 2000	January 29, 1999	February 1, 1998
Net revenue	$25,265	$18,243	$12,327
Gross margin	5,218	4,106	2,722
Operating income	2,263	2,046	1,316
Net income	1,666	1,460	944

Required
Comment on any favorable or unfavorable trends indicated by this data.

E9-5 The inventory records of Acura Corporation indicated the following at December 31, 2000:

	Units	Cost per unit	Total cost
Beginning inventory: 1/1/00	1,000	$7.00	$7,000
Purchases:			
2/2/00	1,000	6.75	6,750
4/1/00	1,500	6.50	9,750
6/30/00	1,400	6.00	8,400
10/31/00	1,000	5.80	5,800
12/31/00	1,200	5.50	6,600
Available for sale	7,100		$44,300

An ending inventory revealed 1,800 units at 12/31/00. From January through June, the company sold 2,500 units for $12 each. From July through December, 2,800 units were sold for $11 per unit.

a. Compute the ending inventory value and cost of goods sold for 2000 under FIFO, LIFO, and average cost flow assumptions. Assume a periodic inventory system.

b.   What would be the gross profit and gross profit percentage under each cost flow assumption?

c.   What are the implications of falling costs and industry over capacity on a company's profitability under each of the cost flow assumptions? How do these results compare with a period of rising prices?

E9-6   Refer to E9-5. Assume that the market price of Acura's inventory falls to $5.30 at December 31, 2000.

Required

a.   Prepare the entry under Lower of Cost or Market assuming the company is using FIFO.

b.   Prepare the entry under Lower of Cost or Market assuming the company is using LIFO.

c.   For firms facing decreasing inventory prices, which method would be preferred? Explain.

E9-7   Jones Company purchased 100 units in its first month of operations at $5 per unit. 80 units were sold at $10 per unit.

Required

a.   Prepare entries to record the sales and cost of inventory sold. Jones uses a perpetual inventory system.

b.   What differences would exist in the entries if Jones used a periodic inventory system?

Problems . . . .

P9-1   Comparative balance sheet and income statement data for Wal-Mart Corporation follow:

(In millions)

	99	98
Inventory at replacement cost	$17,549	$16,845
Less LIFO reserve	473	348
Inventory at LIFO	$17,076	$16,497

(In millions)

	99	98
Sales	$137,634	$117,958
Cost of sales	108,725	93,438
Operating expenses	22,363	19,358
Net income	4,430	3,526

Required

a.   Explain the meaning of the term "LIFO reserve."

b.   Compute Wal-Mart's inventory gross margin percentage, inventory turnover, and days inventory held for 1999.

(Continued)

c. What would Wal-Mart's ending inventory and cost of goods sold have been if the company had used FIFO?

d. What would have been the impact on Wal-Mart's income statement and balance sheet of using FIFO instead of LIFO. Would using FIFO have affected Wal-Mart's cash flows?

e. Compute Wal-Mart's inventory gross margin percentage, inventory turnover, and days inventory held for 1999 if the company had used FIFO. Comment on the difference in the ratios compared to b.

P9-2 LTM Enterprises is a distributor of high tech archaeological tools. Information relative to one of its inventory items for 2001 indicates:

		Units	Cost per unit	Total cost
1/1	Beginning inventory	5,000	$30	$150,000
2/6	Purchase	20,000	34	680,000
7/18	Purchase	17,000	36	612,000
10/20	Purchase	2,000	38	76,000
	Goods available for sale	44,000		$1,518,000

On December 31, 2001, LTM had 3,000 units of the item on hand. During 2001, LTM sold this product at an average of $60 per unit.

Required

a. Compute the value of the ending inventory at December 31, 2001 under FIFO, LIFO and average cost flow assumptions. LTM uses the periodic method of inventory valuation.

b. Compute the gross profit generated during 2001 using FIFO and LIFO.

c. Compute the gross profit percentage generated during 2001 using FIFO and LIFO.

d. Name a practical reason for LTM to use FIFO.

e. Name a practical reason for LTM to use LIFO.

f. If LTM were considering a switch from FIFO to LIFO, it would have to be concerned with the LIFO conformity rule. Explain.

g. Assume LTM uses LIFO and the same number of units were sold. Would the company benefit from purchasing 1,000 units at a cost of $40 each on December 31, 2001? Explain.

h. Would your answer to part g be the same if LTM used FIFO? Explain.

i. If LTM decides to switch from average cost to FIFO, assuming the cost behavior patterns in evidence during the year, would its income be higher or lower than if it had stayed with average cost? Explain.

j. Assume LTM was required to make a lower of cost or market adjustment of $4,000 to its year end inventory. Prepare journal entries showing two alternative approaches for this write-down.

k. Would the entries made in part j result in any differences in LTM's income statement for 2001? Explain.

l. If the inventory written down in part j increased in value $6,000 in 2002, what should LTM do under Generally Accepted Accounting Principles? Explain

P9-3   Aerovox Incorporated (LIFO to FIFO switch)

Aerovox is a leading manufacturer of film, paper, and aluminum electrolytic capacitors. The Company sells its products worldwide, principally to original equipment manufacturers (OEMs) of electrical and electronic products. Applications include air conditioners, fluorescent and high intensity discharge lighting, a variety of appliances including microwave ovens, motors, power supplies, photocopiers, telecommunications, computer and medical equipment, and industrial electrical systems.

In 1996, Aerovox changed its method for costing inventories from LIFO to FIFO. The following end-of-year inventory values were taken from Aerovox annual reports.

	1996	1995	1994	1993
FIFO value	20,910	23,654	20,919	
LIFO reserve		1,024	1,024	?
LIFO value		22,630	19,895	

Excerpts from Aerovox financial statements follow.

Inventories

Inventories are stated at the lower of first-in, first-out (FIFO) cost or market. During the fourth quarter of 1996 the Company changed its method for costing domestic inventories from the last-in, first-out (LIFO) method to the first-in, first-out (FIFO) method. All inventories, both foreign and domestic, are now costed using the FIFO method. The Company will also apply to the Internal Revenue Service to change to the FIFO method of inventory costing for tax purposes.

The Company has been experiencing customer demand for decreasing prices. The establishment of two manufacturing facilities in Mexico several years ago were in response to this trend. The Company expects this pattern to continue with level or decreasing costs well into the future. At the same time, the Company is investing in efforts to increase the turnover of inventories and the reduction of manufacturing cycle times. Accordingly, the Company believes that the FIFO method results in a better matching of current costs with current revenues.

The change has been applied to prior periods by retroactively restating the financial statements as required by generally accepted accounting principles. The effect of this restatement was to increase retained earnings by $640,000 and inventory by $1,024,000 as of December 31, 1993, and to decrease deferred tax assets by $384,000 as of that date. There was no change in the reported net income for the years ended December 31, 1994 and December 30, 1995. Net loss and loss per share for the year ended December 28, 1996 would have been $370,000 and $0.07 greater, respectively, had the Company retained the LIFO method.

Debt

. . . The agreement contains several financial covenants requiring the Company to maintain certain ratios regarding debt, equity, and interest costs. The Company was in violation of one of those covenants on December 28, 1996, for which it received a waiver from the lender. . . .

Required

a.   Make a journal entry to restate the December 31, 1993 balance sheet to FIFO.

b.   What was the LIFO reserve as of December 31, 1993? Explain.

c.   Why was there no change in reported net income, after restatement to FIFO, for the years ended December 31, 1994 and December 30, 1995? Explain.

d. If Aerovox were to compute the LIFO reserve as of the end of 1996, would it be larger or smaller than $1,024? Explain.

e. Comment on the following statement: "the Company believes that the FIFO method results in a better matching of current costs with current revenues." Does it matter if prices of inventoried items are rising or falling?

f. What if any effect does the change in inventory flow assumption have on the debt covenants?

P9-4 Startup Co.: Inventory Accounting

Startup Co. began operations on January 1, 2000. In the year 2000, it made the following purchases of inventory:

Date	Units	Price per unit	Total
January 1	1,000	$ 5	$ 5,000
April 1	1,250	$ 7	$ 8,750
July 1	1,500	$ 8	$12,000
December 1	1,400	$10	$14,000

Startup sold 3,100 units @ $16 per unit during the year. Startup computes ending inventory and cost of goods sold under the *periodic inventory* method. That is, it only makes calculations of these amounts once a year, not perpetually.

Required

a. What is Startup's ending inventory using the FIFO flow assumption?

b. What is Startup's ending inventory using the LIFO flow assumption?

c. The following table contains columns for Startup's income statements using FIFO and LIFO. Fill in the blank cells.

	Startup Co. Income Statements for the year ended December 31, 2000	
	FIFO	LIFO
Sales		
Cost of Goods Sold		
Gross Margin		
Selling, General & Administrative Expenses	(10,000)	(10,000)
Depreciation Expense	(5,000)	(5,000)
Interest Expense	(3,000)	(3,000)
Net Income Before Taxes		
Income Taxes @ 40% of Net Income		
Net Income After Taxes		

P9-5 Refer to P9-4. In the year 2001, Startup made the following purchases of inventory:

Date	Units	Price per unit	Total
February 1	1,800	$12	$21,600
May 1	2,000	$13	$26,000
August 1	2,250	$15	$33,750
November 1	2,500	$16	$40,000

Startup sold 7,000 units @ $25 during the year.

Required

a. What is Startup's ending inventory using the FIFO flow assumption?
b. What is Startup's ending inventory using the LIFO flow assumption?
c. The following table contains columns for Startup's income statements using FIFO and LIFO. Fill in the blank cells.

Startup Co. Income Statements for the year ended December 31, 2001		
	FIFO	LIFO
Sales		
Cost of Goods Sold		
Gross Margin		
Selling, General & Administrative Expenses	(10,000)	(10,000)
Depreciation Expense	(5,000)	(5,000)
Interest Expense	(3,000)	(3,000)
Net Income Before Taxes		
Income Taxes @ 40% of Net Income		
Net Income After Taxes		

P9-6 A firm buys and sells one good. Any cash needed is raised directly and instantly from shareholders' contributions. Any cash generated is paid instantly to shareholders. The firm computes inventory values on a periodic basis.

  All purchases and sales occur at market prices (i.e., the firm is essentially a commodity trader). The market prices for the good through time are given by the following graph:

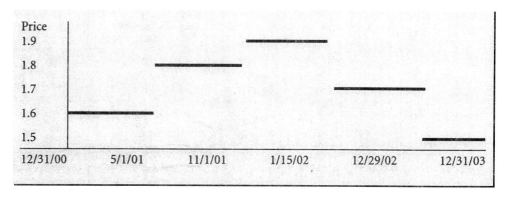

Purchases		
Date	Amount	Price
12/31/00	20 units	$1.6/u
6/15/01	30 units	$1.8/u
2/3/02	50 units	$1.7/u

Sales	
Date	Amount
8/15/01	35 units
1/20/02	15 units
7/1/02	30 units
6/1/03	20 units

Required

a. Prepare a t-account analysis of the inventory account using LIFO and LOCM for the period December 31, 2000 to December 31, 2003.
b. Determine the cost of goods sold and any losses from LOCM inventory write-downs.
c. Compute the amount of inventory on the balance sheets at December 31, 2000, 2001, 2002, and 2003 using LIFO and LOCM.
d. Prepare a t-account analysis of the inventory account using FIFO and LOCM for the period December 31, 2000 to December 31, 2003.
e. Compute the cost of goods sold and any losses from LOCM inventory write-downs.
f. Compute the amount of inventory on the balance sheets at December 31, 2000, 2001, 2002, and 2003 using FIFO and LOCM.
g. Calculate and compare the market-to-book ratios for inventory under FIFO and LIFO. Pay particular attention to the effects of LOCM.

P9-7 A firm buys and sells one good. Any cash needed is raised directly and instantly from shareholders' contributions. Any cash generated is paid instantly to shareholders. The firm computes inventory values on a periodic basis.

All purchases and sales occur at market prices (i.e., the firm is essentially a commodity trader). The market prices for the good through time are given by the following graph:

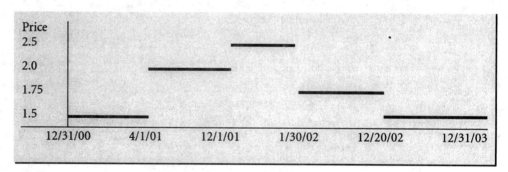

Purchases		
Date	Amount	Price
12/31/00	10 units	$1.50/u
6/1/01	50 units	$2.00/u
2/1/02	60 units	$1.75/u

Sales	
Date	Amount
12/15/01	45 units
1/15/02	15 units
6/1/02	50 units
6/1/03	10 units

Required

a. Prepare a t-account analysis of the inventory account using LIFO and LOCM for the period December 31, 2000 to December 31, 2003 (i.e., show beginning and ending balances in the inventory account for each of the years and the flows in and out of the account).
b. Compute the cost of goods sold and any losses from LOCM inventory write-downs for each of the years.
c. Show balance sheets on December 31, 2000, 2001, 2002, and 2003 using LIFO and LOCM.
d. Prepare a t-account analysis of the inventory account using FIFO and LOCM for the period December 31, 2000 to December 31, 2003 (i.e., show beginning and ending balances in the inventory account for each of the years and the flows in and out of the account).
e. Compute the cost of goods sold and any losses from LOCM inventory write-downs.
f. Prepare balance sheets at December 31, 2000, 2001, 2002, and 2003 using FIFO and LOCM for each of the years.

Cases and Projects ·

C9-1   Jackson Controls, Inc. uses the LIFO cost flow assumption to account for its inventory. The company adopted LIFO during its first year of operation in 1997. At December 31, 1997, the ending inventory under LIFO was 120,000 units @ $5.00 per unit, or $600,000. At the time, the company's accountant, William Zikeck, informed the general manager, Sally Smith, that it would be advisable for the company to maintain an ending inventory of 120,000 units each year. Thus, at the end of each year, the company purchased inventory to ensure that the minimum level was maintained. Purchases and inventory data for 1998 through 2000 are as follows:

	Purchases	Cost	Ending Inventory	Units
1998	200,000	$6.00	$1,200,000	
	100,000	$6.50	650,000	130,000 units
	300,000		$1,850,000	
1999	180,000	$7.00	$1,260,000	
	110,000	$8.00	880,000	135,000 units
	290,000		$2,140,000	
2000	120,000	$9.00	$1,080,000	
	100,000	$9.25	925,000	
	100,000	$9.50	950,000	
	320,000		$2,955,000	138,000 units
2001	300,000	$9.80	$2,940,000	137,000 units
Sales:	*1998*	*1999*	*2000*	*2001*
	$2,900,000	$3,245,000	$4,021,000	$4,214,000

During 2002, Jackson Controls purchased 200,000 units on 6/4 at $13 per unit. During the year, through 12/30, the company sold 300,000 units at $19 per unit. On 12/31/2002, the general manager realized that the inventory was extremely low. If she were to follow Zikeck's advice of maintaining a minimum inventory of approximately 120,000 units, she would have to purchase 100,000 units at the current price of $14. Sally never understood why it was so advisable to maintain the ending inventory at approximately 120,000 units. She decided to analyze the effect of the inventory level on profits by preparing income statements with and without the purchase of the 100,000 units at the end of the period. Sales for 2002 were $5,700,000.

Required

a.   Compute Cost of goods sold and gross profit for 1998 through 2001.

b.   Compute Cost of goods sold and gross profit in 2002 with and without the additional inventory purchase at year-end.

c.   Should the company continue its policy of maintaining an ending inventory of 120,000 units? Why or why not?

C9-2   Lands' End and Coldwater Creek

Lands' End, Inc., is a direct marketer of traditionally styled apparel, domestics (primarily bedding and bath items), soft luggage, and other products. The company manages its businesses in three operating segments consisting of core, specialty, and international, based principally on type of catalog focusing on specific customer needs and market served. The company's primary market is the United States, and other markets include the Pacific Basin area, Europe, and Canada. Financial statements for Lands' End are as follows:

Consolidated Statement of Operations
Lands' End, Inc. & Subsidiaries
(In thousands, except per share data)

	For the period ended		
	January 29, 1999	January 30, 1998	January 31, 1997
Net sales	$1,371,375	$1,263,629	$1,118,743
Cost of sales	754,661	675,138	609,168
Gross profit	$616,714	$588,491	$509,575
Selling, general and administrative expenses	544,446	489,923	424,390
Non-recurring charge	12,600	—	0
Charge from sale of subsidiary	—	—	1,400
Income from operations	$59,668	$98,568	$83,785
Other income (expense):			
Interest expense	$(7,734)	$(1,995)	$(510)
Interest income	16	1,725	1,148
Gain on sale of subsidiary	—	7,805	—
Other	(2,450)	(4,278)	496
Total other income (expense), net	$(10,168)	$3,257	$1,134
Income before income taxes	$49,500	$101,825	$84,919
Income tax provision	18,315	37,675	33,967
NET INCOME	$31,185	$64,150	$50,952

Consolidated Balance Sheets
Lands' End, Inc. & Subsidiaries
(In thousands)

ASSETS	January 29, 1999	January 30, 1998
Current assets:		
Cash and cash equivalents	$6,641	$6,338
Receivables, net	21,083	15,443
Inventory	219,686	241,154
Prepaid advertising	21,357	18,513
Other prepaid expenses	7,589	5,085
Deferred income tax benefits	17,947	12,613
Total current assets	$294,303	$299,146
Property, plant, and equipment, at cost:		
Land and buildings	$102,018	$81,781
Fixtures and equipment	154,663	118,190
Leasehold improvements	5,475	5,443
Construction in progress	0	12,222
Total property, plant, and equipment	$262,156	$217,636
Less—accumulated depreciation and amortization	101,570	84,227
Property, plant, and equipment, net	$160,586	$133,409
Intangibles, net	1,030	917
TOTAL ASSETS	$455,919	$433,472
LIABILITIES AND SHAREHOLDERS' INVESTMENT		
Current liabilities:		
Lines of credit	$38,942	$32,437
Accounts payable	87,922	83,743
Reserve for returns	7,193	6,128
Accrued liabilities	54,392	34,942
Accrued profit sharing	2,256	4,286
Income taxes payable	14,578	20,477
Total current liabilities	$205,283	$182,013
Deferred income taxes	$8,133	$8,747
Shareholders' investment:		
Common stock, 40,221 shares issued	$402	$402
Donated capital	8,400	8,400
Additional paid-in capital	26,994	26,457
Deferred compensation	(394)	(1,047)
Accumulated other comprehensive income	2,003	875
Retained earnings	406,396	375,211
Treasury stock, 10,317 and 9,281 shares at cost, respectively	(201,298)	(167,586)
Total shareholders' investment	$242,503	$242,712
TOTAL LIABILITIES AND SHAREHOLDERS' INVESTMENT	$455,919	$433,472

Consolidated Statements of Cash Flows
Lands' End, Inc. & Subsidiaries
(In thousands)

	For the period ended		
	January 29, 1999	January 30, 1998	January 31, 1997
Cash flows from operating activities:			
Net income	$ 31,185	$ 64,150	$ 50,952
Adjustments to reconcile net income to net cash flows from operating activities:			
Pre-tax non-recurring charge	12,600	—	—
Depreciation and amortization	18,731	15,127	13,558
Deferred compensation expense	653	323	317
Deferred income taxes	(5,948)	(1,158)	994
Pre-tax gain on sale of subsidiary	—	(7,805)	—
Loss on disposal of fixed assets	586	1,127	325
Changes in assets and liabilities excluding the effects of divestitures:			
Receivables	(5,640)	(7,019)	(675)
Inventory	21,468	(104,545)	22,371
Prepaid advertising	(2,844)	(7,447)	4,758
Other prepaid expenses	(2,504)	(1,366)	(145)
Accounts payable	4,179	11,616	14,205
Reserve for returns	1,065	944	629
Accrued liabilities	6,993	8,755	4,390
Accrued profit sharing	(2,030)	1,349	1,454
Income taxes payable	(5,899)	(1,047)	8,268
Other	1,665	64	394
Net cash flows from (used for) operating activities	$ 74,260	$(26,932)	$121,795
Cash flows from (used for) investing activities:			
Cash paid for capital additions	$(46,750)	$(47,659)	$(18,481)
Proceeds from sale of subsidiary	—	12,350	—
Net cash flows used for investing activities	$(46,750)	$(35,309)	$(18,481)
Cash flows from (used for) financing activities:			
Proceeds from short-term borrowings	$6,505	$21,242	$1,876
Purchases of treasury stock	(35,557)	(45,899)	(30,143)
Issuance of treasury stock	1,845	409	604
Net cash flows used for financing activities	$(27,207)	$(24,248)	$(27,663)
Net increase (decrease) in cash and cash equivalents	303	(86,489)	75,651
Beginning cash and cash equivalents	6,338	92,827	17,176
Ending cash and cash equivalents	$ 6,641	$ 6,338	$ 92,827

Coldwater Creek Inc., a Delaware corporation headquartered in Sandpoint, Idaho, is a specialty direct mail retailer of apparel, gifts, jewelry, and home furnishings, primarily marketing its merchandise through regular catalog mailings. The Company also operates full-line retail stores in Sandpoint, Idaho and Jackson Hole, Wyoming where it primarily sells catalog items and unique store merchandise. Additionally, the Company maintains an interactive Internet web site (www.coldwater-creek.com) from which merchandise may be viewed and purchased. Financial statements for Coldwater Creek are as follows:

Coldwater Creek Inc. and Subsidiary
Consolidated Statements
of Operations
(in thousands, except for per share data)

| | Fiscal Year Ended | | |
	February 27, 1999	February 28, 1998	March 1, 1997
Net sales	$325,231	$246,697	$143,059
Cost of sales	156,198	120,126	66,430
GROSS PROFIT	169,033	126,571	76,629
Selling, general, and administrative			
expenses	150,655	107,083	64,463
INCOME FROM OPERATIONS	18,378	19,488	12,166
Interest, net, and other	(697)	57	(153)
INCOME BEFORE PROVISION FOR			
INCOME TAXES	17,681	19,545	12,013
Provision for income taxes	6,990	7,857	1,197
NET INCOME	$ 10,691	$ 11,688	$ 10,816

Coldwater Creek Inc. and Subsidiary
Consolidated Balance Sheets
(in thousands, except for share data)

ASSETS	February 27, 1999	February 28, 1998
Current assets:		
Cash and cash equivalents	$ 149	$ 331
Receivables	2,683	4,019
Inventories	56,474	53,051
Prepaid expenses	1,234	2,729
Prepaid catalog costs	4,274	2,794
Total current assets	64,814	62,924
Deferred catalog costs	3,195	7,020
Property and equipment, net	31,236	26,661
Executive loans	1,376	1,620
TOTAL ASSETS	$100,621	$98,225

(Continued)

LIABILITIES AND STOCKHOLDERS' EQUITY

Current liabilities:		
Revolving line of credit	$ 9,938	$10,264
Accounts payable	17,086	27,275
Accrued liabilities	7,668	10,517
Income taxes payable	4,445	—
Deferred income taxes	1,080	919
Total current liabilities	$ 40,217	$48,975
Deferred income taxes	298	375
Total liabilities	$ 40,515	$49,350
Stockholders' Equity:		
Preferred stock, $.01 par value,		
1,000,000 shares authorized,		
none issued and outstanding	—	—
Common stock, $.01 par value,		
15,000,000 shares authorized,		
10,183,117 and 10,120,118		
issued and outstanding,		
respectively	$ 102	$ 101
Additional paid-in capital	39,287	38,748
Retained earnings	20,717	10,026
Total stockholders' equity	60,106	48,875
TOTAL LIABILITIES AND		
STOCKHOLDERS' EQUITY	$100,621	$98,225

Required

a. You have been asked to provide a preliminary analysis comparing the profitability and efficiency of Lands' End and Coldwater Creek, paying particular attention to cost of goods sold and investment in inventories. Complete the table of ratios that follows:

Ratio	Definition	Lands' End	Coldwater Creek
Cost of goods sold as a % of sales	$\dfrac{\text{CGS}}{\text{Sales}}$		
Current ratio	$\dfrac{\text{Current assets}}{\text{Current liabilities}}$		
Inventory as a % of current assets	$\dfrac{\text{Inventory}}{\text{Current assets}}$		
Inventory as a % of total assets	$\dfrac{\text{Inventory}}{\text{Total assets}}$		
Inventory turnover	$\dfrac{\text{CGS}}{\text{Average inventory}}$		
Days inventory held	$\dfrac{365}{\text{Inventory turnover}}$		
Return on equity	$\dfrac{\text{Net income}}{\text{Average shareholders' equity}}$		

b. Answer the following:

    1. What do these ratios suggest about the relative profitability and efficiencies of the two companies?

    2. What particular further accounting information about inventories would you like to have to improve your analysis?

c. The following information about the accounting policies for inventories is taken from the 10Ks of the two companies.

From Note 1 of Coldwater Creek's 1999 10K:

Inventories primarily consist of merchandise purchased for resale and are stated at the lower of first-in, first-out cost or market.

From Note 1 to the financial statements in Lands' End's 1999 10K:

Inventory, primarily merchandise held for sale, is stated at last-in, first-out (LIFO) cost, which is lower than market. If the first-in, first-out (FIFO) method of accounting for inventory had been used, inventory would have been approximately $26.9 million and $25.1 million higher than reported at January 29, 1999 and January 30, 1998, respectively.

For Lands' End, recompute all of the ratios in the table as if the company had used FIFO instead of LIFO to do its inventory accounting (assume a 35% marginal tax rate).

Ratio	Definition	Lands' End	Coldwater Creek
Cost of goods sold as a % of sales	$\dfrac{\text{CGS}}{\text{Sales}}$		
Current ratio	$\dfrac{\text{Current assets}}{\text{Current liabilities}}$		
Inventory as a % of current as sets	$\dfrac{\text{Inventory}}{\text{Current assets}}$		
Inventory as a % of total assets	$\dfrac{\text{Inventory}}{\text{Total assets}}$		
Inventory turnover	$\dfrac{\text{CGS}}{\text{Average inventory}}$		
Days inventory held	$\dfrac{365}{\text{Inventory turnover}}$		
Return on equity	$\dfrac{\text{Net income}}{\text{Average shareholders' equity}}$		

    d.   Repeat question b1. using the FIFO ratios for the two companies.

    e.   How would the operating cash flow section of the Lands' End Cash Flow Statement change if it had used FIFO rather than LIFO?

    f.   In general, is it true that if the balance sheet values for inventory decrease from the beginning to the end of a period, the physical number of units in inventory must have decreased?

    g.   In question c, should one use the marginal or average tax rate in the analysis?

Chapter ten

Marketable Securities

Questions . . . .

1. What are marketable securities?
2. What are the reasons that companies hold marketable securities?
3. What is a debt security?
4. Give two important characteristics of debt securities.
5. What is an equity security?
6. What is the economic value at any point in time of debt and equity securities?
7. What is a zero-coupon bond?
8. What is the advantage to a company of issuing a zero-coupon bond?
9. What are the three categories of marketable securities classified by Generally Accepted Accounting Principles?
10. How are trading securities valued on the balance sheet?
11. What is an unrealized holding gain or loss?
12. How are unrealized holding gains or losses for trading securities accounted for on the income statement?
13. How are unrealized holding gains or losses for available-for-sale securities accounted for on the income statement?
14. "GAAP for available-for-sale securities are conceptually muddy." Comment.
15. How are available-for-sale securities valued on the balance sheet?
16. What is the treatment of unrealized holding gains or losses on available-for-sale securities?
17. Explain this statement: "GAAP for held-to-maturity securities follow economic values only if events progress exactly as expected."
18. What is the quick ratio? How do marketable securities affect the quick ratio?
19. To what expression does "marked-to-market" refer?
20. Explain this statement: "The GAAP for available-for-sale securities only partially follow the underlying economics."
21. Where does the account Accumulated other comprehensive income (loss) appear?
22. How can transactions involving held-to-maturity securities lead to manipulation of earnings?

Exercises . . . .

E10-1 Determine the selling price of the following marketable securities:

a. A marketable security purchased on January 1, 2002 that is expected to pay off $5,000 on December 31, 2006 when the appropriate interest rate is 9%.

b. A $5,000 zero-coupon bond purchased on January 1, 2002 maturing on December 31, 2006 when the appropriate interest rate is 7%.

(Continued)

c. An investment in a common stock that pays no dividends on January 1, 2002. The common stock is expected to be worth $2,000 on December 31, 2006. Investors expect a 10% return on the investment.

E10-2 AS Company buys a marketable security on January 1, 2002 that is expected to pay off $1,000 on December 31, 2005. AS believes a 7% interest rate is appropriate.

Required

a. Determine how much AS paid for the security.
b. Fill in the following chart with the economic value of the security on the dates indicated, assuming that events unfold as expected:

Date	1/1/02	12/31/02	12/31/03	12/31/04	12/31/05
Value					

E10-3 EKS Corporation purchases a marketable equity security on January 1, 2002. EKS pays $473.01 for the security. On December 31, 2002, the security has a market value of $498.75. EKS considers the security to be a trading security.

Required

a. Prepare the journal entry to record the purchase of the security on January 1, 2002.
b. Prepare the adjustment necessary on December 31, 2002 under Generally Accepted Accounting Principles.
c. Indicate how the security will affect EKS's income statement and balance sheet for 2002.

E10-4 Refer to the information regarding EKS Corporation in exercise E10-3. Prepare answers to requirements a, b, and c, assuming EKS regards the security to be an available-for-sale security.

E10-5 Refer to the information regarding AS Company in exercise E10-2. Assume that the security is a held-to-maturity security.

Required

a. Prepare the journal entry to record the purchase of the security on 1/01/02.
b. Prepare the adjusting entry that would be required on 12/31/02.
   a. How will the accounting for the security affect AS's income statement and balance sheet for 2002?
   b. Assume that the market value of the security is $20.38 higher than the value shown by the company after the 12/31/02 entry. What adjustment would be necessary?

E10-6 Sacks Corporation had the following investments in marketable securities on 12/31/02, after its first year of operation:

	Cost	Market Value on 12/31/02
Marketable equity securities classified as trading	$15,402	$16,407

	Cost	Market Value on 12/31/02
Marketable equity securities classified as available-for-sale	$24,500	$22,408

Required

a.   Prepare the necessary adjusting entry required on 12/31/02 for each category of security to conform to Generally Accepted Accounting Principles.

b.   Indicate how each category of security will affect Sacks Company's income statement and balance sheet for 2002.

c.   Assume that Sacks sells the entire portfolio of trading securities on 1/2/03 for $16,347. Prepare the journal entry to record the sale.

E10-7   Indicate whether each of the following accounts is an income statement account or a balance sheet account.

a.   Unrealized gain on marketable securities—trading   p7 196

b.   Unrealized holding loss on marketable securities—trading

c.   Marketable securities—available-for-sale

d.   Unrealized gain on marketable securities—available-for-sale   p 197

e.   Other accumulated comprehensive income   201

f.   Gain on sale of marketable security—available-for-sale

g.   Gain on sale of marketable security—trading

E10-8   Rogal Corporation held available-for-sale securities in its portfolio on January 2, 2002 that had been purchased for $1470.72 on January 2, 2001. On December 31, 2001, the company had recorded an unrealized gain of $78.56. On January 31, 2002 the securities were sold.

Required

a.   Prepare the entry to record the sale assuming the securities were sold for $1,560.58

b.   Prepare the entry to record the sale assuming the securities were sold for $1,538.20.

c.   Prepare the entry to record the sale assuming the securities were sold for $1,420.00

Problems . . . .

P10-1   The following transactions regarding Smith Company took place during 2001:

February 10	Purchased $15,475 of Marketable Securities classified as trading
June 30	Purchased $27,540 of Marketable Securities classified as trading
September 30	Purchased $18,450 of Marketable Securities classified as available for sale

On December 31, the Market Values of these securities were as follows:

February 10 purchase:	$17,438
June 30 purchase:	$26,540
September 30 purchase:	$18,495

Required

a.   Prepare journal entries for the purchases of the securities.

b.   Prepare the necessary adjusting entries required at December 31, 2001 to conform to Generally Accepted Accounting Principles.

(Continued)

    c.   Indicate the impact of the securities on Smith's income statement, balance sheet, and statement of cash flows for 2001. Be sure to indicate the specific accounts that would be affected.

P10-2   South Company purchased a $10,000 held to maturity security on January 1, 2003. The company was expecting a 7% rate of return. The security matures on December 31, 2005.

Required

    a.   Determine the amount that South would have been willing to pay for the security on January 1, 2003.

    b.   Assume that interest rates remain at 7%. What will be the value of the security on December 31, 2003, December 31, 2004, and December 31, 2005?

    c.   Prepare the entries necessary on the following dates:
        January 1, 2003 for the purchase of the security
        December 31, 2003 adjusting entry
        December 31, 2004 adjusting entry
        December 31, 2005 adjusting entry
        December 31,2005 for the maturity of the security.

    d.   Assume that, instead of remaining stable at 7%, interest rates rise to 9% over the life of the security. What would you expect to happen to the value of the security over its life? Explain your answer. Would it change any of the accounting requirements? Explain your answer.

P10-3   Rhionne Corporation held available-for-sale securities in its portfolio that had been purchased for $2,479.67 on January 2, 2001. On December 31, 2001, the company had an unrealized gain of $278.42.

Required

    a.   Prepare the entry to record the gain.

    b.   Indicate how the securities would affect Rhionne's income statement and balance sheet.

    c.   Assume that the securities were classified as trading securities. Prepare the entry to record the gain.

    d.   Indicate how the securities would affect Rhionne's income statement and balance sheet if they were classified as trading securities.

P10-4   ABC Corporation had the following information about its portfolio of marketable securities purchased on January 15, 2001:

Cost of securities:	$100,000
Market value of securities on:	
12/31/2001	$110,000
12/31/2002	$108,000
12/331/2003	$112,000

The securities were sold for $114,500 on 2/24/04.
The securities were classified as trading securities.

Required

    a.   Prepare the adjusting entries required by GAAP on 12/31/2001, 12/31/2002, and 12/31/2003.

b. Prepare the entry to record the sale of the securities on 2/24/04.

c. What effect did the ownership of the securities have on ABC's income for 2001, 2002, 2003, and 2004?

P10-5 Refer to problem P10-4. Prepare answers to requirements a, b, and c assuming the securities were classified as available for sale securities.

P10-6 The notes to America Online's 1999 annual report include the following:

As of June 30, 1999, the Company had available-for-sale equity investments in public companies with a fair market value of $1,956 million and a cost basis of $1,686 million. The unrealized gain . . . has been recorded as a separate component of stockholders' equity.

Required

a. Recreate the entries that have been made on America Online's books related to the available-for-sale securities.

b. Assume the entire portfolio of securities was sold during July, 1999 for $1,500 million during a dramatic sell-off in the stock market. What entry would have been made by America Online to record the sale of the portfolio?

Cases and Projects ·

C10-1 Jones Company holds a marketable security classified as held-to-maturity. On December 31, 2002, the security has a book value of $1,657.42 and a market value of $1,725. All entries have been made according to Generally Accepted Accounting Principles. At maturity, Jones expects to receive $2,000.

Required

a. Explain how the economic value and the accounting value of the security can be different.

b. Indicate how Jones' management could manipulate earnings and still be following Generally Accepted Accounting Principles.

C10-2 Consider the following information found on the 1999 balance sheets of three high tech companies: one is an Internet service provider, the second a recent start-up provider of affiliate marketing services, assisting e-businesses in promoting goods and services over the Internet, and the third a mature company selling both hardware and software consulting services.

Percent of total assets represented by:

	Company A	Company B	Company C
Cash	65%	6%	16.5%
Marketable securities	23%	1%	10%
Accounts receivable(trade and other)	1%	32%	7.5%
Inventories	0%	5.5%	0%
Prepaid expenses	1%	5.5%	3%
Property, plant, and equipment	9%	20%	12%
Investments		30%	40%
Other	1%	0%	11%
Total	100%	100%	100%

Required

Identify each company. What factors helped you to determine the identity of each?

C10-3   Consider the following balance sheet data for IBM Corporation at 12/31/1999:

(In millions)

Assets		Liabilities and Stockholders' Equity	
Cash and cash equivalents	$5,043	Current liabilities	$39,578
Marketable securities	788	Long term debt	14,124
Notes and accounts receivable	20,039	Other liabilities	13,282
Other receivables	7,579	Total liabilities	$66,984
Inventories	4,868		
Prepaid expenses and other current assets	4,838	Stockholders' equity	20,511
Total current assets	43,155		
Property, plant, and equipment (net)	17,590		
Long term investments	26,087		
Other assets	663		
Total assets	$87,495	Total	$87,495

Required

a.   Compute the following for IBM at 12/31/99:

   1)   Current ratio

   2)   Quick ratio

   3)   Working capital

   4)   Debt-to-Equity ratio

b.   Complete the chart by indicating the impact that the following transactions would have on the ratios listed. All amounts are in millions. Use I for Increase, D for Decrease, and N for no effect:

   1)   Increase in value of marketable securities (trading) from $788 to $810.

   2)   Sale of $50 of inventory for $75.

   3)   Decrease in value of long-term investments (available for sale securities) from $26,087 to $25,992.

   4)   Sale of $500 of land for $400 cash.

   5)   Purchase of $50 inventory for cash.

Transaction	Current Ratio	Quick Ratio	Working Capital	Debt-to-Equity
1				
2				
3				
4				
5				

c.   Indicate the impact that the transactions in part b would have on IBM's net income.

C10-4   **Hosoi Garden Mortuary**

The Company is engaged in one line of business that consists principally of providing mortuary services in the State of Hawaii on the island of Oahu. The financial statements for 1999 and several associated notes follow.

Hosoi Garden Mortuary, Inc. Balance Sheets
(May 31, 1999 and 1998)

	1999	1998
ASSETS		
Current assets		
Cash and cash equivalents	$ 928,162	$ 498,871
Available-for-sale securities, at market		
(Note 5)	847,718	773,464
Accounts receivable, less allowance of		
$62,710 and $78,740	321,453	274,788
Income tax receivable	29,017	255,749
Dividend receivable	—	750,000
Inventories	143,974	149,268
Prepaid expenses and others	58,865	64,787
Deferred income taxes	33,954	43,588
Total current assets	2,363,143	2,810,515
Investments		
Garden Life Plan, Ltd.	2,090,156	1,649,722
Woolsey-Hosoi Mortuary Services, LLC	22,345	—
Cemetery plots	1,350	1,350
Held-to-maturity securities, at cost		
(Note 5)	888,931	842,656
	3,002,782	2,493,728
Property and equipment, at cost, less		
accumulated depreciation (Note 7)	1,506,092	1,524,560
Other assets	101,885	103,921
Total assets	$6,973,902	$6,932,724
LIABILITIES		
Current liabilities		
Accounts payable	$ 259,971	$ 285,445
Accrued liabilities	131,716	135,484
Total current liabilities	391,687	420,929
Deferred income taxes	169,443	172,248
STOCKHOLDERS' EQUITY		
Capital contributed		
Common stock, par value $.20 per share;		
authorized 3,625,000 shares, issued		
2,187,140 shares	437,428	437,428
Less 288,814 and 218,542 reacquired shares	(57,983)	(43,928)
Total capital contributed	379,445	393,500
Retained earnings	6,030,181	5,961,335
Accumulated Other Comprehensive Income		
net of applicable deferred income taxes	84,428	65,994
Treasury stock, 223,785 shares, at cost	(81,282)	(81,282)
Total stockholders' equity	6,412,772	6,339,547
TOTAL LIABILITIES AND		
STOCKHOLDERS' EQUITY	$6,973,902	$6,932,724

Hosoi Garden Mortuary, Inc.
Statements of Income and Comprehensive Income
(Years Ended May 31, 1999 and 1998)

	1999	1998
Revenues		
Sale of urns and other items	$703,411	$742,913
Funeral services	2,043,890	1,921,575
Total revenues	2,747,301	2,664,488
Cost of sales and services	2,053,315	2,100,550
Gross profit	693,986	563,938
Selling, general, and administrative expenses		
Salaries and wages	249,249	241,684
Profit sharing and pension fund contributions	66,816	66,560
Professional services	200,072	241,057
Taxes and licenses	27,309	26,513
Advertising	24,645	37,071
Others	92,035	98,038
Total selling, general, and administrative expenses	660,126	710,923
Operating income (loss)	33,860	(146,985)
Other income and (expenses)		
Interest, dividends, and others	178,788	278,881
Interest and others	(1,643)	(502)
Total other income and (expenses)	177,145	278,379
Income before income taxes and equity in earnings of Garden Life Plan, Ltd.	211,005	131,394
Income taxes	91,554	38,781
Income before equity in earnings of Garden Life Plan, Ltd.	119,451	92,613
Equity in earnings of Garden Life Plan, Ltd., net of deferred taxes of $35,199 and $33,553 (Note 5)	405,235	608,171
Net income	524,686	700,784
Other comprehensive income, net of taxes		
Net unrealized gains on available-for-sale securities	18,434	18,996
Comprehensive income	$543,120	$719,780

Investment securities

Management determines the appropriate classification of securities at the time of purchase. These investments are classified in three categories and accounted for as follows:

- Debt securities that the company intends to hold to maturity are classified as *Securities Held to Maturity* and reported at cost.
- Debt and equity securities that are purchased and held for the purpose of selling in the near term are classified as *Trading Securities* and reported at fair value, with unrealized gains and losses included in income.
- Debt and equity securities not classified as *Securities Held to Maturity* or *Trading Securities* are classified as *Securiites Available for Sale* and reported at fair value, with unrealized gains and losses included in other comprehensive income. *Securities Available for Sale* will be used as part of the Company's asset management strategy and may be sold in response to changes in market values or the need for capital.

Hosoi Garden Mortuary, Inc.
Statements of Cash Flows
(Years Ended May 31, 1999 and 1998)

	1999	1998
Cash Flows from Operating Activities:		
Net income	$524,686	$700,784
Adjustments to reconcile net income to net cash and cash equivalents provided by (used in) operating activities:		
Depreciation	64,053	67,340
Realized gain on sale of investment securities, net	(14,445)	(104,819)
Increase in allowance for doubtful accounts	(16,030)	9,016
Undistributed earnings of affiliate	(440,434)	108,276
Partnership income	(7,345)	—
Cash value of life insurance policies	—	(3,210)
Deferred income taxes	(4,456)	122,096
(Increase) decrease in certain assets:		
Accounts receivable	(30,635)	19,298
Income tax receivable	226,732	(255,749)
Dividend receivable	750,000	(750,000)
Inventories	5,294	(12,322)
Prepaid expenses and other	5,922	(334)
(Decrease) increase in certain liabilities:		
Accounts payable	(25,474)	(67,244)
Accrued liabilities	(3,768)	(233,715)
Income taxes payable	—	(76,716)
Net cash provided by (used in) operating activities	1,034,100	(477,299)
Cash Flows from Investing Activities:		
Purchase of property and equipment	(45,585)	(39,952)
Redemption of life insurance policy	—	27,284
Proceeds from sale of investment securities	1,584,108	4,363,649
Increase in investment securities	(1,660,473)	(3,842,237)
Investment in Woolsey-Hosoi Mortuary Services, LLC	(15,000)	—
Increase in cash value of life insurance policies	2,036	(2,811)
Net cash provided by (used in) investing activities	(134,914)	505,933
Cash Flows from Financing Activities:		
Shares reacquired	(296,407)	(130,289)
Cash dividends paid	(173,488)	(175,569)
Net cash used in financing activities	(469,895)	(305,858)
Net increase (decrease)	429,291	(277,224)
Cash and Cash Equivalents at Beginning of Year	498,871	776,095
Cash and Cash Equivalents at End of Year	$928,162	$498,871

(5) Investment securities

As of May 31, 1999 and 1998, the Company held investments in the following types of securities:

	Gross Amortized Cost	Gross Unrealized Gain	Gross Unrealized Loss	Fair Value
May 31, 1999				
Available-for-sale				
Equity securities	$87,975	$30,962	$3,841	$115,096
Mutual funds	623,628	109,996	1,002	732,622
	711,603	140,958	4,843	847,718
Held-to-maturity				
U.S. Treasury bills	888,931	504	3,711	885,724
Totals	$1,600,534	$141,462	$8,554	$1,733,442
May 31, 1998				
Available-for-sale				
Equity securities	$74,346	$41,132	$1,760	$113,718
Mutual funds	592,721	67,128	103	659,746
	667,067	108,260	1,863	773,464
Held-to-maturity				
U.S. Treasury bills	842,656	850	5,148	838,358
Totals	$1,509,723	$109,110	$7,011	$1,611,822

The maturities of all debt securities held at May 31, 1999 were as follows:

	Available for Sale		Held to Maturity	
	Amortized Cost	Market Value	Amortized Cost	Market Value
Within 1 year	$ —	$ —	$779,601	$778,332
After 1 year through 5 years	—	—	61,229	60,161
After 5 years	—	—	48,101	47,231
			$888,931	$885,724

During the year ended May 31, 1999, the Company sold *Securities Available-for-Sale* for $1,584,108. The net gross realized gain of $14,445 is reflected in earnings. The cost of the securities sold was based on cost of all the shares of each such security held at the time of sale.

The unrealized holding gains on investment securities *Available-for-Sale* during the years ended May 31,1999 and 1998, and reported as a separate component of Stockholders' Equity, are as follows:

	1999	1998
Unrealized holding gains, net of losses	$136,115	$106,396
Deferred income tax on the net unrealized holding gains	(51,687)	(40,402)

Required

a. In which of the three categories, Trading, Available-for-sale, or Held-to-maturity, does Hosoi have investments? How can you tell?

b.   Identify all of the accounts on the balance sheet that relate to Hosoi's investment in securities. Give their exact titles and explain what is being accounted for in each of them.

c.   In the statement of cash flows, $14,445 (realized gain on sale of investment securities) is subtracted from net income in deriving cash flow from operations. The footnote also indicates the securities were sold for $1,584,108.

   1.   Why is the $14,445 subtracted in the cash flow statement?

   2.   Where does the $1,584,108 appear in the cash flow statement?

   3.   Make the journal entry to record the sale of these securities (assume the market value of these securities was equal to their cost at the start of the year.)

d.   The cash flow statement also indicates that $1,660,473 was used to purchase investment securities during 1999.

   1.   Explain how you know that no Held-to-maturity securities were sold during 1999.

   2.   Make the journal entry to explain the increase in Held-to-maturity securities during 1999.

   3.   Make the journal entry to record the purchase of Available-for-sale securities during 1999.

   4.   How is the change in value of the Held-to-maturity securities reflected in the 1999 income statement?

e.   Have interest rates gone up or down since Hosoi purchased the U.S. Treasury bills listed as Held-to-maturity securities? How do you know? What did interest rates do during 1999? How do you know?

f.   Make the journal entry to record the change in the market value of the Available-for-sale securities during fiscal 1999.

g.   Check that the entries you made to the Available-for-sale securities account in (d3), (e), and (f) explain the change in this account balance during fiscal 1999.

h.   Suppose that on June 1, 1999 Hosoi sold all of their Available-for-sale securities for $850,000. Make the journal entry to record the sale.

C10-5   Ford Motor Company

The December 31, 1998 Balance Sheet and the 1998 Income Statement of the Ford Motor Company and subsidiaries follow, as well as Note 2, *Marketable and Other Securities*. A schedule of Comprehensive Net Income for 1998 also follows.

Ford Motor Company and Subsidiaries
Consolidated Statement of Income
For the Years Ended December 31, 1998, 1997, and 1996
(in millions, except amounts per share)

	1998	1997
Automotive		
Sales (Note 1)	$119,083	$122,935
Costs and expenses (Note 1 and 15):		
Costs of sales	104,782	108,907
Selling, administrative, and other expenses	7,616	7,082
Total costs and expenses	112,398	115,989
Operating income	6,685	6,946

Interest income	1,331	1,116
Interest expense	829	788
Net interest income	502	328
Equity in net loss of affiliated companies (Note 1)	(38)	(88)
Net expense from transactions with Financial Services (Note 1)	(191)	(104)
Income before income taxes - Automotive	6,958	7,082
Financial Services		
Revenues (Note 1)	25,333	30,692
Costs and expenses (Note 1):		
Interest expense	8,036	9,712
Depreciation	8,589	7,645
Operating and other expenses	4,618	6,621
Provision for credit and insurance losses	1,798	3,230
Total costs and expenses	23,041	27,208
Net revenue from transactions with Automotive	191	104
Gain on spin-off of The Associates (Note 15)	15,955	—
Gain on sale of Common Stock of a subsidiary)	—	269
Income before income taxes - Financial Services	18,438	3,857
Total Company		
Income before income taxes	25,396	10,939
Provision for income taxes (Note 6)	3,176	3,741
Income before minority interests	22,220	7,198
Minority interests in net income of subsidiaries	149	278
Net income	$22,071	$6,920

Ford Motor Company and Subsidiaries
Consolidated Balance Sheet
(in millions)

	December 31, 1998	December 31, 1997
ASSETS		
Automotive		
Cash and cash equivalents	$3,685	$6,316
Marketable securities (Note 2)	20,120	14,519
Total cash and marketable securities	23,805	20,835
Receivables	2,604	3,097
Inventories	5,656	5,468
Deferred income taxes	3,239	3,249
Other current assets	3,405	3,782
Net current receivable from Financial Services	0	416
Total current assets	38,709	36,847
Equity in net assets of affiliated companies	2,401	1,951
Net property	37,320	34,594
Deferred income taxes	3,175	3,712
Other assets	7,139	7,975
Total Automotive assets	88,744	85,079

Financial Services

Cash and cash equivalents	1,151	1,618
Investments in securities (Note 2)	968	2,207
Net receivables and lease investments	132,567	175,417
Other assets	13,227	4,776
Net receivable from Automotive	888	0
Total Financial Services assets	148,801	194,018
Total assets	$237,545	$279,097

LIABILITIES AND STOCKHOLDERS' EQUITY

Automotive

Trade payables	$13,368	$11,997
Other payables	2,755	2,557
Accrued liabilities	16,925	16,250
Income taxes payable	1,404	1,358
Debt payable within one year	1,121	1,129
Net current payable to Financial Services	70	0
Total current liabilities	35,643	33,291
Long-term debt	8,713	7,047
Other liabilities	30,133	28,899
Deferred income taxes	751	1,210
Net payable to Financial Services	818	0
Total Automotive liabilities	76,058	70,447

Financial Services

Payables	3,555	4,539
Debt	122,324	160,071
Deferred income taxes	5,488	4,347
Other liabilities and deferred income	6,034	7,865
Net payable to Automotive	0	416
Total Financial Services liabilities	137,401	177,238
Company-obligated mandatorily redeemable preferred securities of a subsidiary trust holding solely junior subordinated debentures of the Company	677	678

STOCKHOLDERS' EQUITY

Capital stock:		
Common Stock, par value $1.00 per share (1,151 and 1,132 million shares issued)	1,151	1,132
Class B Stock, par value $1.00 per share (71 million shares issued)	71	71
Capital in excess of par value of stock	5,283	5,564
Accumulated other comprehensive income	(1,670)	(1,228)
ESOP loan and treasury stock	(1,085)	(39)
Earnings retained for use in business	19,659	25,234
Total stockholders' equity	23,409	30,734
Total liabilities and stockholders' equity	$237,545	$279,097

Ford Motor Company and Subsidiaries
Consolidated Statement of Stockholders' Equity For the Year Ended December 31, 1998
(in millions)

	Capital in Excess of Par Capital Stock	Value of Stock	Foreign Retained Earnings	Other Comprehensive Income				
				Minimum Currency Translation	Unrealized Pension Liability	Holding Gain/Loss	Other	Total
Year Ended December 31, 1998								
Comprehensive income:								
Net income (excluding gain on spin-off of The Associates)			6,116					6,116
Gain on The Associates spin-off			15,955					15,955
Foreign currency translation				(53)				(53)
Minimum pension liability (net of tax benefit of $184)					(361)			(361)
Net unrealized holding loss (net of tax benefit of $3)						(6)		(6)
Reclassification adjustments for net gains realized in net income (net of tax of $11)							(22)	(22)
Comprehensive income								$21,629

Note 2. Marketable and Other Securities

Trading securities are recorded at fair value with unrealized gains and losses included in income. Available-for-sale securities are recorded at fair value with net unrealized gains and losses reported, net of tax, in other comprehensive income. Held-to-maturity securities are recorded at amortized cost. Equity securities that do not have readily determinable fair values are recorded at cost. The basis of cost used in determining realized gains and losses is specific identification.

The fair value of substantially all securities is determined by quoted market prices. The estimated fair value of securities, for which there are no quoted market prices, is based on similar types of securities that are traded in the market.

Expected maturities of debt securities may differ from contractual maturities because borrowers may have the right to call or prepay obligations with or without penalty.

Automotive Sector

Investments in securities at December 31 were as follows (in millions):

	Amortized Cost	Unrealized Gains	Unrealized Losses	Fair Value	Book Value
1998					
Trading securities	$19,534	$83	$40	$19,577	$19,577
Available-for-sale securities—					
Corporate securities	543	—	—	543	543
Total investments in securities	$20,077	$83	$40	$20,120	$20,120
1997					
Trading securities	$14,114	$29	$ —	$14,143	$14,143
Available-for-sale securities—					
Corporate securities	395	—	19	376	376
Total investments in securities	$14,509	$29	$19	$14,519	$14,519

During 1997, $365 million of bonds issued by affiliates were reclassified from equity in net assets of affiliated companies to available-for-sale marketable securities; $202 million of the bonds matured in 1998. Proceeds from sales of available-for-sale securities were $586 million in 1998 and $8 million in 1997. In 1998, gross losses of $15 million were reported. Other comprehensive income included net unrealized losses of $5 million in 1998 and net unrealized gains of $28 million in 1997 on securities owned by certain unconsolidated affiliates. The available-for-sale securities at December 31, 1998 had contractual maturities between one and five years.

Financial Services Sector

Investments in securities at December 31, 1998 were as follows (in millions):

	Amortized Cost	Unrealized Gains	Unrealized Losses	Fair Value	Book Value
Trading securities	$231	$3	$4	$230	$230
Available-for-sale securities:					
Debt securities issued by the U.S. government and agencies	153	3	—	156	156
Municipal securities	63	2	—	65	65
Debt securities issued by non-U.S. governments	25	—	—	25	25
Corporate securities	192	3	2	193	193
Mortgage-backed securities	198	3	—	201	201
Equity securities	35	56	1	90	90
Total available-for-sale securities	666	67	3	730	730
Held-to-maturity securities					
Debt securities issued by the U.S. government and agencies	6	—	—	6	6
Corporate securities	2	—	—	2	2
Total held-to-maturity securities	8	—	—	8	8
Total investments in securities	$905	$70	$7	$968	$968

Investments in securities at December 31, 1997 were as follows (in millions):

	Amortized Cost	Unrealized Gains	Unrealized Losses	Fair Value	Book Value
Trading securities	$267	$4	$1	$270	$270
Available-for-sale securities					
Debt securities issued by the U.S. government and agencies	385	4	1	388	388
Municipal securities	13	—	—	13	13
Debt securities issued by non-U.S. governments	36	—	—	36	36
Corporate securities	489	7	1	495	495
Mortgage-backed securities	837	8	1	844	844
Other debt securities	14	—	—	14	14
Equity securities	53	65	2	116	116
Total available-for-sale securities	1,827	84	5	1,906	1,906
Held-to-maturity securities					
Debt securities issued by the U.S. government and agencies	7	—	—	7	7
Corporate securities	15	—	—	15	15
Other debt securities	3	—	—	3	3
Total held-to-maturity securities	25	—	—	25	25
Total investments in securities with readily determinable fair value	2,119	$88	$6	$2,201	$2,201
Equity securities not practicable to fair value	6	—	—	—	6
Total investments in securities	$2,125	$88	$6	$2,201	$2,207

The amortized cost and fair value of investments in available-for-sale securities and held-to-maturity securities at December 31 by contractual maturity were as follows (in millions):

| | Available-for-sale | | Held-to-maturity | |
	Amortized Cost	Fair Value	Amortized Cost	Fair Value
1998				
Due in 1 year or less	$29	$29	$1	$1
Due after 1 year through 5 years	165	167	3	3
Due after 5 years through 10 years	101	102	3	3
Due after 10 years	138	141	1	1
Mortgage-backed securities	198	200	—	—
Equity securities	35	91	—	—
Total	$666	$730	$8	$8
1997				
Due in 1 year or less	$100	$101	$14	$14
Due after 1 year through 5 years	443	446	10	10
Due after 5 years through 10 years	273	276	—	—
Due after 10 years	121	124	1	1
Mortgage-backed securities	837	843	—	—
Equity securities	53	116	—	—
Total	$1,827	$1,906	$25	$25

Proceeds from sales of available-for-sale securities were $2.1 billion in 1998, $2.9 billion in 1997, and $8.4 billion in 1996. In 1998, gross gains of $48 million and gross losses of $3 million were realized on those sales; gross gains of $98 million and gross losses of $8 million were realized in 1997 and gross gains of $43 million and gross losses of $21 million were realized in 1996.

Required

a. What is the total amount of marketable securities held by Ford Motor Company and subsidiaries as of December 31, 1998?

b. Of the total in (a), what is the value of trading securities, held-to-maturity securities, and available-for-sale securities?

c. Why are there no unrealized gains or losses in the held-to-maturity securities?

d. What is the journal entry made by Ford at the end of 1998 to record the unrealized gains or losses on available-for-sale securities?

e. In the December 31, 1998 holdings of available-for-sale securities in the Automotive division, what was the amount by which the December 31, 1998 market value exceeded or was less than the acquisition cost of these securities?

f. In the Automotive division, suppose that the December 31, 1997 carrying value of the available-for-sale securities sold during 1998 reflected an unrealized holding loss of $10 million. What journal entry did Ford make in 1998 to record the sale of these available-for-sale securities?

g. In light of the assumptions in (f), what adjusting journal entry would have been made in the Automotive division to the balance in the *unrealized gains/losses on available-for-sale securities* account on December 31, 1998?

h. What is the fair market value relative to cost of all of the trading securities held by Ford as of December 31, 1998?

Chapter eleven

Long-Lived Assets

▶ **Questions** . . . .

1. What are the major uncertainties that can cause long-lived assets to earn an abnormal positive or negative rate of return?
2. Give five examples of assets that would be considered long-lived assets.
3. Explain why buildings and machinery must be depreciated.
4. What is a liquidating dividend?
5. How is the economic value of long-lived assets determined?
6. How is the **economic depreciation** of a long-lived asset determined?
7. Explain why training and advertising costs are not recognized as assets.
8. What is the accounting treatment for advertising costs and research and development?
9. Give examples of costs that are included in the capitalized cost of a purchased asset.
10. When are interest costs capitalized?
11. What is the accounting definition of depreciation?
12. Explain this statement: "GAAP do not require that economic depreciation be recorded."
13. What is meant by **depreciable cost**?
14. What is meant by **accelerated depreciation**?
15. Give two examples of depreciation methods that are considered accelerated methods of depreciation.
16. How does the presentation of tangible and intangible long-lived assets differ in the balance sheet?
17. Why do most businesses use straight-line depreciation?
18. Explain why the economic values of long-term fixed assets are generally in excess of the book accounting values.
19. How is the gain or loss on sale of a long-term asset determined?
20. Where do gains or losses on sales of long-term assets appear in the financial statements?
21. Explain the term "asset impairment."
22. When must asset impairments be recorded in the financial statements?
23. Give three examples of circumstances that may result in asset impairment.
24. How is depreciation recognized on assets that have been written down because of asset impairment?
25. Why would a company want to avoid an asset impairment charge?

▶ **Exercises** . . . .

E11-1 Indicate whether the following expenditures are considered capital expenditures (C) or are expensed as incurred (E) under GAAP.

    a. Installation cost of a new mainframe computer

    b. Research and development costs to develop a patent

    c.   Purchase cost of a patent from a competitor

    d.   Training costs of new employees

    e.   Transportation of robots to new manufacturing facility

    f.   Insurance policy on robots in transit

    g.   Insurance policy on robots after installation

    h.   Newspaper advertising costs

    i.   Sales tax on new delivery van

    j.   Interest cost on construction of a new manufacturing facility

    k.   Interest cost on loan for delivery van

    l.   Cost of copyright purchased from an author

E11-2   Compute the annual depreciation expense each year for an asset with a cost of $1,200, salvage value of $200, and a useful life of four years under each of the following methods:

    a.   Straight line

    b.   Sum-of-the-years' digits

    c.   Double-declining balance

E11-3   Refer to exercise E11-2. Assume that the company expects the asset in question to produce 100,000 units over the four-year life. The expected output is as follows: Year 1: 40,000, Year 2: 25,000, Year 3: 20,000, and Year 4: 15,000.

Required

    a.   Compute the expected depreciation expense that would result under the units of production method.

    b.   Assume that, instead of the **expected** output, the **actual** output was: Year 1: 50,000, Year 2: 40,000, Year 3: 30,000, and Year 4: 20,000. Compute the depreciation expense that would be recorded each year.

E11-4   Phoenix Corporation purchased equipment on 1/1/2000. The cost was $50,000 and the estimated salvage value was $5,000. The equipment was being depreciated on a straight-line basis with an estimated useful life of 10 years. On 12/31/2002, the equipment was sold. Give the journal entry to record the sale under the following assumptions:

    a.   The asset was sold for $36,500

    b.   The asset was sold for $20,000

    c.   The asset was sold for $41,000

E11-5   Sumner Corporation purchased a molding machine on 1/3/2001. The machine cost $18,000 and has no salvage value. It has an expected useful life of five years. The company uses double-declining balance depreciation, with a switch to straight-line when the straight-line method applied to the remaining depreciable cost results in greater depreciation expense than double-declining balance.

Required

Compute the annual depreciation expense in each of the five years.

E11-6   Jones Company's adjusted trial balance showed the following balances at December 31, 2001:

	Debit	Credit
Equipment	$60,000	
Depreciation expense	7,000	
Accumulated depreciation		$35,000

Required

a.   If the company had been using straight-line depreciation, and the expected useful life of the equipment is eight years, what is the expected salvage value?

b.   What entry was made to record depreciation expense on 12/31/2001?

c.   If the asset were sold on January 2, 2002 for $12,000, what entry would be made?

Problems . . . .

P11-1   Ace containers purchased a new forklift for $20,000 on Jan 1, 2000. The company president and controller are trying to decide which method of depreciation would be better: double-declining balance, straight-line, or units of production. The truck has an expected useful life of five years and is expected to have a salvage value of $2000. It is expected that the forklift will be used 36,000 hours over the five years, broken down as follows: **2000:** 12,000; **2001:** 10,000; **2002:** 8000; **2003:** 4000; **2004:** 2000.

Required

a.   Calculate the depreciation expense, total accumulated depreciation, and book value of the forklift for the first two years under straight-line, double-declining balance, sum-of-the-years' digits, and units of production depreciation methods.

b.   What adjusting entry to record depreciation would be made at December 31, 2001 under the straight-line method?

c.   Provide a theoretical and a practical argument for using each of the three methods.

d.   Notwithstanding the previous answers, assume that the forklift was sold when its book value was $12,000. The company sold the machine for $15,000. Prepare the journal entry to record the sale.

P11-2   Silverman Corporation purchased a new machine on 1/2/00. The machine is expected to last four years and have no salvage value at the end of that time. It will generate annual sales of $10,000 and cost $4,000 annually to run. Silverman's stockholders expect a 12% return on their investment.

Required

a.   How much should Silverman Corporation be willing to pay for the machine?

b.   Prepare a chart showing the economic value of the machine at the end of the year from 2000 to 2003. Assume that all sales revenues and costs of operations occur as expected.

c.   What is the economic depreciation of the asset each year and in total?

d.   What would have been the accounting depreciation each year using straight-line depreciation?

e. Discuss the difference between the economic concept of depreciation and the Generally Accepted Accounting Principles concept of depreciation.

f. Compare the accounting book value and the economic value of the asset at the end of each year. Comment on your findings.

P11-3 Dondero Company began operations on January 2, 2000. The company purchased a long-lived asset for $32,000. The asset had a useful life of four years and no salvage value.

Required

a. Compute depreciation expense for each of the years of the asset's useful life under straight-line depreciation.

b. Compute depreciation expense for each year of the asset's useful life under double-declining balance depreciation.

c. Prepare the journal entry for a and b required at the end of 2000 and 2001.

d. Which method of depreciation will show the highest net income in 2000?

e. Assume that the asset is sold at the end of its third year for $12,000. Prepare the entry to record the sale assuming the company had used straight-line depreciation.

f. Prepare the entry to record the sale assuming the company had used double-declining balance depreciation.

P11-4 The following is the balance sheet for McCormick Corporation at December 31, 2000.

McCormick Corporation
Balance Sheet
As of December 31, 2000

Assets		*Liabilities and Equities*	
Cash	$500	Accounts payable	$630
Accounts receivable	875	Notes payable	1,000
Inventory	769	Accrued liabilities	245
Total current assets	$2,144	Total current liabilities	$1,875
Property plant and equipment		Long-term debt	700
Cost:	$3,840	Total liabilities	$2,575
Less accumulated		Equity:	
depreciation	(920)	Common Stock	300
P, P & E, net	2,920	Retained earnings	2,189
		Total equity	2,489
Total assets	$5,064	Total liabilities and equity	$5,064

McCormick Corporation experienced the following events in 2001:

Old equipment that cost $240 and was fully depreciated was sold for $60.

Depreciation expense was $250

Cash payments for new equipment were $400

Required

a. Prepare the journal entries for 2001 for all events just described.

b. Based on the preceding information, what was McCormick Corporation's net amount of property, plant, and equipment at the end of 2001?

P11-5   Adamo Company began operations on January 2, 2000. The company purchased a long-lived asset for $85,000. The asset had a useful life of 10 years and no salvage value. It is to be depreciated on a straight-line basis.

Required

a.   What will be the book value of the asset on December 31, 2004?

b.   Assume that on December 31, 2004, the company's auditors perform an asset impairment test. What entry will be required if the expected undiscounted future cash flows from the asset are $20,000, and the expected discounted future cash flows are $18,000?

c.   Assuming that the asset's useful life has not changed, what entry will be made for depreciation expense on December 31, 2005?

d.   In general, what circumstances will suggest to a company or its auditors that an asset impairment test should be performed?

e.   Why does the asset impairment test use **undiscounted** future cash flows instead of the **present value** of future cash flows?

P11-6   The operating and investing sections of the cash flow statement of Wallace Computer Services, Inc. and Subsidiaries for the year ended July 31, 2000 follow.

Wallace Computer Services, Inc. and Subsidiaries
Consolidated Statements of Cash Flow—(in thousands)

For the Years Ended July 31, 2000

Cash flows from operating activities:	
Net income	$22,617
Adjustments to reconcile net income to net cash provided by operating activities:	
Depreciation and amortization	77,573
Restructuring charge	31,828
Deferred taxes	4,908
(Gain) loss on disposal of property	(344)
(Gain) on sale of investments	(3,190)
Changes in assets and liabilities, net of effect of acquisitions and divestitures:	
Accounts receivable	(345)
Inventories	(387)
Prepaid taxes	8,940
Advances and prepaid expenses	(1,158)
Other assets	(6,475)
Accounts payable and other liabilities	10,368
Deferred compensation and retirement benefits	4,273
Net cash provided by operating activities	148,608
Cash flows from investing activities:	
Capital expenditures	(53,945)
Proceeds from sales of short-term investments	3,190
Proceeds from disposal of property	6,086
Other capital investments, including acquisitions and divestitures	(10,067)
Net cash used in investing activities	(54,736)

Required

a.   Why are depreciation and amortization added to net income in the operating section?

b.   Why is the gain on disposal of property deducted from net income in the operating section?

c. What was the book value of the property that was sold?

d. Assume that the accumulated depreciation on the property that was sold was $400,000. Prepare the journal entry to record the sale.

P11-7 During 2001, TMC Corporation was expanding its operations into a new manufacturing process for decorating plastic parts. The company was investigating the acquisition of new machinery for its decorating process. During the inquiry, the opportunity to acquire all of the used equipment in a factory located in Kentucky arose. The company placed a bid in a sealed bidding process and was declared the top bidder. The bid was accepted on May 15, 2001 for $200,000. The company was responsible for removal of the equipment at the factory in Kentucky and transportation and installation in its new facility in Pawtucket, Rhode Island. TMC incurred certain additional costs related to this acquisition:

Legal bill related to writing the contract for the equipment	$3,000
Trucking expenses related to rigging company, which disassembled the machinery in Kentucky and transported it to Pawtucket:	104,783
Wages paid to company employees to help unload and install the machinery during regular working hours	10,500
Cost to repair damage from machinery dropped from truck during unloading	6,000
Additional materials, lumber, steel, and other supplies needed in installation	35,400
Interest paid on note to bank used to finance the purchase of machinery	5,540
Casualty insurance policy on new machinery	3,000
Cost of raw materials used during trial runs of machinery	1,000
Cost of advertising the company's new manufacturing capability in national trade magazines	30,000

Installation and testing were completed on September 30, 2001. The company expected the machinery to have a 20-year life with a $30,000 salvage value at the end of that time.

Required

a. Determine the costs that should be capitalized in the machinery account.

b. For any cost that was not capitalized, explain your reasoning.

c. Determine the depreciable cost of the machinery.

d. Compute the depreciation expense for 2001 and 2002 using straight-line depreciation.

e. Compute the depreciation expense for 2001 and 2002 using double-declining balance depreciation.

f. Assume that, during 2004, a large oven used to dry decorated pieces needed a major repair costing $20,000. Should the cost of the repair be capitalized? Why or why not?

Cases and Projects . . . .

C11-1 Recently the Financial Accounting Standards Board proposed that companies that purchase other companies and record goodwill on the balance sheet not be required to amortize the goodwill. That means that the goodwill would remain on the balance sheet until an assessment by the company indicated a permanent impairment, at which time it would be written off. There are differing opinions as to the impact of this ruling on companies' stock prices.

a. Provide one argument as to why a company's stock price should increase under this new regulation.

b. Provide a second argument as to why this new proposal should have no effect on a company's stock price.

C11-2 The following was excerpted from the Wall Street Journal on October 22, 1999:

> Waste Management Inc. is expected to disclose as early as today that a massive audit of its hundreds of dumps and trash-collection operations has uncovered yet another round of accounting problems, requiring a third-quarter charge of as much as $1 billion . . .

The company reported that a significant portion of the charge related to the writing down of the value of dumps. "The value of a dump is essentially the number of tons it can hold, multiplied by the per-ton dumping price, minus costs to build and operate it. The cost of land and improvements is booked as an asset, and then written off, or amortized, over the expected life of the dump."

Required

a. Discuss the GAAP requirements related to asset impairment review. What factors would suggest that an asset impairment review would be necessary?

b. What are some of the uncertainties that could affect the value of Waste Management's dumps?

c. Assume that Waste Management's management had overestimated the number of tons that the dumps could hold when they were acquired. What effect would this error have had on the company's prior years' financial statements?

d. Assume that the amount of the write-down was $800 million. Prepare the journal entry that would be required.

e. How does a write-down affect depreciation expense in subsequent accounting periods?

C 11-3 Mechanical Technology Incorporated

Mechanical Technology Incorporated manufactures and sells precision diagnostic and measurement instruments and incubates alternative energy technology. It conducts business in the areas of fuel cells, and gas and steam powered turbines. It is a leader in the evolution of alternative energy technology.

The balance sheets, income statements and cash flow statements for Mechanical Technology Incorporated for fiscal years 1998 and 1999 are presented on pages 146–148. Supplemental disclosures on pages 148–149 show noncash financing activities and details of the Property, plant, and equipment account.

The *Loss on sale of fixed assets* in the operations section of the cash flow statement refers to the transfer of fixed assets to Plug Power, a company that Mechanical Technology has an equity investment in (that is, it transferred an asset on its own balance sheet to a company that it owns a large investment in, thereby increasing the value of that investment account). This is the only disposal of fixed assets during the year. The $5,861 in "assets contributed to Plug" represents the fair market value of the assets at the time of transfer. The $28 "loss on sale of fixed assets" in the operating section of the cash flow statement refers to this "Plug Company contribution".

Mechanical Technology Incorporated and Subsidiaries
Consolidated Balance Sheets
(Dollars in thousands)

	September 30,	
	1999	1998
Assets		
Current Assets		
Cash and cash equivalents	$ 5,870	$ 5,567
Investments in marketable securities	7,876	—
Accounts receivable, less allowance of		
$113 (1999) and $99 (1998)	3,852	4,959
Other receivables—related parties	105	87
Inventories	3,752	3,748
Taxes receivable	10	8
Note receivable—current	329	327
Prepaid expenses and other current assets	265	472
Net assets of a discontinued operation	—	8
Total Current Assets	22,059	15,176
Property, Plant, and Equipment, net	827	4,467
Note receivable—noncurrent	184	264
Investment in Plug Power	8,710	1,221
Total Assets	$31,780	$21,128
Liabilities and Shareholders' Equity		
Current Liabilities		
Income taxes payable	$ —	$ 5
Accounts payable	614	2,064
Accrued liabilities	2,243	3,328
Contribution payable-Plug Power	—	4,000
Net liabilities of discontinued operations	540	—
Total Current Liabilities	3,397	9,397
Long-Term Liabilities		
Deferred income taxes and other credits	597	607
Total Liabilities	3,994	10,004
Shareholders' Equity		
Common stock, par value $1 per share, authorized		
15,000,000; issued 11,649,959 (1999)		
and 10,773,968(1998)	11,649	10,775
Paid-in capital	42,755	16,274
Deficit	(26,573)	(15,885)
	27,831	11,164
Accumulated Other Comprehensive Loss:		
Unrealized loss on available for sale securities, net	(5)	—
Foreign currency translation adjustment	(11)	(11)
Accumulated Other Comprehensive Loss	(16)	(11)
Common stock in treasury, at cost,		
6,750 shares (1999) and 4,500 shares (1998)	(29)	(29)
Total Shareholders' Equity	27,786	11,124
Total Liabilities and Shareholders' Equity	$31,780	$21,128

Mechanical Technology Incorporated and Subsidiaries
Consolidated Statements of Operations
(Dollars in thousands, except per share)

	For the Years Ended September 30,	
	1999	1998
Net sales	$ 12,885	$21,028
Cost of sales	8,239	12,386
Gross profit	4,646	8,642
Selling, general, and administrative expenses	4,949	5,812
Product development and research costs	1,105	831
Operating (loss) income	(1,408)	1,999
Interest expense	(106)	(102)
Gain on sale of division/subsidiary	—	—
Equity in losses of Plug Power	(9,363)	(3,806)
Other income(expense), net	185	(97)
(Loss)income from continuing operations before extraordinary item and income taxes	(10,692)	(2,006)
Income tax expense	37	25
(Loss)income from continuing operations before extraordinary item	(10,729)	(2,031)
Extraordinary item—gain on extinguishment of debt, net of taxes ($106)	—	—
(Loss)income from continuing operations	(10,729)	(2,031)
Income(loss)from discontinued operations	41	(2,285)
Net(loss)income	$(10,688)	$ (4,316)
Earnings (loss) per share (Basic and Diluted):		
(Loss)income before extraordinary item	$ (.94)	$ (.21)
Extraordinary item	—	—
(Loss)from discontinued operations	—	(.24)
Net(loss)income	$ (.94)	$ (.45)

Mechanical Technology Incorporated and Subsidiaries
Consolidated Statements of Cash Flows
(Dollars in thousands)

	For the Years Ended September 30,	
	1999	1998
Operating Activities		
(Loss)income from continuing operations	$(10,729)	$ (2,031)
Adjustments to reconcile net (loss) income to net cash provided (used) by continuing operations:		
Depreciation and amortization	581	323
Unrealized loss on marketable securities	(5)	
Equity in losses of Plug Power	9,363	3,806
Accounts receivable reserve	14	5
Loss on sale of fixed assets	28	9
Deferred income taxes and other credits	(10)	13
Stock option compensation	55	—

(Continued)

	1999	1998
Changes in operating assets and liabilities net of effects from discontinued operations:		
Accounts receivable	1,093	(1,069)
Accounts receivable—related parties	(18)	—
Inventories	(4)	(362)
Prepaid expenses and other current assets	(174)	(346)
Accounts payable	(1,450)	788
Income taxes	(7)	(76)
Accrued liabilities	(1,085)	(519)
Net cash (used) provided by continuing operations	(2,348)	541
Discontinued Operations:		
Income/(loss) from discontinued operations	41	(2,285)
Adjustments to reconcile income to net cash provided (used) by discontinued operations:		
Changes in net assets/liabilities of discontinued operations	548	3,178
Net assets transferred from discontinued operations	—	(878)
Net cash provided (used) by discontinued operations	589	15
Net cash (used) provided by operations	(1,759)	556
Investing Activities		
Purchases of property, plant, & equipment	(2,738)	(3,166)
Investment in marketable securities	(7,876)	—
Principal payments from note receivable	78	59
Investment in Plug Power	(6,000)	—
Note receivable Plug Power	—	(500)
Net cash (used) provided by investing activities	(16,536)	(3,607)
Financing Activities		
Borrowings under IDA financing, less restricted cash	5,858	—
Proceeds from options exercised	153	225
Proceeds from rights offering	12,820	7,178
Costs of rights offering	(158)	(186)
Debt issue costs	(75)	(28)
Net cash provided (used) by financing activities	18,598	7,189
Effect of exchange rate changes on cash flows	—	8
Increase in cash and cash equivalents	303	4,146
Cash and cash equivalents—beginning of year	5,567	1,421
Cash and cash equivalents—end of year	$ 5,870	$ 5,567

Mechanical Technology Incorporated

Supplemental Disclosures	1999	1998
Noncash Financing Activities		
Conversion of Note Payable to Common Stock:		
Note Payable extinguishment	$ —	$ —
Common stock issued	—	—
Accrued interest - Note Payable	—	—
Additional paid-in capital - Other Investors	14,487	—
Contribution to Plug Power:		
Debt	(6,000)	—
Fixed assets	5,861	—
Prepaid expenses	364	—
Restricted cash	142	—
Net noncash provided (used) by financing activities	$14,854	$ —
Net noncash provided (used) by investing and financing activities	$14,854	$5,000

.

Note (4) Property, Plant, and Equipment
Property, plant, and equipment consists of the following:

(Dollars in thousands)	1999	1998
Land and improvements	$ —	$ 125
Buildings and improvements	26	6,111
Leasehold improvements	470	517
Machinery and equipment	3,686	4,285
Office furniture and fixtures	621	866
	4,803	11,904
Less accumulated depreciation	3,976	7,437
	$ 827	$4,467

Construction in progress, included in buildings and improvements, was approximately $1,371 thousand in 1998.

At the end of 1999, the Company was committed to approximately $387 thousand of future expenditures for new furniture, equipment, and fixtures.

Depreciation expense was $489, $317 and $216 thousand for 1999, 1998, and 1997, respectively. Repairs and maintenance expense was $166, $177 and $175 thousand for 1999, 1998, and 1997, respectively.

Prior to the sale of land and buildings to Plug Power in 1999, the cost and accumulated depreciation of buildings and improvements leased to Plug Power was:

(Dollars in thousands)	1998	1997
Cost	$ 1,547	$ 21
Accumulated depreciation	(660)	(17)
	$ 887	$ 4

Required

a.   Fill in numbers for all of the question marks in the following two t-accounts. Provide a verbal description of each number.

	PP&E (gross)				Accumulated Depreciation	
	Dr.	Cr.			Dr.	Cr.
Beginning balance	?					?	Beginning balance
		?	Subtractions	Subtractions	?	
Additions	?					?	Additions
Ending balance	?					?	Ending balance

b.   Provide journal entries for each of the addition and subtraction numbers in the accounts.

c.   What do the numbers tell you about Mechanical Technology's property, plant, and equipment?

Chapter twelve

Long-Term Liabilities

Questions . . . .

1. Name two major sources of uncertainty for liabilities that can cause their payments to be abnormally high or low.
2. Explain the following statement: GAAP for liabilities are largely historically based.
3. Give examples of liabilities that would be classified as long-term liabilities.
4. What are the four terms commonly specified in a financial instrument agreement?
5. What is meant by coupon rate?
6. What are the two types of payments promised by most notes?
7. What is a floating rate note?
8. What is LIBOR?
9. What is a covenant?
10. Explain the difference between a negative covenant and a positive covenant.
11. How is the current ratio computed?
12. What is meant by technical default?
13. What does it mean when a bond is callable?
14. What does it mean when a bond is convertible?
15. Explain the difference between a secured financial instrument and an unsecured financial instrument.
16. Explain the difference between senior debt and junior debt.
17. What is meant by recourse?
18. Compute the economic rate of return of a bond priced to yield 10%, compounded semi-annually.
19. Explain what would happen to the market price of a $1,000 bond paying 7% interest when interest rates fall from 7% to 6.5%.
20. Explain the following statement: GAAP for bonds do not keep up with changing interest rates.
21. How will discounts on bonds payable be presented on the balance sheet?
22. Explain the difference between an operating lease and a capital lease.
23. What are the three criteria used to distinguish a capital lease from an operating lease?
24. Explain why a "gain on retirement of bonds" may not be in the best interest of a company's stockholders.
25. How is the times-interest-earned ratio computed?
26. What is meant by off-balance sheet financing?
27. What is a zero-coupon bond?
28. Upon issuance, will a zero-coupon bond be more likely to sell for face value, above face value, or below face value? Explain your answer.

Exercises . . . .

E12-1   Indicate the effect on a company's debt/equity ratio as a result of the following transactions:

    a.   Purchased equipment recorded under a capital lease.

    b.   Purchased equipment recorded under an operating lease.

    c.   Purchased inventory for cash.

    d.   Recorded depreciation of equipment leased under a capital lease.

    e.   Issued a bond payable at a discount.

    f.   Market value of bonds increased after the issue date.

    g.   Purchased land and issued a five-year note.

    h.   Paid interest on bonds that were issued at par.

E12-2   On January 1, 2000, Jones Company issued $1,000,000 20-year bonds at 8%. The bonds pay interest on June 30 and December 31 of each year. The issue price was $875,378.

Required

    a.   Was the market interest rate on January 1, 2000 higher, lower, or the same as the coupon rate on the bonds? Explain.

    b.   Prepare the journal entry to issue the bonds.

    c.   Explain how an increase in market interest rates during 2002 will affect:

        1.   Jones Company

        2.   The original bondholders who sell the bonds during 2002

        3.   Investors who purchase the bonds during 2002

E12-3   A.J. Corporation issues a $10,000 bond paying 6% interest (annual coupon) for five years on 1/1/2000. The bond is issued to yield investors 8% interest, selling for $9,201.43.

Required

    a.   Prepare the journal entry to record the sale of the bond on 1/1/2000.

    b.   How will the bond be presented on A.J.'s balance sheet on 1/1/2000?

    c.   Prepare the entry to record the first coupon interest payment on 12/31/2000.

    d.   What will be the economic value of the bond on 12/31/2000, assuming no change in market interest rates?

    e.   How will the bond be presented on the balance sheet on 12/31/2000?

    f.   What will be the amount of the net bond liability on 12/31/2004, the day before the bond matures?

    g.   Prepare the entry that will be made on 1/1/2005, the maturity date of the bond.

E12-4 P.J. Corporation issues a $5,000 bond paying 6% interest annually for five years on 1/1/2000. The bond is issued to yield investors 5% interest, selling for $ 5,216.49.

Required

a. Prepare the journal entry to record the sale of the bond on 1/1/2000.

b. How will the bond be presented on P.J.'s balance sheet on 1/1/2000?

c. Prepare the entry to record the first coupon interest payment on 12/31/2000.

d. What will be the economic value of the bond on 12/31/2000, assuming no change in market interest rates?

e. How will the bond be presented on the balance sheet on 12/31/2000?

f. What will be the amount of the net bond liability on 12/31/2004, the day before the bond matures?

g. Prepare the entry that will be made on 1/1/2005, the maturity date of the bond.

E12-5 On January 2, 2001, Noblick Corporation leased equipment under a three-year lease with payments of $3,000 on each December 31 of the lease term. The present value of the lease payments at a discount rate of 10% is $7,460. If the lease is considered a capital lease, depreciation expense (straight line) and interest expense are recognized. If the lease is considered an operating lease, then rent expense is recognized.

Required

a. What factors must Noblick consider in determining whether the lease is a capital lease or an operating lease?

b. What will be the total expense recognized on Noblick's income statement over the three years if the lease is considered an operating lease?

c. What will be the total expense recognized on Noblick's income statement over the three years if the lease is considered a capital lease?

d. Which lease will result in the highest income in each of the three years? Explain.

e. Which lease will result in the highest cash flow in each of the three years? Explain.

E12-6 On January 1, 2001, Kasper Corporation leased telephone equipment from Telecommunications Company. The lease requires three annual payments of $12,000 on January 1, 2001, 2002, and 2003. The present value of the lease payments at a discount rate of 10% is $32,826. Straight-line depreciation is used on all equipment with no salvage value.

Required

a. If the lease is considered an operating lease, compute the total expense that would be recognized in 2001.

b. If the lease is considered a capital lease, compute the total expense that would be recognized in 2001.

E12-7 Jones Corporation takes out a 30 year, 8.5% fixed rate mortgage of $121,000 on 1/1/2000. The principal and interest payments are $933 per month.

Required

a. Complete the following debt payment schedule for the first three months of the mortgage.

Date	Cash Payment	Interest Expense	Principal Decrease	Unpaid Principal
1/1/2000				
2/1/2000				
3/1/2000				
4/1/2000				

b. Prepare the journal entry to record the mortgage.

c. Prepare the entry for the first payment.

d. What will be the total interest paid over the life of the mortgage?

E12-8 (Appendix)

Sorena Corporation contracts with First Bank to borrow $10,000 on January 2, 2000. The annual interest rate on the loan is 8%. The loan is due in five years. Sorena will pay interest only at the end of each of the next five years and will repay the principal in its entirety at the end of five years.

Required

a. Prepare journal entries to record the issuance of the loan, the interest payments made, and the repayment of the loan.

b. What is the present value of the loan at 8%? Show computations.

c. If interest rates rise to 10% during the life of the loan, how will the entries made in part a be affected? Explain.

E12-9 (Appendix)

Refer to E12-8. Assume that, instead of paying interest annually, First Bank will accept one payment repaying principal and interest at the end of five years.

Required

a. Prepare a schedule computing the amount of the repayment.

b. Prepare a schedule computing the present value of the loan.

c. Prepare journal entries to show the acquisition of the loan on January 2, 2000, and any adjusting entry required on December 31, 2000 and December 31, 2001.

d. What entry will be made on the repayment date?

e. If interest rates fall to 6% during the life of the loan, how will the entries made in parts a through d be affected?

E12-10 (Appendix)

Refer to E12-9. Assume that First Bank requires five annual payments of $2,504.56.

Required

a. Prepare a schedule computing the present value of the loan.

b. Prepare a schedule showing the amount of each payment that will be applied to principal and interest.

c. What will be the total interest expense over the life of the loan?

d. What will be the book value of the loan after the third payment?

e. Prepare journal entries to 1) record the loan, and 2) record the first two interest payments.

Problems ·

P12-1 On January 1, 2000, Gerry Corporation issued $10,000,000 face value 8% bonds paying interest semi-annually at face value. By December 31, 2002, the market value of the bonds had fallen to $9,875,200. Interest payment dates are January 1 and July 1 of each year.

Required

a. Prepare the entry to record the sale of the bonds on January 1, 2000.

b. Prepare the entry made on the first interest payment date of July 1, 2000.

c. What would have been the book value of the bonds on December 31, 2002?

d. What factors would have caused the market value of the bonds to fall below the face value? Explain.

e. What accounting adjustment would be required by Gerry on December 31, 2002?

f. Assume that Gerry retires the bonds on December 31, 2002 by buying the bonds on the open market. What journal entry would be made to retire the bonds?

g. Indicate the impact of the bond retirement on Gerry's net income and debt-to-equity ratio.

h. Explain why management may sometimes retire bonds when it is not in the best interest of the company's stockholders.

P12-2 The balance sheet and income statement of Coca-Cola Company and Subsidiaries at December 31, 1999 are as follows:

Coca-Cola Company and Subsidiaries
Income Statement (in millions)

	For the year ended 12/31/99
Net operating revenues	$19,805
Cost of goods sold	6,009
Gross Profit	13,796
Selling, administrative, and general expenses	9,001
Other operating charges	813
Operating income	3,982
Interest income	260
Interest expense	337
Equity income (loss)	(184)
Other income-net	98
Income before income taxes	3,819
Income taxes	1,388
Net income	$2,431

Coca-Cola Company and Subsidiaries
Consolidated Balance Sheet (in millions)

As of December 31, 1999

ASSETS	
Cash and cash equivalents	$ 1,611
Marketable securities	201
Trade accounts receivable, less allowance of $26	1,798
Inventories	1,076
Prepaid expenses and other assets	1,794
Total current assets	6,480
INVESTMENTS AND OTHER ASSETS	
Equity method investments:	
Coca-Cola Enterprises Inc.	728
Coca-Cola Amatil Ltd.	1,133
Coca-Cola Beverages plc	788
Other, principally bottling companies	3,793
Cost method investments	350
Marketable securities and other assets	2,124
	8,916
PROPERTY, PLANT AND EQUIPMENT	
Land	215
Buildings and improvements	1,528
Machinery and equipment	4,527
Containers	201
	6,471
Less allowances for depreciation	2,204
	4,267
Goodwill and other intangible assets	1,960
Total assets	$21,623
LIABILITIES AND SHARE-OWNERS' EQUITY	
Current	
Accounts payable and accrued expenses	$3,714
Loans and notes payable	5,112
Current maturities of long-term debt	261
Accrued income taxes	769
Total current liabilities	9,856
Long-term debt	854
Other liabilities	902
Deferred income taxes	498
Total liabilities	12,110
SHARE-OWNERS' EQUITY	
Common stock	867
Capital surplus	2,584
Reinvested earnings	20,773
Accumulated other comprehensive income	(1,551)
Less treasury stock, at cost	(13,160)
Total share-owners' equity	9,513
Total liabilities and share-owners' equity	$21,623

Assume that Coca-Cola acquired equipment under a long-term lease on January 2, 2000. The present value of the minimum lease payments is $12,000,000. The life of the lease and the equipment are assumed to be five years, with no residual value. An effective interest rate of 10%

was used to determine the present value of the minimum lease payments. The lease will require five annual payments of $2,877,794, with the first payment due on January 2, 2000.

Required

a. Compute Coca-Cola's debt/equity ratio (using noncurrent liabilities) at December 31, 1999.

b. Prepare the journal entry required to record the first lease payment on January 2, 2000.

c. Prepare the journal entry required to record the second lease payment on January 2, 2001.

d. What will be the effect of the capital lease on Coca-Cola's income statement for 2000?

e. Compute Coca-Cola's debt/equity ratio immediately after acquiring the equipment. Comment on the impact of the lease agreement on Coca-Cola's ability to obtain additional long-term financing.

P12-3 O'Brien Corporation issued $100,000 face-value 8% 10-year bonds on 1/1/01. The bonds pay interest semi-annually and were sold to yield 10%. The final selling price was $87,538. Assume that the market rate of interest stays at 10% over the ten-year period.

Required

a. Explain what factors would cause the bonds to sell at a discount.

b. Prepare the entry that O'Brien made to record the sale of the bonds.

c. Design an Excel spreadsheet to complete the following schedule:

From	To	Beginning Balance	Interest Expense	Coupon Payment	Discount Amortization
1/1/01	6/30/01				
7/1/01	12/31/01				
1/1/02	6/30/02				
7/1/02	12/31/02				
1/1/03	6/30/03				
7/1/03	12/31/03				
1/1/04	6/30/04				
7/1/04	12/31/04				
1/1/05	6/30/05				
7/1/05	12/31/05				
1/1/06	6/30/06				
7/1/06	12/31/06				
1/1/07	6/30/07				
7/1/07	12/31/07				
1/1/08	6/30/08				
7/1/08	12/31/08				
1/1/09	6/30/09				
7/1/09	12/31/09				
1/1/10	6/30/10				
7/1/10	12/31/10				

d.   Prepare the entry to record the first interest payment on 6/30/01.

e.   Show how the bonds would be presented on O'Brien's balance sheet at 12/31/01.

f.   What is the economic value of the bonds on 12/31/01?

g.   What should the liability value and the economic value of the bonds be on 1/1/11, the maturity date of the bonds? Explain.

h.   Prepare the entry to record the retirement of the bonds on 1/1/11.

P12-4   Refer to P12-3. Assume that on 6/30/09, market interest rates soared to 12%.

Required

a.   Compute the economic value of the bonds on 6/30/09.

b.   Comment on any accounting adjustments required by O'Brien Corporation because of the change in market interest rates.

c.   What entry would be made by O'Brien if it retired the bonds on 6/30/09 by purchasing the bonds in the open market?

d.   Explain why the action taken in c may not be in the best interests of O'Brien's stockholders.

P12-5   The following is the GAAP interest amortization schedule for a $1,000 face, 6% semi-annual coupon, 10% market interest rate compounded semi-annually. The bond was issued on 1/1/01 and matures on 12/31/05.

From	To	Beginning Balance	Interest Expense	Coupon Payment	Discount Amortization	Ending Balance
1/1/01	6/30/01	$ 922.78	$ 46.14	$ 40.00	$ 6.14	$ 928.92
7/1/01	12/31/01	928.92	46.45	40.00	6.45	935.36
1/1/02	6/30/02	935.36	46.77	40.00	6.77	942.13
7/1/02	12/31/02	942.13	47.11	40.00	7.11	949.24
1/1/03	6/30/03	949.24	47.46	40.00	7.46	956.70
7/1/03	12/31/03	956.70	47.84	40.00	7.84	964.54
1/1/04	6/30/04	964.54	48.23	40.00	8.23	972.76
7/1/04	12/31/04	972.76	48.64	40.00	8.64	981.40
1/1/05	6/31/05	981.40	49.07	40.00	9.07	990.47
7/1/05	12/31/05	990.47	49.52	40.00	9.52	1,000.00
	Totals		$477.22	$400.00	$ 77.22	

Required

a.   If the bond is retired at maturity, what entry would be made?   *Bonds Payable   1000*
                                                                    Cash   1000

b.   Suppose the company purchased the bond from its holder on 6/30/03 for $935.00. What entry would be made to retire the bonds?

c.   Suppose that the bond was retired on January 1, 2003 by purchasing it in the market for $1,000. What entry would be made to retire the bonds?

d.   What are the GAAP accounting treatments for bonds retired before their maturity date? Discuss the significance of these rules and why they exist.

P12-6 Radley Corporation issued $800,000 face-value 10% 10-year bonds on 1/1/01. The bonds pay interest semi-annually and were sold to yield 8%. The final selling price was $908,723. Assume that the market rate of interest stays at 8% over the ten-year period.

Required
a. Explain what factors would cause the bonds to sell at a premium.
b. Prepare the entry that Radley made to record the sale of the bonds.
c. Design an Excel spreadsheet to complete the following schedule:

From	To	Beginning Balance	Interest Expense	Coupon Payment	Premium Amortization
1/1/01	6/30/01				
7/1/01	12/31/01				
1/1/02	6/30/02				
7/1/02	12/31/02				
1/1/03	6/30/03				
7/1/03	12/31/03				
1/1/04	6/30/04				
7/1/04	12/31/04				
1/1/05	6/30/05				
7/1/05	12/31/05				
1/1/06	6/30/06				
7/1/06	12/31/06				
1/1/07	6/30/07				
7/1/07	12/31/07				
1/1/08	6/30/08				
7/1/08	12/31/08				
1/1/09	6/30/09				
7/1/09	12/31/09				
1/1/10	6/30/10				
7/1/10	12/31/10				

d. Prepare the entry to record the first interest payment on 6/30/01.
e. Show how the bonds would be presented on Radley's balance sheet at 12/31/02.
f. What is the economic value of the bonds on 12/31/02?
g. What should the liability value and the economic value of the bonds be on 1/01/11, the maturity date of the bonds? Explain.
h. Prepare the entry to record the retirement of the bonds on 1/01/11.

P12-7 Refer to P12-6. Assume that on 12/31/07, market interest rates had fallen to 6%.

Required
a. Determine the economic value of the bond on 12/31/07.
b. What entry would be made by Radley Corporation if it retired the bonds on 12/31/07 by purchasing the bonds in the open market?
c. Explain the effect of the bond retirement on Radley's income statement and balance sheet.

P12-8   The following is the balance sheet of Globalstar Telecommunications LP, a provider of global satellite-telephone services, at 12/31/99 and 12/31/98.

Globalstar Telecommunications Ltd
Balance Sheet

	12/31/1999	12/31/1998
ASSETS		
Current assets:		
Cash and cash equivalents	$127,675,000	$56,223,000
Restricted cash	46,246,000	516,000
Insurance proceeds receivable		28,500,000
Production gateways and user terminals	114,980,000	145,509,000
Other current assets	4,001,000	5,540,000
Total current assets	292,902,000	236,288,000
Property and equipment, net	5,128,000	4,958,000
Globalstar System under construction:		
Space segment	2,109,275,000	1,615,485,000
Ground segment	1,071,914,000	686,848,000
Total Globalstar System	3,181,189,000	2,302,333,000
Additional spare satellites	53,467,000	—
Deferred financing costs	151,873,000	15,845,000
Other assets	96,900,000	110,601,000
Total assets	$3,781,459,000	$2,670,025,000
LIABILITIES AND PARTNERS' CAPITAL		
Current liabilities:		
Accounts payable	10,908,000	14,240,000
Payable to affiliates	468,536,000	216,542,000
Vendor financing liability	137,484,000	127,180,000
Accrued expenses	20,841,000	11,679,000
Accrued interest	33,533,000	31,549,000
Total current liabilities	671,302,000	401,190,000
Deferred revenues	25,811,000	25,811,000
Vendor financing liability, net of current portion	256,311,000	243,990,000
Deferred interest payable	595,000	458,000
Term loans payable	400,000,000	—
Senior notes payable ($1,450,000 aggregate principal amount)	1,399,111,000	1,396,175,000
Commitments and contingencies		
Partners' capital:	—	—
8% Series A convertible redeemable preferred partnership interests (4,396,295 interests outstanding at December 31, 1999, $220 million redemption value)	213,393,000	
9% Series B convertible redeemable preferred partnership interests (3,000,000 interests outstanding at December 31, 1999, $150 million redemption value)	145,575,000	
Ordinary partnership interests	516,530,000	573,421,000
Unearned compensation	(16,754,000)	
Warrants	169,585,000	28,980,000
Total partners' capital	1,028,329,000	602,401,000
Total liabilities and partners' capital	$3,781,459,000	$2,670,025,000

Required

a.   Compute Globalstar's debt/equity ratio for 1998 and 1999.

b.   Globalstar's partners' capital account includes redeemable preferred partnership interests. Comment on the inclusion of such interests in partners' equity.

c.   What effect would the removal of the redeemable preferred interests have on Globalstar's debt/equity ratio?

d.   Comment on the financial health of Globalstar.

P12-9   On January 1, 2001 ABC Manufacturing Company signs a three-year lease to acquire a computer. Under the terms of the Lease ABC is to pay Leasing Company $10,000 at the end of the current year and at the end of the subsequent two years.

Required

a.   If the lease is considered an operating lease, what journal entry will ABC Company make at the end of each of the three years of the lease?

b.   If the lease is considered a capital lease and the appropriate interest rate for ABC Manufacturing Company to use is 10%, what is the journal entry made on January 1, 2001 to record the lease?

c.   For the capital lease described in b, make all of the necessary journal entries related to the lease on December 31, 2001; on December 31, 2002; and on December 31, 2003.

d.   Over the life of the lease, how does the total expense associated with the lease compare under operating lease treatment and capital lease treatment?

Cases and Projects . . . .

C12-1   Bell South

On November 29, 1995, the Wall Street Journal reported:

> Bell South yesterday became the second company in a week and the fifth since 1954 to sell 100 year bonds. . . . The so-called Baby Bell that provides telephone services in the nine-state Southeast region, issued $500 million of the century bonds.

Required

a.   What likely conditions existed in the general economy that would have encouraged Bell South to make such an unusual move?

b.   Comment on the likely effect the issuance of 100 year maturity bonds would have on Bell South's financial statements.

c.   Comment on the risks and rewards of investing in such bonds.

C12-2   Verizon Communications

The notes to Consolidated Financial Statements of Verizon Communications at December 31, 2000 include the following information:

We lease certain facilities and equipment for use in our operations under both capital and operating leases. Total rent expense under operating leases amounted to $1,052 million in 2000, $1,008 million in 1999, and $1,020 million in 1998.

Capital lease amounts included in plant, property and equipment are as follows:

	(Dollars in millions)	
	At December 31	
	2000	*1999*
Capital leases	$283	$257
Accumulated amortization	(165)	(155)
Total	$118	$102

The aggregate minimum rental commitments under noncancelable leases for the periods shown at December 31, 2000 are as follows:

	(Dollars in millions)	
Years	*Capital Leases*	*Operating Leases*
2001	$ 38	$ 571
2002	31	500
2003	24	416
2004	15	335
2005	15	254
Thereafter	76	1,224
Total minimum rental commitments	199	$3,300
Less interest and executory costs	(55)	
Present value of minimum lease payments	144	
Less current installments	(32)	
Long-term obligation at December 31, 2000	$112	

Required

a. Discuss the requirements under GAAP that determine whether a lease is accounted for as a capital lease or an operating lease.

b. Would Verizon's operating income be higher or lower if all leases are accounted for as operating leases? Explain.

c. What sections of Verizon's Statement of Cash Flows would be affected by the leases shown above? Explain the impact of the operating and capital leases on the Cash Flow Statement.

d. Would Verizon's times interest earned ratio be higher or lower in 2000 if all of the leases are accounted for as operating leases? Explain.

C12-3 Mendocino Brewing Company, Inc.

Mendocino Brewing Company and its subsidiary operate two breweries, which are in the business of producing beer and malt beverages for the specialty "craft" segment of the beer market. They also own and operate a brewpub and gift store. The breweries are in two locations—Ukiah, California and Saratoga Springs, New York, where the company began operations in December 1997. The brewpub and gift store are located in Hopland, California. The majority of sales for Mendocino Brewing Company are in California. The company brews several brands, of which Red Tail Ale is the flagship brand. In addition, the company performs contract brewing for several other brands.

The following is the current balance sheets, income statements, cash flow statements and several footnotes from the Mendocino Brewing Co. 1999 10K.

Mendocino Brewing Company, Inc. and Subsidiary
Consolidated Balance Sheets
(December 31, 1999 and 1998)

	1999	1998
Assets		
Current assets		
Cash	$ —	$ 42,000
Accounts receivable	1,040,300	679,900
Inventories	1,168,700	978,000
Prepaid expenses	57,200	33,500
Deferred income taxes	43,100	138,300
Total current assets	2,309,300	1,871,700
Property and equipment	14,727,200	15,259,800
Other assets		
Deferred income taxes	2,440,300	1,614,200
Deposits and other assets	22,900	34,600
Intangibles, net of amortization	130,200	142,900
	2,593,400	1,791,700
Total assets	$19,629,900	$18,923,200
Liabilities and Stockholders' Equity		
Current liabilities		
Disbursements in excess of deposits	$ 9,600	$ —
Line of credit	1,159,800	—
Accounts payable	1,708,700	806,700
Accrued wages and related expense	204,600	210,800
Accrued liabilities	130,300	91,000
Current maturities of long-term debt	321,000	322,000
Current maturities of obligations under capital lease	275,700	221,300
Current maturities of notes payable to related party	—	850,600
Total current liabilities	3,809,700	2,502,400
Long-term debt, less current maturities	3,589,600	3,871,800
Line of credit	—	738,000
Obligations under capital lease, less current maturities	1,396,900	1,525,800
Notes payable to related party, less current maturities	576,300	143,400
Total liabilities	9,372,500	8,781,400
Stockholders' Equity		
Preferred stock, Series A, no par value, with aggregate liquidation preference of $227,600; 227,600 shares authorized, issued and outstanding	227,600	227,600
Common stock, no par value; 20,000,000 shares authorized 5,530,177 and 4,497,059 shares issued and outstanding at December 31, 1999 and 1998, respectively	13,834,900	12,413,000
Accumulated deficit	(3,805,100)	(2,498,800)
Total stockholders' equity	10,257,400	10,141,800
Total liabilities and stockholders' equity	$ 19,629,900	$ 18,923,200

Mendocino Brewing Company, Inc. and Subsidiary
Consolidated Statements of Cash Flows
Years Ended December 31, 1999 and 1998

	1999	1998
Cash Flows from Operating Activities		
Net loss	$(1,306,300)	$(1,562,300)
Adjustments to reconcile net loss to net cash		
used by operating activities:		
Depreciation and amortization	794,600	779,400
Induced conversion expense	263,900	—
Gain on sale of assets	—	(3,700)
Deferred income taxes	(730,900)	(1,139,600)
Stock issued for services	102,600	—
Accrued interest converted to stock	61,200	—
Changes in:		
Accounts receivable	(360,400)	(350,200)
Inventories	(190,700)	(433,900)
Prepaid expenses	(23,700)	9,100
Deposits and other assets	11,700	(33,100)
Refundable income taxes	—	106,300
Accounts payable	902,000	78,400
Accrued wages and related expense	39,300	41,100
Accrued liabilities	(6,200)	(157,800)
Net cash used by operating activities	(442,900)	(2,666,300)
Cash Flows from Investing Activities		
Purchases of property, equipment and		
leasehold improvements	(99,800)	(185,900)
Increase in intangibles	—	(63,100)
Proceeds from sale of fixed assets	—	24,000
Net cash used by investing activities	(99,800)	(225,000)
Cash Flows from Financing Activities		
Net borrowings on line of credit	421,800	138,000
Borrowings on long-term debt	—	1,433,600
Principal payments on long-term debt	(283,200)	(153,400)
Payments on obligations under capital lease	(223,800)	(185,200)
Disbursements in excess of deposits	9,600	—
Proceeds from notes payable to related party	576,300	994,000
Net cash provided by financing activities	500,700	2,227,000
Decrease in Cash	(42,000)	(664,300)
Cash, beginning of year	42,000	706,300
Cash, end of year	$ —	$ 42,000

Mendocino Brewing Company, Inc. and Subsidiary
Consolidated Statements of Operations
(Years Ended December 31, 1999 and 1998)

	1999	1998
Sales	$ 9,240,000	$ 6,918,800
Less excise taxes	541,400	389,100
Net sales	8,698,600	6,529,700
Cost of goods sold	5,767,900	4,908,000
Gross profit	2,930,700	1,621,700
Operating Expenses		
Retail operating	417,500	481,900
Marketing	1,691,100	1,311,700
General and administrative	1,652,200	1,901,400
	3,760,800	3,695,000
Loss from operations	(830,100)	(2,073,300)
Other Income (Expense)		
Induced conversion	(263,900)	—
Interest income	500	1,900
Other income (expense)	(95,500)	2,900
Gain on sale of equipment	—	3,700
Interest expense	(846,800)	(636,300)
	(1,205,700)	(627,800)
Loss before income taxes	(2,035,800)	(2,701,100)
Benefit from income taxes	(729,500)	(1,138,800)
Net loss	$(1,306,300)	$(1,562,300)

Note 4: Line of Credit

The Company has available a $3,000,000 line of credit with interest at the prime rate, plus 2.25%. Approximately $1,484,000 was advanced to the Company in the form of a term loan (see Note 5). The bank's commitment under the line of credit matures September 2000. The agreement is secured by substantially all the assets of the Releta Brewing Company, LLC, accounts receivable, inventory, certain securities pledged by a stockholder, and a second position on the real property of Mendocino Brewing Company.

Note 5: Long-Term Debt

	1999	1998
Note payable to bank, in monthly installments of $24,400, including interest at the Treasury Constant Maturity Index, currently 5.83% plus 4.17%; maturing December 2012, with a balloon payment, secured by substantially all the assets of Mendocino Brewing Company	$2,655,800	$2,679,900

Note payable to financial institution,
    in monthly installments of $24,700,
    plus interest at the prime rate plus
    2.25%, currently 10.75%; maturing
    March 2004; secured by substantially
    all the assets of the Releta Brewing
    Company, certain securities pledged
    by a stockholder, accounts receivable,
    inventory and a second position on
    the other assets of Mendocino Brewing
    Company

Note payable to financial institution, ... Company	1,236,600	1,484,000
Note payable, in monthly installments of $1,200, including interest at 5.65%; maturing March 2001; secured by vehicle	18,200	29,900
	3,910,600	4,193,800
Less current maturities	321,000	322,000
	$3,589,600	$3,871,800

Maturities of long-term debt for succeeding years are as follows:

	Year Ending December 31,
2000	$ 321,000
2001	373,900
2002	377,100
2003	384,400
2004	145,000
Thereafter	2,309,200
	$3,910,600

Note 6: Obligations Under Capital Lease

The Company leases brewing and office equipment under various capital lease agreements with various financial institutions.

Future minimum lease payments under these capital lease agreements are as follows:

	Year Ending December 31,
2000	$ 430,800
2001	422,000
2002	402,400
2003	824,900
Thereafter	15,600
	2,095,700
Less amounts representing interest	423,100
Present value of minimum lease payments	1,672,600
Less current maturities	275,700
	$1,396,900

Note 7: Notes Payable to Related Party

	1999	1998
Notes payable consists of convertible notes to United Breweries of America, a related party, with interest at the prime rate plus 1.5%, maturing 18 months after the advances, unsecured, subordinated to bank debt, upon maturity are convertible into common stock at $1.50 per share or may be repaid in 60 monthly installments, notes mature through June 2001, including $11,200 of accrued interest	$576,300	$994,000
Less current maturities	—	850,600
	$576,300	$143,400

Note 16: Statement of Cash Flows

Supplemental cash flow information includes the following:

	1999	1998
Cash paid during the year for:		
Interest	$ 771,600	$ 623,400
Income taxes	$ 1,400	$ 2,300
Non-cash investing and financing activities:		
Seller financed equipment	$ 149,200	$ 224,300
Issuance of stock for intangibles	$ —	$ 45,800
Transfer of liabilities to long-term debt	$ —	$ 80,200
Induced conversion	$1,319,300	$ —
Stock issued for services	$ 102,600	$ —

Required

The following T-accounts relate to long-term liabilities and their associated current portions. Fill in all of the question marks to obtain a complete picture of the financing transactions of Mendocino for the 1999 fiscal year. Because of rounding errors you will not be able to explain the changes exactly in every account. What does the financing activity of the year tell you about Mendocino?

Current maturities of obligations under capital lease		Obligations under capital lease	
	? Beginning balance		? Beginning balance
Subtractions ?		Subtractions ?	
	? Additions		? Additions
	? Ending balance		? Ending balance

**Current maturities of
long-term debt**

		?	Beginning balance
Subtractions	?		
		?	Additions
		?	Ending balance

Long-term debt

		?	Beginning balance
Subtractions	?		
		?	Additions
		?	Ending balance

**Line of credit
(current)**

		?	Beginning balance
Subtractions	?		
		?	Additions
		?	Ending balance

**Line of credit
(long-term)**

		?	Beginning balance
Subtractions	?		
		?	Additions
		?	Ending balance

**Current maturities of
notes payable-related party**

		?	Beginning balance
Subtractions	?		
		?	Additions
		?	Ending balance

**Notes payable
to related party**

		?	Beginning balance
Subtractions	?		
		?	Additions
		?	Ending balance

Chapter thirteen

Equities

Questions . . . .

1. What is a corporate charter?
2. What are the three important rights of owners of a corporation?
3. What are shareholder resolutions?
4. Name two rights of preferred stockholders.
5. Describe the four features that distinguish debt from equity.
6. Explain why preferred stock is often described as a "hybrid" security.
7. What is meant by redeemable preferred stock?
8. What is meant by cumulative preferred stock?
9. What is a stock warrant?
10. Explain the meaning of the terms authorized, issued, and outstanding as they relate to common stock.
11. Explain why the accounts "unearned compensation ESOP" and "accumulated other comprehensive income" appear in the stockholders' equity section of the balance sheet.
12. What is treasury stock?
13. Is the purchase of treasury stock like the retirement of shares? Why or why not?
14. Explain why treasury stock is not an asset.
15. How are gains or losses on the sale of treasury stock accounted for?
16. When do dividends become a liability of a corporation?
17. Give the entry to record the declaration of $100 of cash dividends.
18. Give the entry to record the payment of $100 of cash dividends previously declared.
19. What accounting entry would be made to record a 3-for-1 stock split?
20. How does a 3-for-1 stock split affect a company's income statement and balance sheet?
21. What is a stock dividend?
22. What effect does a 10% stock dividend have on a company's income statement and balance sheet?
23. Explain the difference between basic earnings per share and diluted earnings per share.
24. Explain why preferred dividends are deducted from net income in the computation of earnings per share.
25. What is meant by dilution?
26. What are anti-dilutive securities?

Exercises . . . .

E13-1   A note in the Management's Discussion and Analysis section of the 2000 annual report of the Yankee Candle Company stated:

Partnerships affiliated with Forstmann Little & Co. own approximately 63% of the company's common stock and control the Company.

What are the implications of this disclosure to other stockholders and interested investors of Yankee Candle Company?

E13-2 Gemminger Corporation reported the following stockholders' equity section in its balance sheet at December 31, 2000:

Gemminger Corporation
Stockholders' Equity

	December 31, 2000
4% Cumulative preferred stock, $50 par value	$1,600,000
Common stock, 400,000 shares authorized, 300,000 shares issued	4,500,000
Additional paid-in capital: common	900,000
Retained earnings	6,800,000
Less: treasury stock at cost, 10,000 common shares	(250,000)
Total Stockholders' Equity	$13,550,000

Required

a.   Determine the number of shares Gemminger had outstanding at December 31, 2000.

b.   Determine the average issue price of Gemminger's common stock.

E13-3 Refer to E13-2. Assume that Gemminger declares a cash dividend of $934,000. Determine the amount that an owner of one share of Gemminger's common stock will receive.

E13-4 Refer to E13-2. Assume that Gemminger reissues 1,000 shares of the treasury stock at $28 per share.

Required

a.   Prepare the journal entry made for the reissuance of the treasury stock.

b.   Determine the impact of the reissuance on Gemminger's total assets and total equity.

E13-5 During 2000, Janney Corp. had $2,000,000 of 5% convertible bonds outstanding. The bonds may be converted into a total of 40,000 shares of common stock. The common stock is currently selling for $30 per share. The company's average tax rate is 40%. What is the numerator and denominator effect of the convertible bonds when computing diluted earnings per share?

E13-6 During 2000, Bunneymen Echo Chambers Inc. had 2000 common stock options outstanding. Each option may be used to purchase one share of common stock at $15 per share. The common stock sold at an average price of $25 per share during 2000. What will be the effect of the stock options on the company's basic and diluted earnings per share during 2000?

E13-7 On December 31, 1999, Case, Inc. had 300,000 shares of common stock issued and outstanding. Case issued a 10% stock dividend on July 1, 2000. On October 1, 2000, Case purchased 24,000 shares of its common stock for the treasury, and recorded the purchase by the cost method. What is the number of shares that should be used in computing earnings per share for the year ended December 31, 2000?

E13-8   On May 10, 2001, the Wall Street Journal reported:

Verizon Communications sagged $1.78 to 53.82. The telecommunications service concern unveiled one of the largest convertible debt issues ever, a $3 billion offering of zero-coupon notes.

Explain why the stock market would have such a negative reaction to Verizon's ability to raise $3 billion in financing.

E13-9   South Company had 1,000,000 shares of $5 par value common stock issued and outstanding on January 1, 2001. The following events took place during 2001:

March 15, 2001: Purchased 100,000 shares of treasury stock for $20 per share

June 30, 2001: Reissued 50,000 shares of treasury stock for $23 per share

December 15, 2001: Reissued 10,000 shares of treasury stock for $19 per share

Required
Prepare journal entries for each of the three transactions.

Problems . . . .

P13-1   At December 31, 1999, Volleyballs 'R Us Corp. reported the following in its balance sheet:

Common stock, $10 par value, 200,000 shares issued and outstanding

During 2000, the following equity transactions occurred:

April 1	Issued 400,000 shares of common stock at $40 per share.
May 1	Declared and issued a 10% stock dividend. Market price on the date of issue was $42 per share.
September 1	Declared and issued a 4-1 stock split
October 1	Purchased 50,000 shares at $45 per share of common stock and placed them in the treasury.

Required

a.   Prepare journal entries where required for all 2000 transactions.

b.   Complete the following table. Indicate the impact of each of the transactions on the company's assets, liabilities, and equity. Use I for Increase, D for Decrease, and NE for No effect.

Transaction	Assets	Liabilities	Equity
April 1			
May 1			
September 1			
October 1			

c.   Determine the number of shares that will be outstanding on December 31, 2000.

P13-2   The following was extracted from the balance of Bledsoe Corp. at December 31, 1999:

Stockholders' equity:

8% Cumulative preferred stock, $100 par, 500,000 shares authorized, 300,000 shares issued	$ 30,000,000
Common stock, $10 par value, 2,000,000 shares authorized, 1,500,000 shares issued	15,000,000
Additional paid-in capital	40,000,000
Retained earnings	58,000,000
	143,000,000
Less common treasury shares, 300,000 shares at cost	(1,500,000)
Total stockholders' equity	$ 141,500,000

Required

a.   Assume Bledsoe issued the cumulative preferred at the beginning of 1999 and declared total dividends of $2,000,000 in 1999. How much of a total dividend (both preferred and common) would Bledsoe need to declare in 2000 to be able to pay the common shareholders a $2 per share dividend?

b.   What would be the effect on the following balance sheet items if Bledsoe declares a 25% common stock dividend on the outstanding shares at a time when the stock is selling at $60 per share?

   Common stock:

   Additional paid-in capital:

   Retained earnings:

   Total stockholders' equity:

c.   What would be the effect on the following balance sheet items if Bledsoe declares a 2-1 stock split at a time when the stock is selling at $60 per share?

   Common stock:

   Additional paid-in capital:

   Retained earnings:

   Treasury stock:

P13-3   Total stockholders' equity:

Lyons, Inc. had 1,000,000 authorized shares of $10 par value common stock, of which 400,000 shares were issued and outstanding. The stockholders' equity accounts at December 31, 1999, had the following balances:

Common stock	$4,000,000
Additional paid in capital-common	840,000
Retained earnings	3,800,000
Accumulated other comprehensive income	120,000

Transactions during 2000 and other information relating to the stockholders' equity accounts were as follows:

a.   On January 8, 2000, Lyons issued 30,000 shares of $100 par, 7% cumulative preferred stock at $105 per share. Lyons had 30,000 authorized shares of preferred stock.

b.   On March 1, 2000, Lyons reacquired 10,000 shares of its common stock at a price of $12 per share. Lyons uses the cost method of accounting for treasury stock.

c. On April 8, 2000, Lyons issued 50,000 shares of previously unissued common stock for $600,000.

d. On November 10, 2000, Lyons sold 4,000 shares of treasury stock for $10 per share.

e. Net income for the year ended December 31, 2000 was $748,000.

f. The company experienced a holding loss of $45,000 on its available for sale securities during 2000.

g. On December 31, 2000, the Board of Directors declared the yearly cash dividend on the preferred stock, payable on January 15, 2001 to stockholders of record as of December 31, 2000. The Board of Directors also declared a cash dividend of $.20 per share on the common stock, payable on January 15, 2001 to stockholders of record as of December 31, 2000.

Required

a. Prepare a statement of changes in stockholders' equity for the year ended December 31, 2000 in good form.

b. Prepare the stockholders' equity section of the balance sheet at December 31, 2000 in good form.

P13-4 The following information relates to Morse Inc. at December 31, 2000:

Net income	$5,000,000
Preferred dividend requirement	$ 600,000
Weighted average shares outstanding	400,000

The following analysis has been performed in anticipation of computing earnings per share:

	Numerator effect	*Denominator effect*
Convertible preferred	$600,000	100,000
Convertible bonds	$48,000	4,000
Stock options	—	1,000

Required

a. Compute basic earnings per share.

b. Compute diluted earnings per share.

P13-5 The stockholders equity section of the balance sheet of Papillardo Corporation at December 31, 2000 appears as follows:

Stockholders' equity:

7 % preferred stock, $100 par 100,000 shares authorized, 40,000 shares issued	$4,000,000
Common stock, $1 par, 1,000,000 shares authorized, 600,000 shares issued, of which 50,000 are held in treasury	600,000
Additional paid in capital:	
From issuance of preferred stock	480,000
From issuance of common stock	1,410,000
From treasury stock transactions	25,000
Retained earnings	4,500,000
Less treasury stock (at cost: 50,000 common shares)	(300,000)
Total stockholders' equity	$10,715,000

Required

Answer the following questions related to Papillardo Corporation.

a. What was the average issue price of the preferred stock as of December 31, 2000?

b. How many shares of common stock are outstanding?

c. What journal entry was made when the common stock was issued?

d. If all of the treasury stock was reissued for $400,000, what journal entry would the company make?

e. What is the amount of the total dividend requirement on preferred stock annually?

f. Assuming that there are no dividends in arrears, if the company declared a total cash dividend of $580,000, what would be the dividend per share for the preferred and common stock?

g. Assume the company's common stock is selling for $80 per share. What journal entry would be made if the company issues a 10% common stock dividend?

h. Compute basic earnings per share if the company's net income was $1,560,000 during 2000. Assume no new shares were issued during the year.

i. Refer to the original data. Assume the company declares a 3-for-2 stock split. How many shares of common stock would be outstanding after the split?

j. Refer to the previous requirement. What effect would the stock split have on the company's income statement, balance sheet, and statement of cash flows?

k. If the stock market reacts rationally to the stock split, what would you expect the stock to be selling for after the split? Assume the stock was selling for $80 per share before the split.

P 13-6 At December 31, 2000, Sorena Corp. reported the following in its balance sheet:

Common stock, $5 par value, 400,000 shares issued and outstanding

During 2001, the following equity transactions occurred:

April 1	Issued 600,000 shares of common stock at $40 per share
May 1	Declared and issued a 10% stock dividend
September 1	Declared and issued a 2-1 stock split
October 1	Purchased 100,000 shares of common stock and placed them in the treasury

Required

a. Determine the number of shares outstanding at December 31, 200.

b. Compute the weighted average shares of common outstanding to be used in the calculation of basic earnings per share calculation for ~~2000~~ 2001

Cases and Projects . . . .

C13-1 The balance sheets for Coldwater Creek at 2/27/99 and 2/26/00 are as follows on page 148:

Coldwater Creek Inc.
Balance Sheets
(000's)

	For the years ended	
	02/26/00	02/27/99
ASSETS		
Current Assets:		
Cash and cash equivalents	$7,533	$149
Receivables	5,741	2,683
Inventories	60,203	56,474
Prepaid expenses	1,319	1,234
Prepaid catalog costs	3,994	4,274
Deferred income taxes	915	—
Total Current Assets	79,705	64,814
Deferred catalog costs	2,817	3,195
Property and equipment, net	38,895	31,236
Executive loans	1,453	1,376
Total Assets	$122,870	$100,621
LIABILITIES AND STOCKHOLDERS' EQUITY		
Current Liabilities:		
Revolving line of credit	—	$9,938
Accounts payable	30,098	17,086
Accrued liabilities	13,549	7,668
Income taxes payable	2,140	4,445
Deferred income taxes	—	1,080
Total Current Liabilities	45,787	40,217
Deferred income taxes	513	298
Total Liabilities	46,300	40,515
STOCKHOLDERS' EQUITY:		
Preferred stock, $.01 par value, 1,000,000 shares authorized, none issued and outstanding	—	—
Common stock, $.01 par value, 15,000,000 shares authorized, 10,319,345 and 10,183,117 issued and outstanding, respectively	103	102
Additional paid-in capital	41,579	39,287
Retained earnings	34,888	20,717
Total Stockholders' Equity	76,570	60,106
Total Liabilities and Stockholders' Equity	$122,870	$100,621

Required

Answer the following questions related to Coldwater Creek's Stockholders' Equity:

a.   The company has 1,000,000 shares of preferred stock authorized. What would be a possible explanation as to why the company has not issued any preferred stock?

b. Assuming that the changes in the common stock account were related to sales in the open market during 2000, prepare the journal entry the company made when the shares were issued.

c. Again, assuming that all changes in the common stock account were related to sales in the open market, what was the average market price of new shares issued during 2000?

d. The closing market price per share of Coldwater Creek's common stock on February 26, 2000 was $18.125. What entry would have been made on that date if the company had purchased 600,000 shares of treasury stock in the open market?

e. If the company had purchased 600,000 shares of treasury stock in the open market, what would have been the effect on Coldwater Creek's net income, earnings per share, assets, equity, and cash flows?

f. Assume that Coldwater Creek split its common stock 3-for-1 on February 26, 2000. How would the split have changed the equity section of the balance sheet on February 26, 2000? Would this split affect the balance sheet at February 27, 1999? Explain.

g. How would a 3-for-1 stock split have affected the market value of Coldwater Creek's common stock on February 26, 2000, assuming rational markets?

C13-2 Presented next are seven items that must be disclosed in the statement of stockholders' equity for d'Adamo Corporation for the year ended December 31, 2000. The company began 2000 with 20,000 shares of $1 par per share common stock issued and outstanding. Other balances on January 1, 2000 were:

Additional paid in capital	$800,000
Retained earnings	300,000
Accumulated other comprehensive income	30,000
8% $50 par value cumulative preferred, 3000 shares issued and outstanding	150,000

Additional Information

1. Net income for 2000 was $120,000.

2. All other comprehensive income for the year was due to a holding gain on available-for-sale securities of $22,000.

3. On June 1, 2000, the company issued 3,000 shares of its $1 par common stock in exchange for land with an appraised value of $40,000. The stock was selling on the NASDAQ at $12 per share.

4. On August 1, 2000, the company repurchased 5,000 shares of its common stock at $13 per share.

5. On November 30, 2000, cash dividends were declared on the preferred and the common stock for stockholders of record on December 15 to be paid on January 2, 2001. The entire 2000 dividend along with $2 per share that was in arrears from 1999 was declared for the preferred stock. A $2 per share dividend was declared on the common stock.

6. On December 30, 2000, the company declared and issued a 10% common stock dividend on all outstanding stock. The common stock was selling at $18 per share on December 30, 2000.

7. On September 30, 2000, the company issued 2,000 more shares of its preferred stock at $52 per share. These shares will *not* receive a dividend in 2000.

Required

a. Determine the balances in the following accounts at December 31, 2000:

Common Stock

Additional Paid in Capital

Preferred Stock

Accumulated other comprehensive income

Retained earnings

b. How many shares of common stock were issued and outstanding on December 31, 2000?

C13-3 Minnesota Mining and Manufacturing Company (3M) manufactures a variety of industrial and home products. 3M stock is traded on the New York Stock Exchange. The 3M financial statements follow.

Minnesota Mining and Manufacturing Company and Subsidiaries
Consolidated Balance Sheet
As of December 31, 1992 and 1991
(Dollars in millions)

	1992	1991
Assets		
Current Assets		
Cash and cash equivalents	$ 382	$ 258
Other securities	340	180
Accounts receivable-net	2,394	2,362
Inventories	2,315	2,292
Other current assets	778	635
Total current assets	6,209	5,727
Investments	452	460
Property, Plant and Equipment-net	4,792	4,666
Other Assets	502	451
Total	$ 11,955	$ 11,304
Liabilities and Stockholders' Equity		
Current Liabilities		
Accounts payable	$ 836	$ 809
Payroll	310	376
Income taxes	299	238
Short-term debt	739	709
Other current liabilities	1,057	974
Total current liabilities	3,241	3,106
Other Liabilities	1,428	1,141
Long-Term Debt	687	764
Stockholders' Equity-net	6,599	6,293
Shares outstanding-1992: 219,034,050; 1991: 219,140,359		
Total	$ 11,955	$ 11,304

The accompanying Notes to Financial Statements are an integral part of this statement.

Minnesota Mining and Manufacturing Company and Subsidiaries
Consolidated Statement of Income
For the Years Ended December 31, 1992, 1991 and 1990
(Amounts in millions, except per-share data)

	1992	*1991*	*1990*
Net Sales	$ 13,883	$ 13,340	$ 13,021
Operating Expenses			
Cost of goods sold	8,346	8,058	7,656
Selling, general and administrative expenses	3,557	3,323	3,174
Legal settlement	(129)	—	—
Special charges	115	—	—
Total	11,889	11,381	10,830
Operating Income	1,994	1,959	2,191
Other Income and Expense			
Interest expense	76	97	98
Investment and other income-net	(29)	(15)	(42)
Total	47	82	56
Income Before Income Taxes, Minority Interest			
and Cumulative Effect of Accounting Changes	1,947	1,877	2,135
Provision for Income Taxes	687	691	798
Minority Interest	24	32	29
Income Before Cumulative Effect of			
Accounting Changes	1,236	1,154	1,308
Cumulative Effect of Accounting Changes	3	—	—
Net Income	$ 1,233	$ 1,154	$ 1,308
Per-Share Amounts:			
Income Before Cumulative Effect of			
Accounting Changes	$ 5.65	$ 5.26	$ 5.91
Cumulative Effect of Accounting Changes	(0.02)	—	—
Net Income	$ 5.63	$ 5.26	$ 5.91
Average Shares Outstanding	219.1	219.6	221.4

The accompanying Notes to Financial Statements are an integral part of this statement.

Minnesota Mining and Manufacturing Company and Subsidiaries
Consolidated Statement of Cash Flows
For the Years Ended December 31, 1992, 1991 and 1990
(Dollars in millions)

	1992*	1991	1990
Cash Flows from Operating Activities			
Net income	$ 1,233	$ 1,154	$ 1,308
Adjustments to reconcile net income to net cash provided by operating activities:			
Legal settlement	(129)	—	—
Special charges	115	—	—
Cumulative effect of accounting changes	103	—	—
Depreciation	1,004	884	781
Amortization	83	85	68
Deferred income taxes	(111)	(117)	(69)
Accounts receivable	(142)	(155)	(205)
Inventories	(78)	(21)	(87)
Accounts payable and other liabilities	265	138	449
Other	(66)	(59)	(80)
Net cash provided by operating activities	2,277	1,909	2,165
Cash Flows from Investing Activities			
Capital expenditures	(1,318)	(1,326)	(1,275)
Disposals of property, plant and equipment	78	76	72
Acquisitions	(59)	(35)	(231)
Proceeds from divestitures	63	88	11
Net cash used in investing activities	(1,236)	(1,197)	(1,423)
Cash Flows from Financing Activities			
Net change in short-term debt	(83)	57	209
Repayment of long-term debt	(187)	(162)	(178)
Proceeds from long-term debt	139	140	82
Purchases of treasury stock	(247)	(240)	(420)
Reissuances of treasury stock	177	139	139
Payment of dividends	(701)	(685)	(647)
Other	—	65	37
Net cash used in financing activities	(902)	(686)	(778)
Effect of exchange rate changes on cash	(15)	(62)	(83)
Net increase (decrease) in cash and cash equivalents	124	(36)	(119)
Cash and cash equivalents at beginning of year	258	294	413
Cash and cash equivalents at end of year	$ 382	$ 258	$ 294

*Includes cash flows of international companies for a 14-month period November 1, 1991 to December 31, 1992.

The accompanying Notes to Financial Statements are an integral part of this statement.

Note 9 Stockholders' Equity

Common stock, without par value, of 500,000,000 shares is authorized, with 236,008,264 shares issued in 1992, 1991 and 1990. Treasury shares at year-end totaled 16,974,214 in 1992, 16,867,905 in 1991 and 16,174,861 in 1990. This stock is reported at cost. Preferred stock, without par value, of 10,000,000 shares is authorized but unissued.

(Dollars in millions)

	Common Stock	Retained Earnings	Cumulative Translation	ESOP Unearned Compensation	Treasury Stock	Total
Balance, December 31, 1989	$ 296	$ 6,492	$ (152)	$ (548)	$ (710)	$ 5,378
Net income		1,308				1,308
Dividends paid ($ 2.92 per share)		(647)				(647)
Reacquired stock (5,199,331 shares)					(420)	(420)
Issuances pursuant to stock option and benefit plans (2,288,258 shares)		(47)			186	139
Acquisitions in exchange for stock (80,720 shares)					7	7
Amortization of unearned compensation				18		18
Translation adjustments			327			327
Balance, December 31, 1990	$ 296	$ 7,106	$ 175	$ (530)	$ (937)	$ 6,110
Net income		1,154				1,154
Dividends paid ($ 3.12 per share)		(685)				(685)
Reacquired stock (2,733,416 shares)					(240)	(240)
Issuances pursuant to stock option and benefit plans (2,040,372 shares)		(39)			178	139
Amortization of unearned compensation				14		14
Translation adjustments			(199)			199
Balance, December 31, 1991	$ 296	$ 7,536	$ (24)	$ (516)	$ (999)	$ 6,293
Net income		1,233				1,233
Dividends paid ($ 3.20 per share)		(701)				(701)
Reacquired stock (2,561,689 shares)					(247)	(247)
Issuances pursuant to stock option and benefit plans (2,455,380 shares)		(56)			233	177
Amortization of unearned compensation				18		18
Translation adjustments			(174)			(174)
Balance, December 31, 1992	$ 296	$ 8,012	$ (198)	$ (498)	$ (1,013)	$ 6,599

Required

a. Write the journal entry(ies) 3M would have made in 1992 for (aggregate) treasury stock purchases and sales. Also, provide the journal entries to explain the changes in the retained earnings account for 1992.

b. What impact did treasury stock transactions have on 1992 income before taxes and on 1992's total shareholders' equity?

c. How many treasury shares did 3M purchase in 1992 and at what average price?

d. How many treasury shares did 3M reissue in 1992 and at what average price?

e. What was the average per share acquisition cost of the shares 3M issued from treasury in 1992?

f. Compare the average reissue price of shares issued from treasury in 1992 to their original acquisition price. Do you think it was a good idea for 3M to engage in these share transactions in 1992?

g. Compare the average purchase price of treasury shares in 1992 to the average reissue price of shares issued from treasury in 1992. What is happening?

h. 3M's 1992 annual report disclosed the following concerning its stock price.

1992	1st quarter	2nd quarter	3rd quarter	4th quarter
High	$98.75	$97.38	$103.75	$107.00
Low	87.38	85.50	95.75	97.00

A market to book ratio is either (a) total market value of common equity divided by total book value of equity or (b) market price per common share divided by book value per common share. A firm's total accounting equity is often referred to as total book value and book value per share is the book value per outstanding share. The total market value of a firm's equity is the number of shares outstanding times the market price per share. Compute a high and low market-to-book ratio for 3M during the fourth quarter of 1992. Assume that the number of shares outstanding at the end of the fourth quarter of 1992 was the number outstanding for all of the fourth quarter of 1992. Can you think of any reasons why this ratio would be equal to anything other than one?

Chapter fourteen

Income Taxes

. . . .

1. Explain why deferred tax assets and liabilities appear on the balance sheet.
2. What is a deferred tax liability?
3. What is a deferred tax asset?
4. What is MACRS?
5. What is a tax loss carry-back?
6. What is a tax loss carry-forward?
7. How does the LIFO conformity rule affect accounting for income taxes?
8. What is meant by timing difference?
9. What is meant by permanent difference?
10. Explain why deferred tax items relate only to temporary differences and not to permanent differences.
11. Are leases treated the same under GAAP and TAP?
12. How is TAP depreciation different from GAAP depreciation?
13. Explain how interest on municipal bonds will be treated under GAAP and TAP accounting.
14. Explain how warranty expenses will be treated under GAAP and TAP accounting.
15. Explain how bad debts will be treated under GAAP and TAP accounting.
16. Does TAP produce an income statement and a balance sheet?
17. Do income taxes have an economic value to an organization?
18. What do we mean by the depreciation tax shield?
19. Explain how the accounting for deferred taxes and the mark-to-market approach to accounting for investments are similar.

Exercises . . . .

E14-1 GAAP and TAP accounting often result in differences in the treatment of an accounting item. These differences often are identified as temporary or permanent differences. Some accounting items are handled identically for both GAAP and TAP. Identify whether each of the following will result in a *temporary* difference, a *permanent* difference or *no difference*.

a. Use of MACRS depreciation

b. Interest revenue received on municipal bonds

c. Use of LIFO inventory accounting

d. Warranty expense recognition

e. Asset impairment charges

f.   Accounting for leases

g.   Bad debt recognition

h.   Post-retirement benefits other than pensions

i.   Unrealized gains and losses on marketable securities

j.   Realized gains and losses on marketable securities

E14-2   During 2000, Francis Company sold land, with an original cost of $180,000, for $300,000 and accepted a note for the entire selling price. The note has a term of five years. During 2000, the company received principal payments on the note of $100,000. The company elected the install-ment method for tax purposes, where income taxes due are related to the cash collected on the note receivable. Assume there are no other book-to-tax differences and there is an average tax rate of 40%.

Required
Compute the deferred tax asset or liability that would appear on Francis Company's December 31, 2000 balance sheet.

E14-3   At December 31, 2000, Beach Corporation has a net operating loss carryforward of $200,000. The company believes that $50,000 of the carryforward most likely will never be deducted. Beach has an average tax rate of 40%.

Required
Compute the amount of deferred tax assets that Beach should report on its December 31, 2000 balance sheet.

E14-4   Sylvia Company purchased marketable securities during 2000 for $20,000. At December 31, 2000, the securities had a fair value of $16,000. At December 31, 2001, the Sylvia still owned the same securities and they had a fair value of $19,000. The securities are classified as trading securities on Sylvia's balance sheet.

Required
Explain how the securities will be accounted for under GAAP and TAP in 2000 and 2001.

E14-5   Bliss Corporation purchased a piece of machinery on January 2, 2001 for $200,000. Bliss esti-mated that the machinery had a useful life of 10 years with an estimated salvage value of $20,000. The machinery is considered seven-year property for MACRS depreciation. The com-pany will use straight-line depreciation for GAAP financial statements. Income before any de-preciation under GAAP and TAP is $100,000.

Required
a.   Compute the depreciation expense for GAAP and TAP for 2001.

b.   Compute income tax expense under GAAP and TAP for 2001.

c.   Compute the amount of deferred tax asset or liability that will appear on Bliss' balance sheet at December 31, 2001.

d.   Prepare the journal entry to record income taxes at 12/31/2001.

E14-6 Alera Corporation began operations on January 2, 2000. The company sells computer related equipment, with a two-year warranty on all products sold. The company estimates that 5% of the computers sold will require some warranty repair and that the average repair cost will be $100 per unit. During 2000 and 2001 Alera sold 5,000 and 7,000 computers, respectively. During 2000, 200 computers required repair and during 2001, 325 required repair. Repair costs were consistent with estimates. Assume a tax rate of 40%.

Required

a. Compute the amount of warranty expense that will appear on Alera's GAAP income statement for 2000 and 2001.

b. Compute the amount of warranty expense that will appear on Alera's TAP income statement for 2000 and 2001.

c. Compute the amount of deferred tax assets or liabilities that will appear on Alera's 2000 and 2001 balance sheets.

E14-7 Gecher Corporation earned $5,000,000 in 2000. Included in 2000's net income was an accrual for $400,000 of post-retirement benefits other than pensions in 2000. The actual cash payments for such benefits were $148,000. Assuming a tax rate of 30%, prepare the journal entry that Gecher would make, recognizing any deferred tax asset or liability that would result.

E14-8 Royer Tree Services purchased a new truck in 2001 with a cost of $25,000. The truck is considered five-year property for MACRS. For GAAP accounting, the company will depreciate the truck over five years, using the half-year convention. Income before depreciation expense for both GAAP and TAP was $100,000 in 2001 and $200,000 in 2006. The tax rate was 40%.

Required

a. Compute the amount of depreciation that will be deducted from 2001 to 2006 under GAAP and TAP.

b. Compute the amount of any deferred tax asset or liability that will appear on Royer's balance sheet each year from December 31, 2001 to December 31, 2006.

c. Prepare the journal entry to record income tax expense, including any deferred tax amounts in 2001.

d. Prepare the journal entry to record income tax expense, including any deferred tax amounts in 2006.

E14-9 The 2000 annual report for Starbucks Corporation reported the following assets and liabilities related to deferred taxes:

(In thousands)

	Oct. 1, 2000	Oct. 3, 1999
Current Assets:		
Deferred income taxes, net	$29,304	$21,133
Long-term liabilities:		
Deferred income taxes, net	$21,410	$32,886

Starbuck's deferred tax assets relate to timing differences on TAP deductions versus GAAP deductions related to investments, compensation expense, and inventory related costs. Deferred tax liabilities relate primarily to timing differences between GAAP depreciation and TAP depreciation.

Required

a.   Did Starbucks recognize more deductions related to investments, compensation, and inventory for GAAP or TAP in 2000? Explain.

b.   Did Starbucks recognize more depreciation expense for GAAP or TAP in 2000? Explain.

E14-10   Noreen Corporation was established on 1/1/2001. During 2001, the company experienced the following:

a.   Credit sales $200,000

b.   Collections on credit sales $120,000

c.   Write-offs of accounts deemed uncollectible: $8,000

d.   Aging analysis of accounts deemed uncollectible at 12/31/2001 shows $16,000 of expected uncollectible accounts

e.   Expenses other than bad debts (no difference between GAAP and TAP accounting) were $80,000

Required

a.   Determine GAAP and TAP bad debt expense.

b.   Assuming a tax rate of 30%, determine the amount of any deferred tax asset or liability that Noreen would report at December 31, 2001.

c.   Prepare the year-end entry to recognize income taxes for 2001.

Problems . . . .

P14-1   In its balance sheet at December 31, 2000, the PF Company reported income taxes payable of $11,000 and a noncurrent deferred tax liability of $40,000. This liability was the result of the one temporary book to tax difference:

	GAAP	*TAP*
Plant assets at cost	$200,000	$200,000
Accumulated depreciation	50,000	150,000

The relevant tax rate for 2000 was 40%.

PF Company is preparing its financial statements at December 31, 2001. The following information was extracted from its accounting records relative to 2001:

a.   GAAP income before taxes was $800,000.

b.   The company received $9,000 in municipal bond interest.

c.   The company recorded GAAP depreciation of $40,000 and tax depreciation of $28,000.

d.   The company accrued a contingent loss of $200,000. The company will not pay on the loss until March 2003.

e.   The company made tax payments of $340,000.

f.   There are no other timing or permanent difference items for 2001.

The relevant tax rate in 2001 is 40%. The company believes that most likely it will realize the benefits of any deferred tax assets.

Required

a. Compute current income tax expense under GAAP.

b. Determine the amount of income taxes payable that would appear in the balance sheet at December 31, 2001.

c. Identify the amount of net income that the PF Company will report in its 2001 income statement.

d. Prepare the entry at December 31, 2001 to recognize income taxes.

e. Identify the amounts of deferred tax assets and deferred tax liabilities that will be presented on PF's December 31, 2001 balance sheet. Will these deferred tax assets and liabilities be presented as current or long term?

P14-2 The notes to IBM's 1999 financial statements include the following:

The significant components of activities that gave rise to deferred tax assets and liabilities that are recorded on the balance sheet were as follows:

(Dollars in millions)

	At December 31	
	1999	1998
DEFERRED TAX ASSETS		
Employee benefits	$ 3,737	$ 3,909
Alternative minimum tax credits	1,244	1,169
Bad debt, inventory and warranty reserves	1,093	1,249
Infrastructure reduction charges	918	863
Capitalized research and development	880	913
Deferred income	870	686
General business credits	605	555
Foreign tax loss carryforwards	406	304
Equity alliances	377	387
Depreciation	326	201
Sales and local tax loss carryforward	227	212
Intracompany sales and services	153	182
Other	2,763	2,614
Gross deferred tax assets	13,599	13,244
Less: Valuation allowance	647	488
Net deferred tax assets	$12,952	$12,756
DEFERRED TAX LIABILITIES		
Retirement benefits	$ 3,092	$ 2,775
Sales-type leases	2,914	3,433
Depreciation	1,237	1,505
Software costs deferred	250	287
Other	2,058	1,841
Gross deferred tax liabilities	$ 9,551	$ 9,841

Required

a. Explain briefly why the following items have resulted in deferred tax assets for IBM:

    1. Bad debts

    2. Inventory write-downs

    3. Warranty reserves

    4. Employee benefits

b. Why did IBM deduct $647 million as a valuation allowance from the deferred tax assets in 1999?

c. Explain briefly why the following have resulted in deferred tax liabilities for IBM:

1. Retirement benefits

2. Depreciation

3. Software costs deferred

P14-3 Zorro Corporation purchased an asset on 1/2/2001 for $575 in cash. The asset is classified as a five-year asset under MACRS. It will be depreciated straight-line for financial reporting purposes, with no salvage value. The asset is expected to generate before-tax cash flows of $220 in each of the five years. The company requires a rate of return on investments of 8%.

Required

a. Compute the after-tax cash flows generated by the asset throughout its useful life.

b. Compute the depreciation tax shield in 2002.

c. Prepare a schedule detailing the after-tax cash flows in 2002, isolating the effect of the depreciation tax shield.

d. Explain how the economic value of the asset would be computed.

P14-4 Be Free, Inc. is an Internet firm that acts as a full-service performance marketing partner and intermediary, tracking transactions and reporting results back to merchants and affiliates. The company was founded in 1997. A footnote in its 1999 annual report contains the following.

Income Taxes

Deferred income taxes include the net tax effects of temporary differences between the carrying amounts of assets and liabilities for financial reporting purposes and the amounts used for income tax purposes. The components of the company's deferred tax assets are as follows:

| | December 31 | |
	99	98
Startup costs	$ 171,880	$ 240,633
Other temporary differences	288,533	277,788
Net operating losses	8,026,263	1,563,194
Total net deferred tax asset	8,486,676	2,081,615
Valuation allowance	(8,486,676)	(2,081,615)
Net deferred taxes	$ —	$ —

The company had net operating loss carryforwards of approximately $19,931,000 and $3,882,000 at December 31, 1999 and 1998, respectively. These net operating loss carryforwards begin to expire in 2010.

Required

a. Explain why startup costs would result in a deferred tax asset.

b. What other activities might have resulted in the "other temporary differences" deferred tax assets?

c. Explain why Be Free has established a valuation allowance equal to its total deferred tax asset account.

d. Why is there a difference between the components of the deferred tax assets related to operating losses and the amount of net operating loss carryforwards?

e. If Be Free earned a profit before taxes of $10,000,000 in 2000 and $30,000,000 in 2001, compute the amount of income taxes to be paid, taking into account *only* the net operating loss carryforward. Assume a tax rate of 35%.

f. Notwithstanding your answer in e, assume that Be Free was able to realize $2,000,000 of tax savings in 2000 because of the net operating loss carryforward. Prepare the journal entry that Be Free would make to recognize this benefit.

g. Compute the estimated tax rate used to determine the net operating loss component of the deferred tax asset.

P14-5 The following are four adjusting entries made by Jeremiah Corporation for its GAAP financial statements in 2000, its first year of operations:

```
Depreciation expense ....................................10,000
        Accumulated depreciation ...........................................10,000
Cash ........................................................5,000
        Interest on municipal bonds  .........................................5,000
Bad debt expense .........................................20,000
        Allowance for doubtful accounts ...................................20,000
Warranty expense ........................................12,000
        Warranty payable .................................................12,000
```

Other Information

The company's before tax income was $200,000

MACRS depreciation was $15,000

Bad debts written off due to customer bankruptcy were $3,000

Actual cash paid for warranty repairs during the year was $8,000

The company's income tax rate is 35%

Required

Prepare the journal entry required at year-end to record income taxes, including any deferred tax assets and liabilities.

Cases and Projects . . . .

C14-1 Manatron, Inc.

Manatron, Inc. and its subsidiaries design, develop, market, install, and support a family of Web-based and client/server application software products for county, city, and municipal governments. These products support both back-office processes for government agencies as well as "virtual courthouse" needs providing Internet access to information for industry professionals and the public. The company also provides mass appraisal services, assessing residential, commercial, and other types of properties to ensure updated and equitable property valuations. The company's business primarily is concentrated in the midwest and southeast regions of the United States.

The financial statements and part of a note on taxes for Manatron, Inc. follow.

Manatron, Inc. and Subsidiaries
Consolidated Balance Sheets
As of April 30,

	2000	*1999*
ASSETS		
Current Assets:		
Cash and equivalents	$ 608,062	$ 6,511,266
Accounts receivable, less allowances of		
$1,190,000 in 2000 and $1,298,000 in 1999	7,818,663	4,646,911
Revenues earned in excess of billings		
and retainages on long-term contracts	3,824,887	3,920,928
Notes receivable	1,179,119	780,420
Inventories	363,588	415,341
Deferred tax assets	2,195,664	1,750,000
Other current assets	170,960	347,124
Total current assets	16,160,943	18,371,990
Net Property and Equipment	3,047,946	1,207,140
Other Assets:		
Notes receivable, less current portions	1,254,477	1,080,037
Officers' receivable	—	232,969
Computer software development costs,		
net of accumulated amortization	1,445,600	1,507,178
Goodwill, net of accumulated amortization	4,777,115	715,503
Deferred tax assets	—	82,000
Other, net	38,644	31,612
Total other assets	7,515,836	3,649,299
	$26,724,725	$23,228,429
LIABILITIES AND SHAREHOLDERS' EQUITY		
Current Liabilities:		
Current portion of long-term debt	$ 50,000	$ 155,000
Line of credit borrowings	474,336	—
Accounts payable	1,337,099	1,726,397
Billings in excess of revenues earned on		
long-term contracts	3,057,534	3,308,140
Billings for future services	5,659,960	5,914,071
Restructuring reserve	24,953	189,942
Accrued liabilities:		
Payroll and employee benefits	3,331,375	2,563,195
Income taxes	570,355	1,835,320
Accrued commissions	367,808	511,996
Other	128,927	190,523
Total current liabilities	15,002,347	16,394,584
Deferred Income Taxes	242,878	—
Long-Term Debt, less current portion	—	50,000
Other Long-Term Liabilities	23,733	—
SHAREHOLDERS' EQUITY		
Common stock, no par value, 7,500,000 shares		
authorized, 3,518,245 and 2,973,970 shares		
issued and outstanding at April 30, 2000 and		
1999, respectively	8,707,431	5,672,530
Retained earnings	3,072,212	1,468,367
Deferred compensation	(298,876)	(232,052)
Unearned ESOP shares	(25,000)	(125,000)
Total shareholders' equity	11,455,767	6,783,845
	$26,724,725	$23,228,429

Manatron, Inc. and Subsidiaries
Consolidated Statements of Operations
For the Years Ended April 30,

	2000	1999	1998
Net Revenues:			
Hardware, software, and			
supply sales	$ 9,913,119	$ 9,026,170	$ 5,894,325
Service fees	33,732,258	28,523,094	18,897,556
Total net revenues	43,645,377	37,549,264	24,791,881
Cost of Revenues:			
Hardware, software, and			
supplies	5,980,875	5,432,965	3,561,354
Services	23,078,047	19,111,157	11,757,453
Total cost of revenues	29,058,922	24,544,122	15,318,807
Gross profit	14,586,455	13,005,142	9,473,074
Selling, General, and			
Administrative Expenses	12,506,825	11,753,302	9,070,234
Income from operations	2,079,630	1,251,840	402,840
Other Income (Expense):			
Interest expense	(41,712)	(50,199)	(140,794)
Other	305,927	102,929	51,725
	264,215	52,730	(89,069)
Income before provision			
for federal income taxes	2,343,845	1,304,570	313,771
Provision for Federal Income Taxes	740,000	—	—
Net Income	$ 1,603,845	$ 1,304,570	$ 313,771
Basic Earnings Per Share	$ .49	$ .45	$ .11
Diluted Earnings Per Share	$ .45	$ .41	$ .11

Manatron, Inc. and Subsidiaries
Consolidated Statements of Shareholders' Equity
For the Years Ended April 30, 2000, 1999, and 1998

	Common Stock	Retained (Deficit) Earnings	Deferred Compensation	Unearned ESOP Shares	Total Shareholders' Equity
Balance at April 30, 1997	$5,418,203	$(149,974)	$(117,562)	$(325,000)	$4,825,667
Net income	—	313,771	—	—	313,771
Repurchase of 95,200 shares by the Company	(201,027)	—	—	—	(201,027)
Issuance of 52,814 shares under employee stock plans	98,134	—	—	—	98,134
Compensation expense	(40,180)	—	14,250	100,000	74,070
Balance at April 30, 1998	5,275,130	163,797	(103,312)	(225,000)	5,110,615
Net income	—	1,304,570	—	—	1,304,570
Repurchase of 18,500 shares by the Company	(75,480)	—	—	—	(75,480)
Issuance of 160,529 shares under employee stock plans	431,823	—	(194,250)	—	237,573
Compensation expense	41,057	—	65,510	100,000	206,567
Balance at April 30, 1999	5,672,530	1,468,367	(232,052)	(125,000)	6,783,845
Net income	—	1,603,845	—	—	1,603,845
Repurchase of 7,315 shares by the Company	(49,819)	—	—	—	(49,819)
Issuance of 251,590 shares under employee stock plans and tax benefit from stock option exercise	1,042,976	—	(192,758)	—	850,218
Compensation expense	97,744	—	125,934	100,000	323,678
Issuance of 300,000 shares related to ProVal acquisition	1,944,000	—	—	—	1,944,000
Balance at April 30, 2000	$8,707,431	$3,072,212	$(298,876)	$(25,000)	$11,455,767

Manatron, Inc. and Subsidiaries
Consolidated Statements of Cash Flows
For the Years Ended April 30,

	2000	1999	1998
Cash Flows from Operating Activities:			
Net income	$ 1,603,845	$ 1,304,570	$ 313,771
Adjustments to reconcile net income to net cash and equivalents provided by operating activities:			
Gain on sale of assets	(139,632)	—	—
Depreciation and amortization	2,037,233	2,095,741	1,583,855
Deferred income taxes	(94,799)	(1,542,000)	(3,000)
Deferred compensation expense	323,678	206,567	74,070
Decrease (increase) in current assets:			
Accounts and notes receivable	(3,077,021)	482,292	8,735
Revenues earned in excess of billings and retainages	96,041	(1,197,357)	49,134
Inventories	51,753	(118,921)	(21,278)
Other current assets	212,757	(84,869)	58,176
Increase (decrease) in current liabilities:			
Accounts payable and accrued liabilities	(1,214,267)	2,926,339	716,318
Billings in excess of revenues earned	(250,606)	1,964,650	(405,610)
Billings for future services	(544,864)	1,166,840	1,519,366
Restructuring reserve	(164,989)	(60,892)	13,106
Net cash and equivalents provided by (used for) operating activities	(1,160,871)	7,142,960	3,906,643
Cash Flows from Investing Activities:			
Proceeds from sale of property and equipment	$ 343,261	$ —	$ —
Decrease (increase) in long-term receivables	61,672	(402,060)	81,091
Net additions to property and equipment	(2,303,723)	(621,731)	(542,089)
Investments in computer software development	(728,359)	(1,103,956)	(1,010,188)
Decrease (increase) in other, net assets	(223,045)	(98,895)	23,734
Acquisition of ProVal, net of cash received	(1,235,607)	—	—
Acquisition of CPS	(1,800,000)	—	—
Net cash and equivalents used for investing activities	(5,885,801)	(2,226,642)	(1,447,452)
Cash Flows from Financing Activities:			
Repayments of long-term debt	$ (155,000)	$ (20,000)	$ (100,000)
Repurchase of common stock	(49,819)	(75,480)	(201,027)
Purchases of common stock by stock plans and tax benefit from stock option exercises	850,218	237,573	98,134
(Decrease) increase in line of credit borrowings	474,336	—	(885,000)
(Decrease) increase in other long-term liabilities	23,733	(160,814)	(215,320)
Net cash and equivalents provided by (used for) financing activities	1,143,468	(18,721)	(1,303,213)
Cash and Equivalents:			
Increase (decrease)	(5,903,204)	4,897,597	1,155,978
Balance at beginning of year	6,511,266	1,613,669	457,691
Balance at end of year	$ 608,062	$ 6,511,266	$ 1,613,669

(Continued)

Supplemental Disclosures of
cash flow information:

Interest paid on debt	$ 34,000	$ 51,000	$ 140,000
Income taxes paid	$ 2,127,000	$ 254,000	$—

Tax Note

Required

Answer the following questions, which pertain to the tax note.

The tax effect and type of significant temporary differences that gave rise to the future tax bene-fits and deferred income taxes as of April 30 are approximately as follows:

	2000	1999
Deferred tax assets (liabilities):		
Valuation reserves not currently deductible	$ 1,208,000	$ 980,000
Accrued liabilities not currently deductible	851,000	832,000
Alternative minimum tax credit carryforward	—	163,000
Lease accounting method differences	8,000	83,000
Restructuring reserves not currently deductible	8,000	46,000
Property and equipment depreciation	(23,000)	44,000
Valuation allowance	—	(219,000)
Software development costs expensed for tax purposes	(307,000)	(274,000)
Other	208,000	177,000
Net deferred tax asset	$ 1,953,000	$ 1,832,000

As of April 30, 1997, the company recorded a valuation allowance totaling $912,000 against cer-tain of its future tax benefits, including its tax loss carryforward, due to the uncertainty of their ultimate realization. Approximately $219,000, $527,000, and $166,000 of this valuation al-lowance was utilized in fiscal 2000, 1999, and 1998, respectively, to offset the provision for fed-eral income taxes related to the pretax income for each year.

a. Give an example of what "valuation reserves not currently deductible" are. The number has increased from 1999 to 2000. What does that imply?

b. Explain why "accrued liabilities not currently deductible" are a deferred tax asset.

c. Assume a tax rate of 35%. How much more or less depreciation expense did Manatron re-port in its financial statements than in its tax return?

d. How are the "software development costs" referred to in the tax note treated in the financial statements?

e. In general, what does the large net deferred tax asset on Manatron's balance sheet say about the relative amounts of financial statement income versus taxable income since their incorporation?

C14-2 Refer to the Mendocino Brewing Company Case (Case 12-3, page 161) financial statements and notes.

Required

Answer the following questions related to Mendocino Brewing Company's income tax accounting.

a. Why does Mendocino report a "benefit from income tax" in its 1999 income statements when the company earned no income?

b. Using the information provided in the financial statements and footnotes, prepare a schedule showing how the company arrived at the benefit from income taxes of $729,500.

c. Based on the information provided in the financial statements and footnotes, prepare the journal entry made by Mendocino related to income taxes in 1999.

d. Why did Mendocino deduct deferred income taxes of $730,900 from net income in the statement of cash flows?

e. Why is the deduction of $730,900 in the statement of cash flows different from the income tax benefit of $729,500 shown in the income statement?

Chapter fifteen

Active Investments in Corporations

Questions ·

1. Name three reasons why a company may make an active investment in another company.
2. What is meant by consolidation in financial reporting?
3. What do we mean by minority interest?
4. What percent ownership of a corporation would require a company to mark investments to market?
5. What percent ownership of a corporation would require a company to use the equity method of accounting?
6. Give the entry to record the declaration of a dividend by a subsidiary that is accounted for using the equity method.
7. What percent ownership of a corporation would require consolidated financial statements?
8. When is goodwill recorded in financial statements?
9. How is minority interest in earnings of subsidiaries accounted for on a company's statement of cash flows? Explain your answer.
10. How is an outside minority interest in earnings of subsidiaries accounted for on a company's income statement? Explain your answer.
11. Explain how the earnings and dividends of subsidiaries are accounted for under the equity method of accounting.
12. Where does the account *minority interest* appear on the balance sheet?
13. How does a consolidated balance sheet differ from a balance sheet in which the equity method of accounting was used?
14. Explain the difference in the consolidated balance sheet in an acquisition accounted for by pooling of interest and one accounted for by purchase accounting.
15. Explain the difference in the consolidated income statement in an acquisition accounted for by pooling of interest and one accounted for by purchase accounting.
16. Will total assets be higher or lower if purchase accounting is used instead of pooling of interests? Explain your answer.
17. What difference in depreciation expense will there be between business combinations accounted for under purchase accounting versus those accounted for as pooling of interests? Explain.
18. Explain this statement: "The numbers under pooling grossly underestimate the true economic values, and make analysis of the reports more difficult."

Exercises ·

E15-1 On January 1, 2000, Lopez Fashions purchased a 30% stake in the voting stock of Aguillera Jewelry Corp.'s common stock for $9,000,000 cash. During 2000, Aguillera reported total net income of $20,000,000 and declared dividends of $15,000,000.

a. Prepare the entry to record the original purchase of the stock.

b. Prepare the journal entries that Lopez would record relative to its investment in Aguillera during 2000.

c. How would your answers to a and b have differed if Lopez had purchased 15% of the voting stock of Aguillera instead of 30%?

E15-2 On January 2, 2001, Conner Corporation purchased 5,000 shares of Aleski Corporation for $26.50 per share. Aleski had 100,000 shares outstanding on January 2, 2001. During 2001, Aleski earned $500,000 and declared and distributed $50,000 in cash dividends. On December 31, 2001, Aleski's stock was selling for $27.56 per share.

Required

Prepare all journal entries that Conner Corporation would make during 2001 related to its investment in Aleski Corporation.

E15-3 Refer to E15-2. Assume that, instead of 100,000 shares outstanding on January 2, 2001, Aleski had only 20,000 shares outstanding. Prepare all journal entries that Conner Corporation would make during 2001 related to its investment in Aleski Corporation.

E15-4 On December 31, 2001, Jones Corporation acquired 100% of the common stock of Seleka Corporation. Saleka had 10,000 shares issued and outstanding on the date of acquisition, for which Jones paid $52.50 per share. The stockholders' equity section of Saleka's balance sheet at December 31, 2001 is as follows:

Stockholders' equity:

Common Stock, $1 par value, 10,000 shares issued and outstanding	$10,000
Paid in capital in excess of par value	42,000
Retained earnings	473,000
Total stockholders' equity	$525,000

Saleka's assets consisted of $50,000 in cash and $775,000 in land. Saleka had $300,000 in accounts payable and no other liabilities on the date of acquisition.

Required

a. Prepare the entry Jones made to record the acquisition.

b. Prepare the eliminating entries necessary to prepare a consolidated balance sheet at December 31, 2001.

E15-5 Refer to E15-4. Assume that instead of $52.50 per share, Jones paid $75 per share to acquire 100% of Saleka's common stock. An appraisal indicated that the land was worth $825,000 on December 31, 2001.

Required

a. Prepare the entry Jones made to record the acquisition.

b. Prepare the eliminating entries necessary to prepare a consolidated balance sheet at December 31, 2001.

E15-6   Refer to E15-4. Assume that instead of $52.50 per share, Jones paid $75 per share to acquire 90% of Saleka's common stock. An appraisal indicated that the land was worth $825,000 on December 31, 2001.

Required

a.   Prepare the entry Jones made to record the acquisition.

b.   Prepare the eliminating entries necessary to prepare a consolidated balance sheet at December 31, 2001.

E15-7   Polarma Corporation paid $600,000 for 100% of the outstanding common stock of Stavis Company on January 2, 2001. At that time, Stavis had the following condensed balance sheet:

	Carrying amounts
Current assets	$ 80,000
Plant and equipment, net	760,000
Liabilities	400,000
Stockholders' equity	440,000

The fair value of the plant and equipment was $120,000 more than its recorded carrying amount. The fair values and carrying amounts were equal for all other assets and liabilities.

Required

What amount of goodwill, related to Stavis's acquisition, should Polarma report in its consolidated balance sheet?

E15-8   On January 2, 2001, Reese Corporation purchased 25% of Francis Corporation's common stock for $150,000. During 2001, Francis recorded income of $60,000 and paid total dividends of $40,000. Reese uses the equity method to account for this investment.

Required

a.   Compute the income that Reese will report in its 2001 income statement related to the Francis investment.

b.   Compute the balance in the investment account that Reese will report on its December 31, 2001 balance sheet related to the investment in Francis.

E15-9   On December 31, 2000, Cornelia Inc. acquired a 35% share of Dawson Corporation's common stock, paying $600,000. During 2001, Dawson reported net income of $400,000 and paid dividends of $60,000. The fair value of Cornelia's 35% investment in Dawson's stock at December 31, 2001 was $580,000. Cornelia mistakenly accounted for the investment using the fair value method, considering the Dawson stock to be available-for-sale securities, instead of using the equity method.

Required

a.   How much higher or lower would Cornelia's assets and equity have been if it had properly accounted for the investment under the equity method of accounting?

b.   How much higher or lower would Cornelia's 2001 net income have been if it had properly accounted for the investment under the equity method of accounting?

Problems ·

P15-1   D&K Healthcare Resources, Inc.

D&K Healthcare is a full-service, regional wholesale drug distributor. From facilities in Missouri, Kentucky, Minnesota, South Dakota, and Florida, the company distributes a broad range of pharmaceutical products, health and beauty aids, and related products to its customers in more than 24 states. The company focuses primarily on a target market sector, which includes independent retail, institutional, franchise, chain store, and alternate site pharmacies in the midwest and south.

The long-lived asset accounts on D&K's balance sheets show an *Investment in Affiliates* account with a balance of $5,199,000 and $4,111,000 on June 30, 2000 and June 30, 1999, respectively.

D&K's consolidated statement of cash flows is shown below.

D&K Healthcare Resources, Inc. and Subsidiaries
Consolidated Statements of Cash Flows
(In thousands)
For the Years Ended

		June 30,	
	2000	*1999*	*1998*
Cash Flows from Operating Activities			
Net income	$ 8,199	$ 6,625	$ 3,942
Adjustments to reconcile net income to net cash flows from operating activities:			
Depreciation and amortization	3,118	1,647	1,468
Amortization of debt issuance costs	375	188	59
Gain from sale of assets	(16)	(9)	(32)
Equity in net income of PBI	(634)	(332)	(389)
Deferred income taxes	270	492	1,241
(Increase) decrease in receivables, net	(15,034)	41,182	(16,500)
Increase in inventories	(36,839)	(42,437)	(48,791)
(Increase) decrease in prepaid expenses and other current assets	(403)	242	633
Increase (decrease) in accounts payable	(7,526)	39,297	31,491
Increase (decrease) in accrued expenses	548	(7,729)	312
Other, net	(427)	(157)	432
Net cash flows from operating activities	(48,369)	39,009	(26,134)
Cash Flows from Investing Activities			
Payments for acquisitions, net of cash acquired	—	(13,961)	(1,256)
Investment in affiliates	(804)	—	—
Cash dividend from PBI	350	350	350
Purchases of property and equipment	(3,270)	(879)	(863)
Proceeds from sale of assets	16	752	32
Net cash flows from investing activities	(3,708)	(13,738)	(1,737)

(Continued)

Cash Flows from Financing Activities			
Borrowings under revolving line of credit	538,303	487,844	429,431
Repayments under revolving line of credit	(479,767)	(513,714)	(397,997)
Proceeds from equipment loan	965	—	—
Payments of long-term debt	(283)	(1,973)	(1,571)
Payments of capital lease obligations	(118)	(9)	—
Proceeds from exercise of stock options			
and warrants	814	822	413
Purchase of treasury stock	(4,602)	(944)	—
Payments of deferred debt costs	(282)	(640)	—
Net cash flows from financing activities	55,030	(28,614)	30,276
Increase (decrease) in cash	2,953	(3,343)	2,405
Cash, beginning of period	708	4,051	1,646
Cash, end of period	$ 3,661	$ 708	$ 4,051

Required

a. What method is D&K using to account for the investments included in the *Investment in Affiliates* account? Justify your answer.

b. Construct a complete set of journal entries that explains the change in the *Investment in Affiliates* account from the beginning to the end of the period.

c. What might be the justification for accounting for this investment in the manner D&K does in the cash flow statement? How is it different from what was presented in the chapter?

P15-2 Grant Corp. purchased 100% of the voting stock of Bergman Inc. on January 2, 2000, for $25,000,000. On that date, an analysis of Bergman's balance sheet revealed:

	Book value	Fair value
Current assets	$ 1,000,000	$ 950,000
Plant assets	20,000,000	25,000,000
Intangible assets (no goodwill)	1,500,000	2,700,000
Current liabilities	400,000	500,000
Long-term liabilities	10,000,000	10,000,000
Stockholders' equity	12,100,000	

The difference in fair value of the current assets is due to accounts receivable and inventory that Grant believes is worthless and Grant believes that accrued expenses were undervalued at January 2. The plant assets and intangible assets have estimated remaining lives of eight years and five years, respectively. Grant amortizes goodwill over 20 years.

a. Determine the amount of goodwill that should be recorded in this transaction.

b. Prepare the journal entry necessary to record the purchase.

c. Identify the accounts and amounts relative to this investment that would appear in Grant's balance sheet at December 31, 2000, for $25,000.

P15-3 Refer to P15-2. Assume that, instead of acquiring 100% of the stock of Bergmann, Grant purchased 90% on January 2, 2000, for $25,000,000.

Required
Repeat parts a through c.

P15-4 On December 31, 2001, Peter Corporation paid $400 cash to acquire Sorena Corporation. Peter made the following entry to record the transaction:

Investment in Sorena Corporation 400

Cash 400

Sorena Corporation had the following balance sheet on the date of acquisition:

Sorena Corporation
Balance Sheet
December 31, 2001

Assets		*Liabilities and Stockholders' Equity*	
Cash	$ 80	Liabilities:	
Accounts receivable	140	Accounts payable	$180
Inventory	340	Notes payable	160
Fixed assets—net	360	Other current	
Total assets	$920	liabilities	40
		Long term liabilities	140
		Total liabilities	520
		Stockholders Equity:	
		Common Stock	280
		Retained Earnings	120
		Total Equity	400
		Total Liabilities & Equity	$920

Required

Complete the worksheet to produce a consolidated balance sheet for Peter Corporation at December 31, 2000.

Peter Corporation Worksheet to Produce a Consolidated Balance Sheet as of December 31, 2001						
Accounts	Individual Company Statements		Combined Balance Sheet	Eliminations		Consolidated Balance Sheet
	Peter	Sorena		Debit	Credit	
Cash	400					
Accounts receivable	218					
Notes receivable	170					
Inventory	300					
Investment in Sorena	400					
Fixed assets (net of accumulated depreciation)	1,210					
	2,698					
Accounts payable	200					
Notes payable	78					
Other current liabilities	190					
Long-term liabilities	320					
Common stock	800					
Retained earnings	1,110					
	2,698					

P15-5   Refer to P15-4. Assume that, instead of paying $400 for all of Sorena's common stock, that Peter paid $600. An appraisal indicated that the fixed assets of Sorena have a fair value of $520. No other differences exist between the book value and fair value of Sorena's assets and liabilities.

Required

Complete the worksheet to consolidate the financial statements.

Peter Corporation
Worksheet to Produce a Consolidated Balance Sheet
as of December 31, 2001

Accounts	Individual Company Statements		Combined Balance Sheet	Eliminations		Consolidated Balance Sheet
	Peter	Sorena		Debit	Credit	
Cash	200					
Accounts receivable	218					
Notes receivable	170					
Inventory	300					
Investment in Sorena	600					
Fixed assets (net of accumulated depreciation)	1,210					
	2,698					
Accounts payable	200					
Notes payable	78					
Other current liabilities	190					
Long-term liabilities	320					
Common stock	800					
Retained earnings	1,110					
	2,698					

P15-6   Cisco Systems, Inc. is a worldwide leader in networking for the Internet. The company provides hardware, software, and service offerings to individuals, companies, and countries. Founded in 1986, the company has experienced tremendous growth. From 1997 to 1999, sales increased 88% to $12.2 billion, and net income increased 99% to 2.096 billion. During that time, total assets increased 168% to $14.725 billion and shareholders' equity increased 170% to $11.678 billion.

A significant part of Cisco's growth can be attributed to acquisitions. The notes to the 1999 financial statements of Cisco Systems contain the following:

In June 1999, the Company announced definitive agreements to purchase TransMedia Communications, Inc. . . . and StratumOne Communications, Inc. . . . . In August 1999, the Company announced definitive agreements to purchase Calista Inc.; MaxComm Technologies, Inc.; Cerent Corporation; and Monterey Networks, Inc. . . . The terms of the pending business combinations are as follows (in millions):

Entity name	Consideration	Accounting Treatment
Transmedia Communications, Inc.	$ 407	Pooling of interests
StratumOne Communications, Inc.	435	Pooling of interests
Calista, Inc	55	Purchase
MaxComm Technologies, Inc.	143	Purchase
Cerent Corporation	6,900	Pooling of interests
Monterey Networks, Inc	500	Purchase

Consideration for each of these transactions will be the company's common stock.

Required

a. Explain how the acquisitions accounted for under the pooling of interests method will affect Cisco's income statement and balance sheet in the year of acquisition.

b. Explain how the acquisitions accounted for under the purchase method will affect Cisco's income statement and balance sheet in the year of acquisition.

c. Explain how the acquisitions will affect Cisco's statement of cash flows in the year of acquisition.

d. Of the total acquisitions of $8.4 billion, Cisco is accounting for 92% using pooling of interests and only 8% using purchase accounting. Why do you think Cisco structured the majority of transactions as pooling of interests?

e. What are the implications of Cisco using its common stock as consideration for the acquisitions instead of cash? Cisco's common stock ranged from $21.94 per share to $67.06 per share during 1999.

f. The Financial Accounting Standards Board has announced that, effective June 30, 2001, the pooling of interests method of accounting for acquisitions will be eliminated. Purchase accounting will be required in all business combinations. Instead of writing down goodwill with each income statement, companies will be allowed to use an impairment test to determine whether goodwill needs to be written down. However, the FASB postponed until late 2001 a rule that would enable companies to exclude the amortization of already existing goodwill from their balance sheets. (Barron's, May 21, 2001). What are the implications of this announcement for publicly held companies?

P15-7 Selected information from the separate consolidated balance sheets and income statements of Pace Corporation and its subsidiary, Spartus Company, as of December 31, 2001 and for the year then ended is as follows:

	Pace	Spartus	Consolidated
Balance Sheet accounts:			
Notes receivable	$52,000	$19,000	$67,000
Investment in Spartus	67,000	—	—
Goodwill	—	—	30,000
Minority interest			10,000
Stockholders equity	154,000	50,000	154,000
Income statement accounts:			
Amortization of goodwill			2,000

Additional information:

Pace acquired its interest in Spartus on January 2, 2001. Pace's policy is to amortize goodwill by the straight-line method.

Required:

Show all computations.

a.   At December 31, 2001, what was the amount of Spartus' notes payable to Pace?

b.   Without regard to your answer in a, assume that Spartus owes Pace $20,000. What would be the entry required on the consolidating worksheet?

c.   What is the percent of minority interest ownership in Spartus?

d.   Over how many years has Pace chosen to amortize goodwill?

Cases and Projects ·

C15-1   Coors Brewing Company

Coors Brewing Company (CBC) produces, markets, and sells high-quality malt-based beverages. CBC concentrates on distinctive premium and above-premium brands that provide higher-than-average margins. Most of CBC's sales are in U.S. markets; however, the company is committed to building profitable sales in international markets. Sales of malt beverages totaled 21.2 million barrels in 1998, 20.6 million barrels in 1997, and 20.0 million barrels in 1996.

Coors' financial statements are shown below and on pages 201–204.

Adolph Coors Company and Subsidiaries
Consolidated Statements of Income
For the years ended
(In thousands, except per share data)

	December 27, 1998	December 28, 1997	December 29, 1996
Sales—domestic and international	$2,291,322	$2,207,384	$2,121,146
Less: beer excise taxes	391,789	386,080	379,311
Net sales	1,899,533	1,821,304	1,741,835
Costs and expenses:			
Cost of goods sold	1,158,887	1,131,610	1,131,470
Marketing, general and administrative	617,432	573,818	523,250
Special charges (credits)	19,395	(31,517)	6,341
Total operating expenses	1,795,714	1,673,911	1,661,061
Operating income	103,819	147,393	80,774
Other income (expense):			
Interest income	12,136	8,835	2,924
Interest expense	(9,803)	(13,277)	(14,212)
Miscellaneous – net	4,948	3,942	5,489
Total	7,281	(500)	(5,799)
Income before income taxes	111,100	146,893	74,975
Income tax expense	43,316	64,633	31,550
Net income	67,784	82,260	43,425

Adolph Coors Company and Subsidiaries
Consolidated Balance Sheets
(In thousands)

	December 27, 1998	December 28, 1997
Assets		
Current assets:		
Cash and cash equivalents	$ 160,038	$ 168,875
Short-term investments	96,190	42,163
Accounts and notes receivable:		
Trade, less allowance for doubtful accounts of $299 in 1998 and $557 in 1997	106,962	89,731
Affiliates	11,896	19,677
Other, less allowance for certain claims of $584 in 1998 and $1,500 in 1997	7,751	15,077
Inventories:		
Finished	38,520	44,729
In process	24,526	20,119
Raw materials	34,016	35,654
Packaging materials, less allowance for obsolete inventories of $1,018 in 1998 and $1,049 in 1997	5,598	5,977
Total inventories	102,660	106,479
Other supplies, less allowance for obsolete supplies of $3,968 in 1998 and $4,165 in 1997	27,729	32,362
Prepaid expenses and other assets	12,848	18,224
Deferred tax asset	22,917	24,606
Total current assets	548,991	517,194
Properties, at cost and net	714,441	733,117
Excess of cost over net assets of businesses acquired, less accumulated amortization of $6,727 in 1998 and $5,726 in 1997	23,114	22,880
Long-term investments	31,444	47,100
Other assets	142,608	91,792
Total assets	$1,460,598	$1,412,083
Liabilities and Shareholders' Equity		
Current liabilities:		
Current portion of long-term debt	$ 40,000	$ 27,500
Accounts payable:		
Trade	132,193	113,864
Affiliates	11,706	18,072
Accrued salaries and vacations	54,584	58,257
Taxes, other than income taxes	48,332	52,805
Federal and state income taxes	10,130	13,660
Accrued expenses and other liabilities	86,967	74,988
Total current liabilities	383,912	359,146
Long-term debt	105,000	145,000
Deferred tax liability	65,779	76,219
Postretirement benefits	74,469	71,908
Other long-term liabilities	56,640	23,242
Total liabilities	685,800	675,515

(Continued)

Shareholders' equity:
  Capital stock:

Class A common stock, voting, $1 par value, (authorized, issued and outstanding: 1,260,000 shares)	1,260	1,260
Class B common stock, non-voting, no par value, $0.24 stated value (authorized: 100,000,000 shares; issued and outstanding: 35,395,306 in 1998 and 35,599,356 in 1997)	8,428	8,476
Total capital stock	9,688	9,736
Paid-in capital	10,505	—
Retained earnings	756,531	730,628
Accumulated other comprehensive income	(1,926)	(3,796)
Total shareholders' equity	774,798	736,568
Total liabilities and shareholders' equity	$1,460,598	$1,412,083

Adolph Coors Company and Subsidiaries
Consolidated Statements of Cash Flows
(In thousands)
For the years ended

	December 27, 1998	December 28, 1997	December 29, 1996
Cash flows from operating activities:			
Net income	$ 67,784	$ 82,260	$ 43,425
Adjustments to reconcile net income to net cash provided by operating activities:			
Equity in net earnings of joint ventures	(33,227)	(15,893)	(11,467)
Reserve for severance	8,324	—	—
Reserve for joint venture investment	—	21,978	—
Depreciation, depletion and amortization	115,815	117,166	121,121
Loss on sale or abandonment of properties and intangibles, net	7,687	5,594	12,535
Impairment charge	2,219	10,595	—
Deferred income taxes	(8,751)	(15,043)	17,696
Change in operating assets and liabilities:			
Accounts and notes receivable	2,140	(10,971)	2,232
Inventories	4,176	14,051	18,076
Other assets	8,977	3,742	(2,128)
Accounts payable	9,899	9,599	(8,175)
Accrued expenses and other liabilities	(3,898)	37,475	(3,712)
Net cash provided by operating activities	181,145	260,553	189,603
Cash flows from investing activities:			
Purchases of investments	(101,682)	(122,800)	(5,958)
Sales and maturities of investments	62,393	39,499	—
Additions to properties and intangible assets	(104,505)	(60,373)	(65,112)
Proceeds from sale of properties and intangibles	2,264	3,273	8,098
Distributions from joint ventures	22,438	13,250	5,000
Other	(4,949)	(775)	6,569
Net cash used in investing activities	(124,041)	(127,926)	(51,403)

(Continued)

Cash flows from financing activities:			
Issuances of stock under stock plans	9,823	24,588	4,674
Purchases of stock	(27,599)	(60,151)	(6,975)
Dividends paid	(21,893)	(20,523)	(18,983)
Payments of long-term debt	(27,500)	(20,500)	(38,000)
Other	1,140	4,544	—
Net cash used in financing activities	(66,029)	(72,042)	(59,284)
Cash and cash equivalents:			
Net (decrease) increase in cash and cash equivalents	(8,925)	60,585	78,916
Effect of exchange rate changes on cash and cash equivalents	88	(2,615)	(397)
Balance at beginning of year	168,875	110,905	32,386
Balance at end of year	$160,038	$168,875	$110,905

Adolph Coors Company and Subsidiaries— Notes to Consolidated Financial Statements

Summary of Significant Accounting Policies

Principles of consolidation: The consolidated financial statements include the accounts of Adolph Coors Company (ACC); its principal subsidiary, Coors Brewing Company (CBC); and the majority-owned and controlled domestic and foreign subsidiaries of both ACC and CBC (collectively referred to as "the Company"). All significant intercompany accounts and transactions have been eliminated. The equity method of accounting is used for the Company's investments in affiliates over which the Company has the ability to exercise significant influence. The Company has other investments that are accounted for at cost.

Excess of cost over net assets of businesses acquired: The excess of cost over the net assets of businesses acquired in transactions accounted for as purchases is being amortized on a straight-line basis, generally over a 40-year period. During 1998, CBC recorded a $2.2-million impairment charge, which has been classified as a special charge in the accompanying statements of income, related to long-lived assets at one of its distributorships. The long-lived assets were considered impaired in light of both historical losses and expected future, undiscounted cash flows. The impairment charge represented a reduction of the carrying amounts of the impaired assets to their estimated fair market values, which were determined using a discounted cash flow model.

Investments in marketable securities: ACC invests excess cash on hand in interest-bearing debt securities. At December 27, 1998, $96.2 million of these securities were classified as current assets and $31.4 million were classified as non-current assets, as their maturities exceeded one year. All of these securities were considered to be available-for-sale. At December 27, 1998, these securities have been recorded at fair value, based on quoted market prices, through other comprehensive income. Maturities on these investments range from 1999 through 2001.

Equity method investments: The Company has investments in affiliates that are accounted for using the equity method of accounting. These investments aggregated $62.3 million and $51.7 million at December 27, 1998, and December 28, 1997, respectively. These investment amounts are included in Other assets on the Company's consolidated balance sheets.

Summarized condensed balance sheet and income statement information for the Company's equity method investments are as follows:

Summarized condensed balance sheets:

	As of	
	December 27, 1998	December 28, 1997
Current assets	$90,092	$76,260
Non-current assets	94,508	78,829
Current liabilities	55,312	40,859
Non-current liabilities	123	4,437

Summarized condensed statements of operations:

| | *For the years ended* | | |
	December 27, 1998	December 28, 1997	December 29, 1996
Net sales	$453,246	$372,479	$357,273
Gross profit	97,478	39,459	37,372
Net income	59,650	22,384	19,289
Company's equity in operating income	33,227	15,893	11,467

The Company's share of operating income of these non-consolidated affiliates is primarily included in Sales and Cost of goods sold on the Company's consolidated statements of income.

Required

Answer the following:

a. Does Coors Brewing have majority-owned investments in the common stock of other companies? How do you know?

b. Where is goodwill listed in the balance sheet?

c. Did Coors add to its investment in consolidated subsidiaries during 1998? How do you know? (Hint: Analyze the *Goodwill* account.)

d. Analyze the following account as best you can. It is part of *other assets* in the consolidated balance sheet.

Equity in Earnings of Unconsolidated Affiliates

Beginning balance	???		
		??	Decreases
Increases	??		
Ending balance	???		

You will not be able to analyze it exactly. What are some other possible explanations for the little portion of the change which you cannot explain?

e. Assuming Coors was able to and had used the pooling of interests method to account for its consolidated acquisitions, how would its financial statements differ (describe in general terms)?

f. Where does the income from the equity method investments show up in the consolidated income statement?

15-2 Amazon.com

The financial statements for Amazon.com for the fiscal years ended 12/31/99 and 12/31/98 are shown on pages 206–208. The business is described in its annual report as follows: Amazon.com. Inc., an Internet retailer, was incorporated in July, 1994, and opened its virtual doors on the Web in July, 1995. Amazon.com offers book, music DC, video, DVD, computer game, and other titles on its Web sites.

Required

Answer the following questions related to Amazon.com's investments.

a. What accounts on Amazon.com's income statement, balance sheet, and cash flow statement represent activities related to investments for which Amazon.com has less than a 20% interest?

b. What accounts on Amazon.com's income statement, balance sheet, and cash flow statement represent activities related to investments for which Amazon.com has between 20% and 50% interest?

c. What accounts on Amazon.com's income statement, balance sheet, and cash flow statement represent activities related to investments for which Amazon.com has greater than 50% interest?

d. Analyze the following account as best you can:

Investments in
Equity-Method Investees

Beginning balance	???			
		??	Decreases	
Increases	??			
Ending balance	???			

You will not be able to analyze it exactly. What are some other possible explanations for the little portion of the change that you cannot explain?

e. Why is "equity in losses of equity-method investees" added back to Amazon.com's net loss in the Statement of Cash flows?

f. Prepare the entry made by Amazon.com to record the 1999 equity in losses of equity-method investees.

g. Did Amazon.com pay cash for all of its investments? Explain.

h. By approximately how much more than fair market value did Amazon.com pay for its investments that were consolidated? What additional information would you need to determine the exact amount?

Amazon.com Inc
Income Statement
For the year ended:

	12/31/99	12/31/98
Net sales	$1,639,839,000	$609,819,000
Cost of sales	1,349,194,000	476,155,000
Gross profit	290,645,000	133,664,000
Operating expenses:		
Marketing and sales	413,150,000	132,654,000
Technology and content	159,722,000	46,424,000
General and administrative	70,144,000	15,618,000
Stock-based compensation	30,618,000	1,889,000
Amortization of goodwill and other intangibles	214,694,000	42,599,000
Merger, acquisition and investment-related costs	8,072,000	3,535,000
Total operating expenses	896,400,000	242,719,000
Loss from operations	(605,755,000)	(109,055,000)
Interest income	45,451,000	14,053,000
Interest expense	(84,566,000)	(26,639,000)
Other income, net	1,671,000	—
Net interest income (expense) and other	(37,444,000)	(12,586,000)
Loss before equity in losses of equity-method investees	(643,199,000)	(121,641,000)
Equity in losses of equity-method investees	(76,769,000)	(2,905,000)
Net loss	($719,968,000)	($124,546,000)
Basic and diluted loss per share	($2.20)	($0.42)
Shares used in computation of basic and diluted loss per share	326,753,000	296,344,000

Amazon.com Inc
Balance Sheet

	As of:	
	12/31/99	*12/31/98*
Current assets:		
Cash and cash equivalents	$133,309,000	$71,583,000
Marketable securities	572,879,000	301,862,000
Inventories	220,646,000	29,501,000
Prepaid expenses and other current assets	85,344,000	21,308,000
Total current assets	1,012,178,000	424,254,000
Fixed assets, net	317,613,000	29,791,000
Goodwill, net	534,699,000	174,052,000
Other purchased intangibles, net	195,445,000	4,586,000
Investments in equity-method investees	226,727,000	7,740,000
Other investments	144,735,000	0
Deferred charges and other	40,154,000	8,037,000
Total assets	$2,471,551,000	$648,460,000
Liabilities and stockholders' equity		
Current liabilities:		
Accounts payable	$463,026,000	$113,273,000
Accrued expenses and other		
current liabilities	126,017,000	34,413,000
Accrued advertising	55,892,000	13,071,000
Deferred revenue	54,790,000	0
Interest payable	24,888,000	10,000
Current portion of long-term debt		
and other current liabilities	14,322,000	808,000
Total current liabilities	738,935,000	161,575,000
Long-term debt and and other	1,466,338,000	348,140,000
Commitments and contingencies		
Stockholders' equity:		
Preferred stock, $0.01 par value:		
Authorized shares—150,000		
Issued and outstanding		
shares—none	$0	$0
Common stock, $0.01 par value:		
Authorized shares—1,500,000		
Issued and outstanding shares—		
345,155 and 318,534 shares at		
December 31, 1999 and		
1998, respectively	3,452,000	3,186,000
Additional paid-in capital	1,195,540,000	298,537,000
Note receivable for common stock	(1,171,000)	(1,099,000)
Stock-based compensation	(47,806,000)	(1,625,000)
Accumulated other comprehensive		
income (loss)	(1,709,000)	1,806,000
Accumulated deficit	(882,028,000)	(162,060,000)
Total stockholders' equity	266,278,000	138,745,000
Total liabilities and stockholders' equity	$2,471,551,000	$648,460,000

Amazon.com Inc
Cash Flow Statement

	For the year ended:	
	12/31/99	12/31/98
Operating Activities:		
Net loss	($719,968,000)	($124,546,000)
Adjustments to reconcile net loss to net cash provided (used) in operating activities:		
Depreciation and amortization of fixed assets	36,806,000	9,421,000
Amortization of deferred stock-based compensation	30,618,000	2,386,000
Equity in losses of equity-method investees	76,769,000	2,905,000
Amortization of goodwill and other intangibles	214,694,000	42,599,000
Non-cash merger, acquisition, and investment related costs	8,072,000	1,561,000
Non-cash revenue for advertising and promotional services	(5,837,000)	0
Loss on sale of marketable securities	8,688,000	271,000
Non-cash interest expense	29,171,000	23,970,000
Net cash used in operating activities before changes in operating assets and liabilities	($320,987,000)	($41,433,000)
Changes in operating assets and liabilities, net of effects from acquisitions:		
Inventories	(172,069,000)	(20,513,000)
Prepaid expenses and other current assets	(60,628,000)	(16,758,000)
Accounts payable	330,166,000	78,674,000
Accrued expenses and other current liabilities	65,121,000	21,615,000
Accrued advertising	42,382,000	9,617,000
Deferred revenue	262,000	0
Interest payable	24,878,000	(167,000)
Net cash provided by changes in operating assets and liabilities, net of effects from acquisitions	230,112,000	72,468,000
Net cash provided (used) in operating activities	($90,875,000)	$31,035,000
Investing Activities:		
Sales and maturities of marketable securities	2,064,101,000	227,789,000
Purchases of marketable securities	(2,359,398,000)	(504,435,000)
Purchases of fixed assets	(287,055,000)	(28,333,000)
Acquisitions and investments in businesses, net of cash acquired	(369,607,000)	(19,019,000)
Net cash used in investing activities	($951,959,000)	($323,998,000)
Financing Activities:		
Proceeds from issuance of capital stock and exercise of stock options	64,469,000	14,366,000
Proceeds from long-term debt	1,263,639,000	325,987,000
Repayment of long-term debt	(188,886,000)	(78,108,000)
Financing costs	(35,151,000)	(7,783,000)
Net cash provided by financing activities	$1,104,071,000	$254,462,000
Effect of exchange rate changes	$489,000	($35,000)
Net increase (decrease) in cash and cash equivalents	61,726,000	(38,536,000)
Cash and cash equivalents at beginning of period	71,583,000	110,119,000
Cash and cash equivalents at end of period	133,309,000	71,583,000
Supplemental Cash Flow Information:		
Fixed assets acquired under capital leases	$25,850,000	
Fixed assets acquired under financing agreements	$5,608,000	$0
Stock issued in connection with business acquisitions	$774,409,000	$217,241,000
Equity securities of other companies received for non-cash revenue for advertising and promotional services	$54,402,000	$0
Cash paid for interest, net of amounts capitalized	$59,688,000	$26,629,000

Chapter sixteen

Financial Statement Analysis and the Valuation of Common Stock

1. Chapter 6 covered expected present values; what is a present value?
2. What is usually the first thing projected when projecting future cash flow?
3. Why must changes in the current asset and current liability accounts be included in estimating future cash flows?
4. What business is Coldwater Creek in?
5. Are there any unusual items on Coldwater Creek's recent balance sheets? If so, what are they?
6. Where did we find Coldwater's depreciation and amortization expense? Why did we need it?
7. What role can the indirect method for cash flow statements play in making projections of future cash flows?
8. What is the forecast horizon we used in our analysis of Coldwater Creek?
9. What contributes more to our estimate of Coldwater's value: projected cash flows over the forecast horizon or projected cash flows beyond the forecast horizon? Why?
10. Why begin an examination of financial statements by reading the auditors' opinion?
11. What is a benchmark? What is a time-series benchmark?
12. What is a cross-sectional benchmark?
13. What does cross-sectional analysis add to time-series analysis?
14. What information does the current ratio provide about a company?
15. How does the quick ratio differ from the current ratio?
16. What are SIC codes?
17. How do SIC codes aid in financial statement analysis?
18. Why is assessing sales growth important in projecting future cash flows?

Exercises . . . .

E16-1 The Topps Company, Inc. is an international marketer of entertainment products—principally candy, collectible trading cards, and sticker album collections. It is well known for such products as Topps Ring Pops, Bazooka bubble gum, Pokemon merchandise, and collectible sports products, particularly baseball cards. Presented next are the comparative income statement and balance sheet data along with selected notes from Topps' 2001 annual report for the years 1997 to 2001.

(In thousands, except per share data)

	2001	2000	1999	1998	1997
OPERATING DATA					
Net sales	$439,268	$374,193	$229,414	$241,250	$268,975
Gross profit	215,344	178,835	94,791	79,709	90,121
SGA expense	96,391	84,738	72,288	78,437	75,974
Income (loss) from operations	121,917	94,852	26,658	(2,020)	(14,475)
Interest income (expense)	5,717	1,712	(454)	(1,585)	(1,942)
Net income (loss)	88,489	59,215	15,571	(4,572)	(10,943)
Per share	$1.97	$1.28	$0.34	$(0.10)	$(0.23)
BALANCE SHEET DATA					
Cash and equivalents	$158,741	$75,853	$41,728	$22,153	$24,199
Working capital	138,079	71,128	24,919	20,971	18,716
PP & E, net	11,181	9,181	7,429	10,148	12,900
Long-term debt, less current portion	—	—	5,158	22,617	27,450
Total assets	280,272	203,313	151,453	159,148	177,939
Stockholders' equity	$196,542	$129,175	$77,224	$61,609	$68,052

Notes to financial statements:

Note 10: Long-term debt

On June 26, 2000, the company entered into a credit agreement with Chase Manhattan Bank and LaSalle Bank National Association. The agreement provides for a $35 million unsecured credit facility to cover revolver and letter of credit needs, and expires on June 26, 2004. Interest rates are variable and a function of the company's EBITDA. The credit agreement contains restrictions and prohibitions of a nature generally found in loan agreements of this type and requires the company, among other things, to comply with certain financial covenants; limits the company's ability to repurchase its shares, sell or acquire assets, or borrow additional money; and prohibits the payment of dividends. The credit agreement may be terminated by the company at any point over the four-year term (provided the company repays all outstanding amounts thereunder) without penalty.

Required

a. Prepare percentage income statements for the five years presented.

b. Comment on any favorable or unfavorable trends. Cite any factors that may be explanations for those trends.

c. Comment on environmental factors that must be considered in looking at Topps as a potential investment.

d. The financial statements indicate that, for the quarter ended March 3, 2001, the company's common stock traded in a price range of $7.88 to $10.69 per share. Given the results presented in Topps' income statements, would this stock appear to be selling at a relatively high valuation, low valuation, or fair valuation? Give reasons for your answer.

E16-2   Refer to E16-1. Topps reported inventory of $19,526,000 and $20,738,000 on March 3, 2001 and on February 26, 2000, respectively. If Topps' sales are expected to grow 15% in fiscal 2002, estimate the amount of inventory Topps could expect to have on hand on February 28, 2002.

E16-3   Refer to E16-1.

Required

a.   Prepare a comparative analysis of Topps' balance sheet data from 1997 to 2001. Comment on any findings, with possible explanations for any favorable or unfavorable trends.

b.   Assume that Topps will access the entire $35 million in credit discussed in the note on March 5, 2001. Assume the debt is classified as long-term debt. The company's balance sheet contained the following at March 3, 2001(in thousands):

Total current assets: $210,779

What impact would such a move have on the following ratios?

1.   Current ratio

2.   Quick ratio

3.   Debt-to-equity ratio

4.   Long-term debt-to-equity ratio

E16-4   X and Y are competing companies in the same industry. X had sales of $1 million and Y had sales of $5 million in 2000. Presented below are selected data from the income statement and balance sheets of the two companies for 2000.

	X	Y
INCOME STATEMENTS		
Sales	$1,000,000	$5,000,000
Cost of goods sold	400,000	2,250,000
Gross Profit	600,000	2,750,000
Operating expenses	200,000	1,500,000
Income before taxes	400,000	1,250,000
Income taxes	120,000	375,000
Net income	280,000	875,000
BALANCE SHEETS		
Current assets	$400,000	$800,000
Plant and Equipment, net	600,000	3,200,000
Total assets	$1,000,000	$4,000,000
Current Liabilities	$200,000	600,000
Long-term debt	100,000	2,000,000
Total liabilities	300,000	2,600,000
Equity	700,000	1,400,000
Total liabilities & Equity	$1,000,000	$4,000,000

Required

a. Prepare a comparative analysis of the financial statements in percentage terms.

b. What information does the percentage analysis reveal that might aid in analyzing the results of the two companies?

c. What key ratios might also be used to compare these two companies?

E16-5 Presented below are selected data from the 2000 annual reports from Motorola Corporation, a manufacturer of wireless phones and communications processors; Pfizer, a major manufacturer of prescription medicines; and Kmart, a national discount retailer.

Amounts in millions

	A	B	C
INCOME STATEMENT			
Revenues	$29,574	$37,580	$37,028
Cost of goods sold	1,907	23,628	29,658
Selling and administrative expenses	11,442	5,141	7,415
Net income	$3,726	$1,318	($244)
BALANCE SHEET			
Current assets	17,187	19,885	7,624
Inventories	2,702	5,242	6,412
Current liabilities	11,981	16,257	3,799
Total assets	33,510	42,343	14,630
Total equity	16,076	18,612	6,083
CASH FLOW STATEMENT			
Cash dividends paid	2,197	333	—
Purchases of P,P&E	2,191	4,131	1,087
Cash flow from operations	6,195	(1,164)	1,039

Required

Based on your analysis of the information presented, identify each company. Use ratios and other financial analysis techniques presented in the text to justify your choices.

Problems ....

P16-1 Lands' End, Inc., is a direct marketer of traditionally styled apparel, domestics (primarily bedding and bath items), soft luggage, and other products. The company manages its businesses in three operating segments: core, specialty, and international, based principally on type of catalog focusing on specific customer needs and market served. The company's primary market is the United States, and other markets include the Pacific Basin area, Europe, and Canada. The income statement, balance sheet, and cash flow statement for Lands' End and Subsidiaries for the year ended January 29, 1999 are presented on pages 187–189.

Required

a.   Assume that Lands' End will have sales growth of 12% for the year ended January 31, 2000. Project Lands' End estimated cost of goods sold for the year ended January 31, 2000. Be sure to state your assumptions.

b.   Based on the 12% estimated sales growth, prepare a projected income statement for the year ended January 31, 2000 and a projected balance sheet for January 31, 2000. Be sure to state the assumptions used in your projections.

c.   Lands' End has been using free cash flow to purchase treasury stock. Based on your projections in a and b, project the total amount of free cash flow that Lands' End would have available to purchase treasury stock for the year ended January 31, 2000. Be sure to state your assumptions.

d.   Prove the projected free cash flow from requirement c. by preparing a projected free cash flow report using the indirect method.

Lands' End, Inc. & Subsidiaries
Consolidated Statement of Operations
(In thousands, except per share data)

	For the period ended		
	January 29, 1999	January 30, 1998	January 31, 1997
Net sales	$1,371,375	$1,263,629	$1,118,743
Cost of sales	754,661	675,138	609,168
Gross profit	$616,714	$588,491	$509,575
Selling, general and administrative expenses	544,446	489,923	424,390
Non-recurring charge	12,600	—	—
Charge from sale of subsidiary	—	—	1,400
Income from operations	$59,668	$98,568	$83,785
Other income (expense):			
Interest expense	$(7,734)	$(1,995)	$(510)
Interest income	16	1,725	1,148
Gain on sale of subsidiary	—	7,805	—
Other	(2,450)	(4,278)	496
Total other income (expense), net	$(10,168)	$3,257	$1,134
Income before income taxes	$49,500	$101,825	$84,919
Income tax provision	18,315	37,675	33,967
Net income	$31,185	$64,150	$50,952

Lands' End, Inc. & Subsidiaries
Consolidated Balance Sheets
(In thousands)

	For the period ended	
	January 29, 1999	January 30, 1998
ASSETS		
Current assets:		
Cash and cash equivalents	$ 6,641	$ 6,338
Receivables, net	21,083	15,443
Inventory	219,686	241,154
Prepaid advertising	21,357	18,513
Other prepaid expenses	7,589	5,085
Deferred income tax benefits	17,947	12,613
Total current assets	$294,303	$299,146
Property, plant and equipment, at cost:		
Land and buildings	$102,018	$81,781
Fixtures and equipment	154,663	118,190
Leasehold improvements	5,475	5,443
Construction in progress	—	12,222
Total property, plant and equipment	$262,156	$217,636
Less accumulated depreciation and amortization	101,570	84,227
Property, plant and equipment, net	$160,586	$133,409
Intangibles, net	1,030	917
Total assets	$455,919	$433,472
LIABILITIES AND SHAREHOLDERS' INVESTMENT		
Current liabilities:		
Lines of credit	$38,942	$32,437
Accounts payable	87,922	83,743
Reserve for returns	7,193	6,128
Accrued liabilities	54,392	34,942
Accrued profit sharing	2,256	4,286
Income taxes payable	14,578	20,477
Total current liabilities	$205,283	$182,013
Deferred income taxes	$8,133	$8,747
Shareholders' investment:		
Common stock, 40,221 shares issued	$402	$402
Donated capital	8,400	8,400
Additional paid-in capital	26,994	26,457
Deferred compensation	(394)	(1,047)
Accumulated other comprehensive income	2,003	875
Retained earnings	406,396	375,211
Treasury stock, 10,317 and 9,281 shares at cost, respectively	(201,298)	(167,586)
Total shareholders' investment	$242,503	$242,712
Total liabilities and shareholders' investment	$455,919	$433,472

Lands' End, Inc. & Subsidiaries
Consolidated Statements of Cash Flows
(In thousands)

	For the period ended		
	January 29, 1999	January 30, 1998	January 31, 1997
Cash flows from operating activities:			
Net income	$31,185	$64,150	$50,952
Adjustments to reconcile net income to net cash flows from operating activities—			
Pre-tax non-recurring charge	12,600	—	—
Depreciation and amortization	18,731	15,127	13,558
Deferred compensation expense	653	323	317
Deferred income taxes	(5,948)	(1,158)	994
Pre-tax gain on sale of subsidiary	—	(7,805)	—
Loss on disposal of fixed assets	586	1,127	325
Changes in assets and liabilities excluding the effects of divestitures:			
Receivables	(5,640)	(7,019)	(675)
Inventory	21,468	(104,545)	22,371
Prepaid advertising	(2,844)	(7,447)	4,758
Other prepaid expenses	(2,504)	(1,366)	(145)
Accounts payable	4,179	11,616	14,205
Reserve for returns	1,065	944	629
Accrued liabilities	6,993	8,755	4,390
Accrued profit sharing	(2,030)	1,349	1,454
Income taxes payable	(5,899)	(1,047)	8,268
Other	1,665	64	394
Net cash flows from (used for) operating activities	$74,260	$(26,932)	$121,795
Cash flows from (used for) investing activities:			
Cash paid for capital additions	$(46,750)	$(47,659)	$(18,481)
Proceeds from sale of subsidiary	—	12,350	—
Net cash flows used for investing activities	$(46,750)	$(35,309)	$(18,481)
Cash flows from (used for) financing activities:			
Proceeds from short-term borrowings	$6,505	$21,242	$1,876
Purchases of treasury stock	(35,557)	(45,899)	(30,143)
Issuance of treasury stock	1,845	409	604
Net cash flows used for financing activities	$(27,207)	$(24,248)	$(27,663)
Net increase (decrease) in cash and cash equivalents	303	(86,489)	75,651
Beginning cash and cash equivalents	6,338	92,827	17,176
Ending cash and cash equivalents	$6,641	$6,338	$92,827

P16-2 Financial Statement Analysis and Articulation

Frisby Technologies, Inc. is engaged in the development and commercialization of innovative branded thermal management products for use in a broad range of consumer and industrial products such as gloves, boots, athletic footwear, apparel, protective and temperature retardant equipment, medical equipment, electronics cooling systems, packaging materials, and coating substances. The company's Thermasorb® and ComforTemp® products utilize licensed patents and the company's proprietary microencapsulated phase change material (MicroPCM) technology to enhance thermal characteristics (i.e., insulation, cooling, or temperature control properties). For example, when Thermasorb® additives and ComforTemp® foams are incorporated into ski gloves, the skier's hands would remain within a constant, pre-set temperature range without the typical accumulation of moisture. Also, if a firefighter were to wear flame retardant clothing incorporating ComforTemp® foam, the firefighter would remain cooler and be able to fight fires longer and more safely than a firefighter wearing flame retardant clothing without ComforTemp® foam. The company's balance sheet and income statement for the 1998 fiscal year are presented below and on page 191.

Frisby Technologies, Inc.
Balance Sheet

	December 31, 1998
ASSETS	
Current assets:	
Cash and cash equivalents	$6,516,138
Marketable securities	1,555,683
Accounts receivable	1,045,975
Accounts receivable — unbilled	58,159
Inventory	671,569
Prepaid expenses and other current assets	595,998
Total current assets	$10,443,522
Property and equipment, net	277,494
Intangible assets, less accumulated amortization of $51,300	2,000,700
Other assets	391,516
Total assets	$13,113,232
LIABILITIES AND STOCKHOLDERS' EQUITY	
Current liabilities:	
Accounts payable	$868,649
Accrued expenses and other current liabilities	385,533
Payable to Triangle Research and Development Corporation	400,000
License fees payable	189,726
Deferred license revenues	85,000
Total current liabilities	$1,928,908
Accrued license agreement costs	120,250
Deferred license revenues	46,250
Other liability	1,300,000
Total liabilities	$3,395,408

(Continued)

STOCKHOLDERS' EQUITY

Preferred Stock, 1,000,000 shares authorized; 587,500 shares issued and outstanding	$2,479,000
Common Stock, $.001 par value; 10,000,000 shares authorized; 5,120,613 shares issued and outstanding	5,121
Additional paid-in capital	12,199,828
Accumulated other comprehensive income	21,000
Retained Earnings	(4,987,125)
Total stockholders' equity	$9,717,824
Total liabilities and stockholders' equity	$13,113,232

Frisby Technologies, Inc.
Statement of Operations

	Year ended
	December 31, 1998
Revenues:	
Product sales	$2,198,275
Research and development projects	196,345
Licenses and royalties	474,519
Total revenues	$2,869,139
Cost of sales:	
Product sales	$2,125,730
Research and development projects	158,856
Licenses and royalties	234,403
Total cost of sales	$2,518,989
Gross profit	$350,150
Selling and marketing expense	2,234,499
General and administrative expense	2,400,930
Loss from operations	$(4,285,279)
Interest income (expense), net	366,635
Net loss	$(3,918,644)

Required

a. "Property and equipment, net" appears on the balance sheet. What does "net" refer to?

b. What does "Deferred license revenues" likely refer to and why is it listed on the balance sheet? Why are there two "Deferred license revenues" listed on the balance sheet?

c. Total revenues are $2,869,139 on the income statement. Accounts receivable were $1,769,507 on December 31, 1997. Did Frisby collect more or less than $2,869,139 in cash from its customers during 1998?

d. On Frisby's balance sheet, $58,159 is listed as "Accounts receivable-unbilled." What do you think it means? What other account was likely changed when the unbilled receivables were recognized?

e. Suppose no dividends were paid in 1998. What was the balance in Retained Earnings on December 31, 1997?

f. What is Frisby's primary source of revenue?

g. Why are there two items labeled "Licenses and royalties" on Frisby's income statement?

h. What was the cost of Frisby's "Intangible assets"?

i. What is the major component of Frisby's expenses?

j. What is Frisby's most profitable product?

k. Frisby reported expenses associated with "Product sales" of $2,125,730 for 1998. Is this how much cash Frisby paid in 1998 for the products it sold? Justify your answer.

l. Compute the current ratio and quick ratio at December 31, 1998. What do these ratios tell you about the company?

m. Compute the debt-to-equity ratio at December 31, 1998. What does this ratio tell you about the company?

n. Suppose that you were an investor interested in purchasing the common stock of Frisby Technologies at December 31, 1998. Provide reasons both for and against investing in this company?

o. What additional information would an investor need to make a rational investment decision on Frisby Technologies?

P16-3 Selected financial data from the Quarterly filings (10Q) of NUKO Information Systems for December 31, 1995 and June 30, 1996 follows. You will also find the copy of an SEC filing called an 8-K.

Required

a.   Perform an analysis of NUKO's 10Q's using analytical techniques mentioned in the chapter. As a potential investor in this company's stock, state five reasons for concern. Cite specifics to justify your answer.

b.   Explain why the SEC requires registrants to file an 8K under certain circumstances.

From NUKO Information Systems, Inc. 10Q:

NUKO Information Systems, Inc.
Condensed Consolidated Balance Sheets

	June 30, 1996	December 31, 1995
ASSETS:		
Current Assets:		
Cash and cash equivalents	$6,374,415	$11,255,820
Short-term investments	2,654,273	
Accounts receivable, trade	1,061,895	120,000
Receivables from officers/directors		27,931
Share subscriptions receivable including interest of $30,567 at December 31, 1995		341,967
Inventories (net)	1,497,092	758,552
Other current assets	364,669	110,762
Total Current Assets	11,952,344	12,615,032
Property and Equipment (Net)	1,637,041	459,497
Other Assets	9,783	253,340
Total Assets	$13,599,168	$13,327,869
LIABILITIES AND STOCKHOLDERS' EQUITY		
Current Liabilities:		
Accounts payable	$2,823,790	$1,319,959
Accrued liabilities		108,719
Current portion—capital lease obligation	125,701	95,273
Total current liabilities	2,949,491	1,523,951
Senior notes		325,000
Capital lease obligation	100,106	101,686
Total liabilities	3,049,597	1,950,637
SHAREHOLDERS' EQUITY:		
Common stock, $0.001 par value, 20,000,000 shares authorized: 10,409,098 shares issued and outstanding at June 30, 1996; and 9,128,418 shares issued and outstanding at December 31, 1995	10,409	9,128
Additional paid-in capital	20,507,113	15,741,718
Accumulated deficit	(9,967,951)	(4,373,614)
Total shareholders' equity	10,549,571	11,377,232
Total Liabilities and Shareholders' Equity	$13,599,168	$13,327,869

NUKO Information Systems, Inc.
Condensed Consolidated Statements of Operations

	Three Months Ended June 30,	
	1996	1995
Net sales	$2,162,867	$—
Cost and Expenses:		
Cost of sales	1,389,909	—
Research and development	1,524,143	233,155
Selling, general and administrative expenses	1,890,342	154,501
	4,804,394	387,656
Loss from operations	(2,641,527)	(387,656)
Other income (expense), net	111,965	(35,870)
Net loss	(2,529,562)	(423,526)
Net loss per share	($0.25)	($0.17)
Weighted average shares outstanding	10,256,785	2,528,000

NUKO Information Systems, Inc.
Condensed Consolidated Statements of Operations

	Six Months Ended June 30,	
	1996	1995
Net sales	$2,637,280	$—
Cost and Expenses:		
Cost of sales	1,532,230	—
Research and development	3,712,190	561,752
Selling, general and administrative expenses	3,196,022	247,171
	8,440,442	808,923
Loss from operations	(5,803,162)	(808,923)
Other income (expense), net	208,825	(56,584)
Net Loss	(5,594,337)	(865,507)
Net loss per share	($0.62)	($0.35)
Weighted average shares outstanding	8,976,242	2,496,000

NUKO Information Systems, Inc.
Condensed Consolidated Statements of Cash Flows

	Six Months Ended June 30,	
	1996	1995
Operating activities		
Net cash used in operating activities	$(5,663,406)	$(758,792)
Investing activities:		
Purchase of short-term investments—Net	(2,654,273)	—
Acquisitions of property and equipment	(1,345,789)	(38,658)
Net cash used in investing activities	(4,000,062)	(38,658)
Financing activities:		
Issuance of common stock	5,108,643	4,000
Proceeds (repayment) from notes payable and long-term debt	(326,580)	1,050,000
Net cash provided by (used) in financing activities	4,782,063	1,054,000
Decrease in cash and cash equivalents	(4,881,405)	256,550
Cash and cash equivalents at beginning of period	11,255,820	372
Cash and cash equivalents at end of period	$6,374,415	$256,922

United States
Securities and Exchange Commission
Washington, D.C. 20549

Form 8-K/A

Amendment No. 1
To
Current Report

Pursuant to Section 13 or 15(b) of the Securities Exchange Act of 1934

Date of Report: August 16, 1996

Nuko Information Systems, Inc.
(Exact name of registrant as specified in its charter)

New York
(State or other jurisdiction of incorporation)

| 2-31438 | 16-0962874 |
| (Commission File No.) | (I.R.S. Employer Identification No.) |

2235 Qume Drive
San Jose, CA 95131
(Address of principal executive offices)
(408) 526-0288
(Registrant's telephone number, including area code)

The undersigned Registrant hereby amends Item 4. Change In Registrant's Certifying Accountant on its current report on Form 8-K dated August 2, 1996 as originally filed, with respect to the dismissal of Grant Thornton as its principal independent accountant.

Item 4. Change in Registrant's Certifying Accountant

(a)Dismissal of Independent Accountant. On July 22, 1996, the Registrant's Board of Directors, upon recommendation of its Audit Committee, dismissed Grant Thornton LLP ("Grant Thornton") as the Registrant's principal independent accountant engaged to audit the Registrant's financial statements.

The independent auditor's report of Grant Thornton on the consolidated financial statements of the Registrant for the eight months ended December 31, 1995, and for the years ended April 30, 1994 and 1995, included in the Form 10-K for December 31, 1995, contained no adverse opinion or disclaimer of opinion and was not qualified as to uncertainty, audit scope or accounting principle.

In connection with the Registrant's audit for the eight months ended December 31, 1995, and for the fiscal years ended April 30, 1994 and 1995, and in the subsequent interim period prior to Grant Thornton's dismissal on July 22, 1996, (i) there were no disagreements with Grant Thornton on any matter of accounting principles or practices, financial statement disclosure, or auditing scope or procedure which disagreements, if not resolved to the satisfaction of Grant Thornton, would have caused Grant Thornton to make reference to the subject matter of the disagreement in connection with their report; and (ii) the matters stated in item 304 (a) (iv) (B) of Regulation S-B where applicable.

The Registrant has requested Grant Thornton to furnish the Registrant with a letter addressed to the Securities and Exchange Commission stating whether it agrees with the statement made by the Registrant above, and if not, to state the respects in which it does not agree. The Registrant shall provide Grant Thornton with a copy of this Form 8-K no later than on the day this Form 8-K is filed with the Securities and Exchange Commission. As Grant Thornton is unavailable to supply the letter described above at the time of filing this 8-K, the Registrant will request Grant Thornton to provide the letter as promptly as possible so that the Registrant can file the letter with the SEC within ten (10) business days after the filing of this Form 8-K.

Signature

Pursuant to the requirements of the Securities Exchange Act of 1934, the Registrant has duly caused this report to be signed on its behalf by the undersigned hereunto duly authorized.

Nuko Information Systems, Inc.
Date: August 1, 1996 By: John H. Gorman

Subsequent to the date that the Registrant originally reported the dismissal of Grant Thornton on a Form 8-K, Grant Thornton notified the Registrant that it believed that Registrant did not have a comprehensive system of internal control in place and that the Registrant was notified of this on April 10, 1996. Grant Thornton has notified the Registrant that it believes that this consituted [*sic*] a reportable condition and Registrant agreed to amend this report. Subsequent to April 10, 1996, the Registrant hired a Chief Financial Officer and expanded its staff to strengthen its internal controls and a letter from Grant Thornton is included as an Exhibit to this report.

Exhibit 2

Certifying Accountant's Response to Registrant's Response
August 16, 1996

Securities and Exchange Commission
Washington, DC 20549

Re: NUKO Information Systems, Inc.
File No. 2-31438

Dear Sir or Madam:

We have read Item 4 of the Form 8-K/A of NUKO Information Systems, Inc. dated August 16, 1996 and agree with the statements contained therein.

Very truly yours,

/s/ Grant Thornton LLP

P16-4   Statement Analysis, Impairment, and Articulation

Sun Healthcare Group, Inc., through its direct and indirect subsidiaries (collectively referred to herein as "Sun" or the "Company"), is one of the largest providers of long-term, subacute, and related specialty healthcare services in the United States and the United Kingdom. The Company also has operations in Spain, Germany, and Australia. The Company operates through four principal business segments: (i) inpatient services, (ii) rehabilitation and respiratory therapy services, (iii) pharmaceutical and medical supply services, and (iv) international operations. In October 1999, the Company commenced cases under Chapter 11 of the U.S. Bankruptcy Code and is currently operating its business as a debtor-in-possession subject to the jurisdiction of the Bankruptcy Court for the District of Delaware.

Income statements, balance sheets, statements of cash flows, and selected footnotes from SUN Healthcare's 1999 10K are presented on pages 197–198.

Required

Review Sun's financial statements and notes. Answer the following questions:

a.   What are reorganization costs? Why are they added to net earnings in order to obtain cash flow from operations?

b.   What event caused Sun to conclude that the values of their long-lived assets were impaired?

c.   What is the total impairment loss in 1999? In 1998? In 1997? How much of these losses were paid in cash? How are these costs shown in the operating cash flow section of the cash flow statement? Why? What percentage of total assets were written off each year?

d. Which assets were written down the most because of impairment? How did those assets arise and what has happened to decrease their values?

e. Explain what the major components of the $27.4 million 1999 restructuring cost are related to. What is your best guess as to the cash outflow for restructuring costs in 1999? Explain.

f. In fiscal 1998, was there any adjustment in the operating section of the cash flow statement necessary for restructuring costs? Why or why not? If there is a necessary adjustment, what is the amount and where is it?

g. What is the amount of the restructuring liability as of December 31, 1999? Where is it in the balance sheet?

h. What is the company's debt-to-equity ratio on December 31, 1998? How should mandatorily redeemable convertible preferred securities affect this ratio?

i. Prove the change in the accumulated deficit account from 1998 to 1999.

j. How much bad debt expense was recognized by the company in 1999? How many accounts were written off as uncollectible? Compute the allowance for doubtful accounts as a percentage of gross accounts receivable at December 31, 1998 and December 31, 1999. Comment on your findings and provide an explanation for any significant change.

Sun Healthcare Group, Inc. and Subsidiaries
(Debtor-in-Possession)
Consolidated Statements of Earnings (Losses)
For the Years Ended December 31, 1999, 1998 and 1997
(In Thousands Except Per Share Data)

	1999	1998	1997
Total net revenues	$2,529,039	$3,088,460	$2,010,820
Costs and expenses:			
Operating costs	2,477,713	2,629,485	1,662,818
Impairment loss	457,449	397,492	—
Corporate general and administrative	159,671	180,934	98,169
Interest, net (contractual interest expense $166,101)	129,054	135,411	74,482
Provision for losses on accounts receivable	123,217	83,083	15,839
Depreciation and amortization	81,325	102,515	56,630
Loss on sale of assets, net	78,673	206,205	7,000
Restructuring costs	27,353	4,558	—
Loss on termination of interest rate swaps	2,488	—	—
Legal and regulatory matters, net	38	22,456	—
Total costs and expenses before reorganization items	3,536,981	3,762,139	1,914,938
Dividends on convertible preferred securities of subsidiary	20,407	16,163	—
Earnings (losses) before reorganization costs, income taxes, extraordinary loss and cumulative effect of change in accounting principle	(1,028,349)	(689,842)	95,882
Reorganization costs, net	48,132	—	—
Earnings (losses) before income taxes, extraordinary loss and cumulative effect of change in accounting principle	(1,076,481)	(689,842)	95,882
Income taxes	161	53,577	41,153
Earnings (losses) before extraordinary loss and cumulative effect of change in accounting principle	(1,076,642)	(743,419)	54,729
Extraordinary loss from early extinguishment of debt, net of income tax benefit of $3,700 and $9,815 in 1998 and 1997, respectively	—	(10,274)	(19,928)
Cumulative effect of change in accounting principle	(12,816)	—	—
Net earnings (losses)	$(1,089,458)	$(753,693)	$34,801

Cash Flows from Operating Activities:

	1999	1998	1997
Net earnings (losses)	$(1,089,458)	$(753,693)	$34,801
Adjustments to reconcile net earnings (losses) to net cash provided by (used for) operating activities:			
Extraordinary loss	—	10,274	19,928
Loss on sale of assets, net	78,673	206,205	7,000
Impairment loss	457,449	397,492	—
Cumulative effect of change in accounting principle	12,816	—	—
Reorganization costs, net	48,132	—	—
Depreciation and amortization	81,325	102,515	56,630
Provision for losses on accounts receivable	123,217	83,083	15,839
Other, net	18,055	9,068	3,312
Changes in operating assets and liabilities:			
Accounts receivable	160,864	(61,679)	(164,966)
Other current assets	8,412	(19,557)	(6,323)
Other current liabilities	72,607	(41,530)	24,228
Income taxes payable	35,430	22,242	31,284
Net cash provided by (used for) operating activities before reorganization costs	7,522	(45,580)	21,733
Net cash paid for reorganization costs	(269)	—	—
Net cash provided by (used for) operating activities	7,253	(45,580)	21,733

Consolidated Balance Sheets
As of December 31, 1999 and 1998
(In Thousands)

	1999	1998
ASSETS		
Cash and cash equivalents	$25,047	$27,504
Accounts receivable, net of allowance for doubtful accounts of $151,841 and $79,015 at December 31, 1999 and 1998, respectively	254,464	538,329
Other receivables, net	15,916	48,073
Inventory, net	42,983	48,862
Prepaids and other assets	15,087	13,091
Income tax receivables	—	15,874
Total current assets	353,497	691,733
Property and equipment, net	446,176	601,270
Goodwill, net	475,567	795,945
Notes receivable, net of allowance of $6,556 and $1,712 at December 31, 1999 and 1998, respectively	22,698	32,334
Assets held for sale	70,609	192,447
Other assets, net	69,941	148,309
Deferred tax assets	—	6,000
Total assets	$1,438,488	$2,468,038

(Continued)

LIABILITIES AND STOCKHOLDERS' EQUITY (DEFICIT)

Current liabilities:		
Current portion of long-term debt	$44,776	$812,621
Current portion of obligations under capital leases	433	3,703
Accounts payable	53,787	94,143
Accrued compensation and benefits	84,117	102,091
Accrued interest	2,972	26,095
Accrued self-insurance obligations	59,075	54,865
Other accrued liabilities	116,489	137,851
Income tax payables	9,130	—
Total current liabilities	370,779	1,231,369
Long-term debt, net of current portion	100,765	705,653
Obligations under capital leases, net of current portion	65,675	103,679
Other long-term liabilities	36,794	41,061
Liabilities subject to compromise (see Note 2)	1,558,518	—
Total liabilities	2,132,531	2,081,762
Minority interest	5,979	7,517
Company-obligated mandatorily redeemable convertible preferred securities of a subsidiary trust holding solely 7% convertible junior subordinated debentures of the Company	344,119	345,000
Stockholders' equity (deficit):		
Common stock of $.01 par value, authorized 155,000,000 shares, 63,937,302 and 61,930,159 shares issued and outstanding as of December 31, 1999 and 1998, respectively	639	619
Additional paid-in capital	777,164	774,860
Accumulated deficit	(1,785,507)	(696,049)
Accumulated other comprehensive income (loss)	(5,017)	2,902
	(1,012,721)	82,332
Less:		
Unearned compensation	(3,966)	(8,552)
Common stock held in treasury, at cost, 2,212,983 and 2,124,868 shares as of December 31, 1999 and 1998, respectively	(27,376)	(26,967)
Grantor stock trust, at market, 1,915,935 and 1,989,132 shares as of December 31, 1999 and 1998, respectively	(78)	(13,054)
Total stockholders' equity (deficit)	(1,044,141)	33,759
Total liabilities and stockholders' equity (deficit)	$1,438,488	$2,468,038

Restructuring Costs

In the fourth quarter of 1998, the Company initiated a restructuring plan focused primarily on reducing the operating expenses of its United States operations. Related to the 1998 corporate restructuring plan, the Company recorded a 1998 fourth-quarter charge of approximately $4.6 million. The 1998 corporate restructuring plan included the elimination of approximately 7,500 positions, primarily in the Company's rehabilitation and respiratory therapy operations and also included the closure of approximately 70 divisional and regional offices. The 1998 corporate restructuring charge consists of approximately $3.7 million related to employee terminations and approximately $0.9 million related to lease termination costs. As of December 31, 1998, the Company had terminated 1,440 employees, and paid approximately $1.4 million and $0.1 million in termination benefits and lease termination costs, respectively. As of December 31, 1998, the Company's 1998 corporate restructuring costs reserve balances relating to employee terminations and lease termination costs were approximately $2.3 million and $0.8 million, respectively. During 1999 the Company paid approximately $1.1 million relating to employee terminations. As of

December 31, 1999, approximately $1.2 million of the 1998 corporate restructuring costs reserve balance of approximately $2.0 million is composed of prepetition severance accruals that are classified as liabilities subject to compromise in the Company's consolidated balance sheets. In 1999, the Company's 1998 corporate restructuring plan was substantially complete.

In the first quarter of 1999, the Company initiated a second corporate restructuring plan focused on further reducing the operating expenses of its United States operations. Related to the 1999 corporate restructuring plan, the Company recorded a first quarter charge of approximately $11.4 million. The 1999 corporate restructuring plan included the termination of approximately 3,000 employees, primarily in its rehabilitation and respiratory therapy services operations. The 1999 restructuring plan also includes the closure of approximately 23 divisional and regional offices. In addition, the plan included the relocation of the management of the Company's medical supply subsidiary and temporary therapy services subsidiary to the Company's corporate headquarters in Albuquerque, New Mexico. As part of the relocation, the Company terminated 96 employees of these subsidiaries. The 1999 corporate restructuring charge consisted of approximately $9.1 million related to employee terminations, approximately $1.4 million related to lease termination costs, and $0.9 million related to asset disposals or write-offs. The amounts paid out during 1999 were consistent with the charges recorded in 1999. As of December 31, 1999, the Company's 1999 corporate restructuring plan was complete.

During 1999, the Company recorded financial restructuring costs of approximately $16.0 million—primarily professional fees, related to the Company's activities in response to the defaults under the Senior Credit Facility, the 9-3/8% Subordinated Notes, and the 9-1/2% Subordinated Notes and in preparation for its filing for protection under Chapter 11 of the U.S. Bankruptcy Code.

Reorganization Costs

Reorganization costs under Chapter 11 are items of expense or income that are incurred or realized by the Company because it is in reorganization. These include, but are not limited to, professional fees and similar types of expenditures incurred directly relating to the Chapter 11 proceeding, loss accruals or realized gains or losses resulting from activities of the reorganization process, and interest earned on cash accumulated by the Company because it is not paying its prepetition liabilities.

For the period from the Filing Date to December 31, 1999, reorganization costs, net, were $48.1 million, and the components are as follows:

Amount Reorganization Cost (in thousands)

Write-off of debt discounts and deferred issuance costs	$37,614
Loss on sale of assets	7,085
Professional fees	4,115
Less interest earned on accumulated cash	(682)
Total	$48,132

7 (A): Impairment of Long-Lived Assets

SFAS 121 requires impairment losses to be recognized for long-lived assets used in operations when indications of impairment are present and the estimate of undiscounted future cash flows is not sufficient to recover long-lived asset carrying amounts. SFAS 121 also requires that long-lived assets held for disposal be carried at the lower of carrying value or fair value less costs of disposal, once management has committed to a plan of disposal.

The Balanced Budget Act of 1997 established, among other things, a new Medicare PPS (Prospective Payment System: a system under which skilled nursing facilities were reimbursed a fixed dollar amount per day for a patient in a certain category, which replaced a "cost plus" reimbursement system) for skilled nursing facilities. PPS became effective for the Company's facilities acquired from RCA on July 1, 1998, and for the Company's remaining facilities on

January 1, 1999. The Company's revenues from its Inpatient Services Division, Rehabilitation and Respiratory Therapy Services Division, and Pharmaceutical and Medical Supply Services Division were significantly and adversely impacted by the amount of the federally established reimbursement rates. In the first quarter of 1999, the Company became aware that these reductions were expected to have a material adverse impact on net revenues in 1999 and the decline was other than temporary. This served as an indication to the Company that the carrying values of the long-lived assets of its Inpatient Services Division, Rehabilitation and Respiratory Therapy Services Division, and its Pharmaceutical and Medical Supply Services Division were impaired.

During the second quarter of 1999, the Company revised its projections of future cash flows for its various business units, as current operating results were worse than planned. The significant write-down of goodwill and other long-lived assets resulted from the continued adverse impact of PPS on the level of Medicare reimbursement and occupancy and the demand for the Company's rehabilitation and respiratory therapy and pharmaceutical and medical supply services. Additionally, certain of the United Kingdom facilities have not achieved profitability targets established upon their acquisition.

The following is a summary of the impairment loss by segment for the year ended December 31, 1999 and 1998 (in thousands):

1999:	Goodwill	Property and Equipment	Other Assets	Total
Inpatient Services	$192,459	$88,852	$13,701	$295,012
Rehabilitation and Respiratory Therapy	49,529	11,005	11	60,545
Pharmaceuticals and Medical Supply Services	29,133	2,417	—	31,550
International Operations	29,322	31,959	—	61,281
Other Operations	5,327	1,794	1,940	9,061
	$305,770	$136,027	$15,652	$457,449
1998:				
Inpatient Services	$223,241	$55,736	$14,168	$293,145
Rehabilitation and Respiratory Therapy	36,734	60	4,216	41,010
Pharmaceuticals and Medical Supply Services	2,784	233	31	3,048
International Operations	26,520	10,151	—	36,671
Other Operations	23,590	28	—	23,618
	$312,869	$66,208	$18,415	$397,492

Sun Healthcare Group, Inc. and Subsidiaries
(Debtor-in-Possession)
Valuation and Qualifying Accounts

	Beginning Balance	To costs and expenses	To other accounts	Deductions	Ending Balance
Year ended December 31, 1999:					
Allowance for doubtful accounts	$79,015	$118,373 (3)	$—	$(45,547)	$151,841
Exit costs for acquired businesses.	$4,240	$—	$—	$(4,240)	$—
Notes receivable reserve	$1,712	$4,844 (3)	$—	$—	$6,556
Reserve for assets held for sale	$159,828	$85,758	$—	$(174,355)	$71,231
1998 corporate restructure reserve	$3,138	$—	$—	$(1,174)	$1,964
1999 restructure reserve	$—	$27,353	$—	$(27,353)	$—

(Continued)

	Beginning Balance	To costs and expenses	To other accounts	Deductions	Ending Balance
Year ended December 31, 1998:					
Allowance for doubtful accounts	$34,433	$81,371 (3)	$10,726 (1)	$(47,515)	$79,015
Exit costs for acquired businesses	$4,800	$—	$3,828 (2)	$(4,388)	$4,240
Notes receivable reserve	$—	$1,712 (3)	$—	$—	$1,712
Reserve for assets held for sale	$—	$206,205	$—	$(46,377)	$159,828
1998 corporate restructure reserve	$—	$4,558	$—	$(1,420)	$3,138

(1) Represents the allowance for doubtful accounts of acquired entities at the date of acquisition.
(2) Exit costs for acquired businesses are included in the purchase price allocation.
(3) Charges included in provision for losses on accounts receivable.

P16-5 JPM Company is a leading independent manufacturer of cable assemblies and wire harnesses for original equipment manufacturers and contract manufacturers in the computer, networking, and telecommunications sectors of the electronics industry. The information below and on pages 203–209 was filed in JPM's December 31, 2000 10Q, along with selected footnotes from the company's December 31, 2000 annual report and the audit opinion of PricewaterhouseCoopers.

Required

Assume that you were the loan officer for a large regional bank near the company's headquarters in Lewisburg, PA. John Mathias, Chairman and Chief Executive Officer of JPM has approached you about establishing a banking relationship. This relationship would involve refinancing significant portions of JPM's existing liabilities. Review the financial statements and notes and indicate whether you feel that this decision would be beneficial to the bank. Compute key ratios that might be of concern in making your credit decision. Cite specific reasons why you would grant or deny the loan.

JPM CO
Income Statement

	Three Month Ending	
	2000/12/31	1999/12/31
Net sales	$44,632,000	$45,419,000
Cost of sales	$41,340,000	$38,070,000
Gross profit	$3,292,000	$7,349,000
Selling, general and administrative expenses	$3,560,000	$4,129,000
Operating profit (loss)	($268,000)	$3,220,000
Other expense		
Interest expense	($2,359,000)	($1,308,000)
Other, net	($1,955,000)	($163,000)
	($4,314,000)	($1,471,000)
Income (loss) before income taxes and minority interest	($4,582,000)	$1,749,000
Provision for income taxes	$615,000	$659,000
Income (loss) before minority interest	($5,197,000)	$1,090,000
Minority interest	$516,000	$60,000
Net income (loss)	($5,713,000)	$1,030,000
Basic earnings (loss) per common share	($0.77)	$0.14
Diluted earnings (loss) per common share	($0.77)	$0.14
Weighted average number of shares of Common Stock outstanding (basic)	7,400,000	7,364,000
Weighted average number of shares of Common Stock outstanding (diluted)	7,400,000	7,527,000

The JPM Company
Condensed Consolidated Balance Sheet

	December 31, 2000	September 30, 2000 (unaudited)
ASSETS		
Current assets:		
Cash and cash equivalents	$5,902,000	$1,838,000
Accounts receivable (net of allowance of		
$1,385,000 and $1,448,000)	$24,682,000	$25,373,000
Inventories, net	$36,492,000	$37,052,000
Other current assets	$6,729,000	$7,972,000
Total current assets	$73,805,000	$72,235,000
Property, plant and equipment, net	$26,941,000	$27,442,000
Excess of cost over fair value of net assets		
acquired and other tangible assets, net	$27,307,000	$27,794,000
Other assets	$4,374,000	$4,493,000
	$132,427,000	$131,964,000
LIABILITIES AND SHAREHOLDERS' EQUITY		
Current liabilities:		
Current maturities of long-term debt	$73,613,000	$1,931,000
Notes payable	$2,000,000	$2,000,000
Accounts payable	$22,821,000	$20,262,000
Accrued expenses	$7,892,000	$7,938,000
Deferred income taxes	$3,462,000	$3,462,000
Total current liabilities	$109,788,000	$35,593,000
Long-term debt	$4,446,000	$73,602,000
Deferred compensation liability	$1,687,000	$1,687,000
Deferred income taxes	$1,255,000	$1,229,000
Minority interest	$1,647,000	$1,131,000
Other long-term liabilities	$807,000	$0
	$119,630,000	$113,242,000
Commitments and contingencies	$0	$0
SHAREHOLDERS' EQUITY:		
Preferred Stock, no par value, 10,000,000 shares		
authorized, Class A, $31.43 stated value,		
no shares issued and outstanding	$0	$0
Common Stock, $.000067 par value, 40,000,000		
shares authorized, 7,400,000 shares issued	$0	$0
Additional paid-in capital	$20,443,000	$20,443,000
Retained earnings (accumulated deficit)	($5,624,000)	$89,000
Accumulated other comprehensive loss	($2,022,000)	($1,810,000)
Total shareholders' equity	$12,797,000	$18,722,000
	$132,427,000	$131,964,000

1. Summary of Business and Significant Accounting Policies

The JPM Company (the "Company") is an independent manufacturer of cable assemblies and wire harnesses for original equipment manufacturers in the telecommunications, networking, computer, and business automation sectors of the global electronics industry.

A substantial portion of the Company's products are sold to a limited number of customers. Accordingly, a significant decrease in business from, or the loss of, any major customer would have a material adverse effect on the Company. The Company continuously seeks to expand the number of products it supplies to existing customers, as well as to develop similar relationships with new customers. Because of the complexity of these relationships, sales cycles can be long, sometimes taking up to 18 months or more to develop. As the Company becomes a qualified supplier for new products and as its customers' products progress through their life cycles, the Company's operating results can fluctuate significantly both annually and quarterly.

A summary of the Company's significant accounting policies follows.

Principles of Consolidation

The consolidated financial statements include the accounts of the Company and its wholly-owned and majority-owned subsidiaries. All significant intercompany transactions and balances have been eliminated.

Cash and Cash Equivalents

Cash and cash equivalents represent cash and highly liquid short-term investments with original maturities of three months or less.

Inventories

Inventories are valued at the lower of cost or market as determined on the first-in, first-out basis. Cost includes raw materials, direct labor, and manufacturing overhead. The Company generally provides reserves for inventory considered to be in excess of the previous 12 months of usage or sale, as well as inventory in excess of forecasted future demand.

Property, Plant, and Equipment

Property, plant, and equipment are recorded at cost and are depreciated on a straight-line basis over the estimated useful lives of the respective assets.

Revenue Recognition Policy

Sales are recorded upon shipment of product. Provision is made for returns and allowances, and for estimated warranty costs, in the period of sale.

Long-lived and Intangible Assets

Assets and liabilities acquired in connection with business combinations accounted for under the purchase method are recorded at their respective fair values. Deferred taxes have been recorded to the extent of differences between the fair value and the tax basis of the assets acquired and liabilities assumed. The excess of the purchase price over the fair value of the net assets acquired is amortized on a straight-line basis over 20 years. Intangible assets include the ISO 9002 certification of an acquired plant, which is being amortized on a straight-line basis over five years.

The carrying value of long-lived assets and certain identifiable intangible assets will be evaluated whenever changes in circumstances indicate the carrying amount of such assets may not be recoverable. In performing such review for recoverability, the Company will compare the expected future cash flows to the carrying value of long-lived assets and identifiable intangibles. In addition, on a quarterly basis, the carrying value of the excess of cost over fair value of net assets acquired is subject to a separate evaluation.

2. Acquisitions

In November 1998, the Company acquired 60% of the stock of AF Datalink Equipamentos de Telecomunicacao, Ltda. ("Datalink"), a Sao Paulo, Brazil-based manufacturer of wire harnesses and cable assemblies for $6,000 in cash, $2,500 in stock (256,000 shares of JPM stock), and one-year notes for $2,000 with interest at 8.75%. The transaction has been accounted for as a purchase in accordance with APB 16.

In June 1998, the Company acquired all of the stock of Antrum Interface 725, Ltd. ("Antrum"), manufacturers and assemblers of cable and wire harnesses, for cash consideration of approximately $16,500. The stock purchase agreement also provided for contingent cash consideration of up to $4,500 based on achievement of operating profit targets, as defined, for the period from June 1, 1997 through November 30, 2000. The contingent cash consideration of $4,500 was paid in September 2000 and has been treated as additional purchase price. The transaction has been accounted for as a purchase in accordance with APB 16.

The results of operations on an unaudited pro forma basis as if Datalink and Antrum had been acquired on October 1, 1997 are as follows:

| | Year Ended September 30, | |
	1999	1998
Net sales	$166,917	$149,582
Operating income	13,203	14,871
Net income	5,417	3,200
Net income per basic common share	$0.72	$0.44
Net income per diluted common share	$0.69	$0.42

3. Write-Down of Long-Lived Assets

The Company accounts for impairment of long-lived assets in accordance with Statement of Financial Accounting Standards No. 121 (SFAS 121), "Accounting for the Impairment of Long-Lived Assets and for Long-Lived Assets to be Disposed of." SFAS 121 requires that long-lived assets be reviewed for impairment whenever events or changes in circumstances indicate that the book value of the asset may not be recoverable.

During the year ended September 30, 2000, the Company recorded a $2,530 write-down of its investment in ERP implementation due to the decision to cease manufacturing at its San Jose facility and suspend implementation of the ERP manufacturing model at the Company's other facilities.

4. Closing of South Carolina Manufacturing Facility

On March 27, 1998, the Company announced plans to cease operations at its Winnsboro, S.C. manufacturing location and subsequently transfer all business to other plants in Pennsylvania, California, and Mexico.

The plant ceased production on June 26, 1998. Supervisory and breakdown crews remained at the facility until July 17, 1998. The Company accrued expenses totaling $1,412 and $178 in 1998 and 1999, respectively, for closing and severance costs. These costs are reflected in the income statement as a separate line item described as "Plant shutdown costs." All activity has ceased and the Company is seeking a buyer for the physical facility.

5. Major Customers and Suppliers

Net sales to Nortel, IBM, Hewlett-Packard, and Lucent amounted to 35%, 13%, 10%, and 10% of total sales, respectively, for fiscal 2000. Net sales to Nortel, IBM, Hewlett-Packard, and Lucent amounted to 28%, 14%, 11%, and 11% of total sales, respectively, for fiscal 1999. Net sales to Nortel, IBM, Hewlett-Packard, and Diebold amounted to 21%, 16%, 13%, and 11% of total sales, respectively, for fiscal 1998. Aggregate net sales to major customers, each of which exceeded 10% of total net sales, were 68%, 64%, and 61% of total net sales in 2000, 1999, and 1998, respectively. At September 30, 2000 and 1999, aggregate accounts receivable from these customers represented 71% and 63% of total accounts receivable, respectively. To reduce its credit risk, the Company reviews its customers' financial position before extending credit and periodically thereafter.

Historically, the Company has purchased a significant portion of its wire, cable, and connectors from a limited number of suppliers. Although the Company believes that its raw materials generally are available from several domestic and international sources, customers often specify that the Company purchase certain components from particular manufacturers. Accordingly, the loss of any of the Company's key suppliers could have a material adverse impact on the Company.

6. Inventories

	September 30,	
	2000	1999
Finished goods	$10,604	$10,392
Work-in-process	4,323	5,134
Raw materials and supplies	26,718	23,039
Valuation reserve	(4,593)	(1,338)
	$37,052	$37,227

7. Property, Plant, and Equipment, Net

	September 30,		Estimated
	2000	1999	Useful Lives
Land	$343	$400	
Buildings and improvements	12,500	13,511	10–25 years
Machinery and equipment	15,733	13,867	5–10 years
Furniture and fixtures	10,384	7,953	5–10 years
Vehicles	394	451	3–5 years
Construction in progress	2,606	6,371	
	41,960	42,553	
Less: Accumulated depreciation	(14,518)	(11,389)	
	$27,442	$31,164	

Depreciation expense was $3,224, $2,587, and $2,212 for fiscal 2000, 1999, and 1998, respectively.

The Company leases certain equipment under capital leases. Property, plant, and equipment includes $2,119 and $1,898 of capital leases at September 30, 2000 and 1999. Accumulated depreciation includes $375 and $152 at September 30, 2000 and 1999, respectively, related to these capital leases. The following is a schedule by years of future minimum lease payments under capital leases together with the present value of net minimum lease payments:

Year ending September 30:

2001	$514
2002	453
2003	364
2004	182
Total net minimum lease payments	1,513
Less amount representing interest	(129)
Present value of net minimum lease payments	$1,384

The Company also leases certain office and manufacturing facilities, office equipment, and vehicles under operating leases. Rent expense under operating leases was $2,063, $1,054, and $1,116 for fiscal 2000, 1999, and 1998, respectively. Future minimum lease payments under operating leases are:

2001	$2,203
2002	1,863
2003	1,264
2004	979
2005	939
Thereafter	1,521
Total minimum payments required	$8,769

8. Accounts Payable and Accrued Expenses

	September 30,	
	2000	1999
Salaries and benefits	$3,532	$3,523
Other	4,406	1,230
Total accrued expenses	$7,938	$4,753

Included in accounts payable at September 30, 2000 and 1999 are book overdrafts totaling $2,544 and $2,906, respectively.

9. Financing Arrangements

	2000	1999
Mortgage payable to Pennsylvania Industrial Development Authority; at a fixed rate of 5.75%; payable in monthly installments of $4 through May 2014; secured by land, buildings and improvements in Beaver Springs, PA with a net book value of $1,720 at September 30, 2000	$452	$472
Mortgage payable to bank; bank prime rate (9.50% at September 30, 2000 and an average of 8.83% for fiscal 2000) installments of $19 through January 2002; secured by land, buildings and improvements in Lewisburg, PA with a net book value of $528 at September 30, 2000	299	479
Mortgage payable to bank; at a fixed rate of 7.75%; payable in monthly installments of $6 through December 2011; secured by land, buildings and improvements in Beaver Springs, PA with a net book value of $1,720 at September 30, 2000	511	537
Mortgage payable to bank; at a fixed rate of 7.25%; payable in monthly installments of $24 through January 2013; secured by land, building and improvements in Lewisburg, PA with a net book value of $3,533 at September 30, 2000	2,338	2,437
Mortgage payable to bank; bank prime rate plus .75% (7.50% at September 30, 2000 and an average rate of 6.95% for fiscal 2000); payable in monthly installments of $4 through December 2002; secured by land and building in Pickering, Ontario, Canada with a net book value of $1,236 at September 30, 2000	587	648
Debt under a line of credit facility; $71,002 at a weighted average LIBOR-based rate of 10.66% at September 30, 2000 less short-term invested funds of $1,040 at September 30, 2000	69,962	47,668
Capital lease obligations, payable through June 2003	1,384	1,603
	75,533	53,844
Less: Current maturities	(1,931)	(744)
	$73,602	$53,100

Maturities of long-term debt, subsequent to September 30, 2000 are as follows:

Year ending September 30,

2001	$1,931
2002	69,643
2003	1,031
2004	389
2005	227
Thereafter	2,312
	$75,533

Interest paid in fiscal 2000, 1999, and 1998 on short-term borrowings and long-term debt totaled $5,965, $4,003, and $1,440, respectively.

Effective September 16, 2000, the Company amended its bank revolving line of credit to increase the facility by $5,000 to a total of $75,000. This amendment also waived any loan defaults existing at the time and accelerated the due date of all outstanding funds to December 31, 2000. Borrowings are collateralized by substantially all of the Company's assets. The interest rate on the line is the bank's prime lending rate, 9.5% at September 30, 2000, plus 3.0% or a LIBOR-based rate, approximately 6.62% at September 30, 2000, plus 3.75%. The commitment fee on the unused portion of the line is 0.5%. At September 30, 2000, the Company had $4,540 available under the bank agreement and was in compliance with all provisions of its loan agreement. The weighted average interest rate at September 30, 2000 on outstanding borrowings under the line of credit was $10.66%.

On December 22, 2000 and January 23, 2001, the Company further amended its loan agreement. These amendments extended the due date of all outstanding funds to December 31, 2001, and include an interest rate at the banks' prime lending rate plus 1.0% or, at the Company's election, a LIBOR-based rate plus 3.0%. The commitment fee on the unused portion of the line is 0.5%. The amendment requires mandatory principal payments of $50 per month for January through March 2001 and $150 per month for April through December 2001. In addition, certain other principal payments are required should the Company sell certain assets or collect certain accounts receivable. The amendment includes a number of reporting requirements and financial covenants commencing January 2001 based on monthly net income or net loss projections and three-month rolling EBITDA projections. Because the financial covenants are based on monthly computations with look-back and look-forward provisions, the Company believes there is doubt that it will be able to remain in compliance with the debt covenants through October 1, 2001, and as a result, substantially all of the Company's debt would be callable. If the Company does not remain in compliance with the debt covenants, it would expect to negotiate with its bank group to amend the loan agreement. At December 31, 2000, the Company had $1,878 available under the bank agreement.

The Company remains highly leveraged and as a result, access to additional funding sources is limited. If the Company's operating results deteriorate, or product sales and margins do not improve, or the Company is not in compliance with its covenants, or the Company is not successful in refinancing its bank line of credit, the Company could be in default under its loan agreement and any such default, not resolved, could lead to curtailment of certain of its business operations, sale of certain assets, or the commencement of insolvency proceedings by its creditors.

10. Comprehensive Income (Loss)

The components of comprehensive income (loss) are as follows:

	Year Ended September 30,		
	2000	*1999*	*1998*
Net income (loss)	$(18,821)	$5,296	$2,570
Other comprehensive income (loss):			
Change in accumulated translation adjustment	(1,400)	(45)	(365)
Total comprehensive income (loss)	$(20,221)	$5,251	$2,205

Auditor's Opinion:

To the Board of Directors and Shareholders of The JPM Company

In our opinion, the consolidated financial statements listed in the index appearing under Item 14 (a) (1) on page 15 present fairly, in all material respects, the financial position of The JPM Company and its subsidiaries (the "Company") at September 30, 2000 and 1999, and the results of their operations and their cash flows for each of the three years in the period ended September 30, 2000, in conformity with accounting principles generally accepted in the United States of America. In addition, in our opinion, the financial statement schedule listed in the index appearing under Item 14 (a) (2) on page 16 presents fairly, in all material respects, the information set forth therein when read in conjunction with the related consolidated financial statements. These financial statements and financial statement schedule are the responsibility of the Company's management; our responsibility is to express an opinion on these financial statements and financial statement schedule based on our audits. We conducted our audits of these statements in accordance with auditing standards generally accepted in the United States of America, which require that we plan and perform the audit to obtain reasonable assurance about whether the financial statements are free of material misstatement. An audit includes examining, on a test basis, evidence supporting the amounts and disclosures in the financial statements, assessing the accounting principles used and significant estimates made by management, and evaluating the overall financial statement presentation. We believe that our audits provide a reasonable basis for our opinion.

The accompanying financial statements have been prepared assuming that the Company will continue as a going concern. As discussed in Note 9 to the financial statements, the Company modified its debt agreement on December 22, 2000 and January 23, 2001. The Company has concluded it may not be able to remain in compliance through October 1, 2001, with certain of the covenants included in the modified debt agreement, and as a result, substantially all of the Company's debt would be callable. Accordingly, substantial doubt exists about the Company's ability to continue as a going concern. Management's plans in regard to this matter are also discussed in Note 9. The financial statements do not include any adjustments that might result from the outcome of this uncertainty.

PricewaterhouseCoopers LLP
Philadelphia, PA
January 24, 2001

Cases and Projects ·

C16-1   Financial Statement Analysis Project

The primary purpose of this project is to provide you with an in-depth look at a company's annual report and the industry in which it operates, and to familiarize you with searching on the Internet. In particular, you will conduct analyses of the financial statements contained in the report and relate your analysis to the business environment and industry in which the company operates.

Required

a.   Obtain a copy of the most recent annual report of a publicly held company.

b.   Research the company's current operating environment. Provide a discussion of the current state of the company and the industry in which it operates. You may want to comment on any relevant economic, technical, legal, political, or international considerations that may affect the future performance of this company. Are there positive or negative economic trends that will help or hurt this company in the near future?

c. Analyze the company's comparative income statements for the last three years and comparative balance sheets for the last two years. Prepare a percentage analysis. Comment on any positive or negative trends.

d. Identify the primary sources and uses of cash for the most recent year. What does this tell you about the company?

e. Find an Internet Web site or library reference tool that provides industry averages for the industry in which your company operates.

f. Throughout the text, we have cited financial ratios that are helpful in analyzing the condition of the company. Provide a comparative chart showing key ratios for your company compared to the industry average. Comment on any major differences and cite possible explanations for these differences.

g. Answer the following questions regarding your company:

1) If you were a bank responsible for deciding whether or not to lend $30 million to the company in a revolving line of credit, would you grant the credit line? Why or why not? Cite reasons for your answers.

2) If the company issued $200 million of 30-year bonds, would you purchase $10,000 of the bonds? Cite reasons for your answers.

3) If you had $5,000 to invest, would you purchase the common stock of this company? Cite reasons for your answer.

C16-2 Free Cash Flow Projection

Refer to Case 16-1.

Required

a. Using the information provided in the annual report, project the estimated growth rate in sales for your company.

b. Using the estimated growth rate that you computed in a, prepare forecasted income statements for the next five years and beyond. Use Exhibits 16.10 and 16.11 as your guide. Be sure to state your assumptions.

c. Using Exhibits 16.12 and 16.13 as your guide, prepare projected balance sheets for the next five years and beyond for your company. Be sure to state your assumptions.

d. Using Exhibit 16.5 as your guide, project the free cash flows for the next five years and beyond for your company.

e. Using a discount rate of 10%, compute the present value of the free cash flows. What is the estimated value per share of common stock?

f. Compare the estimated value per share of common stock to the current market price of the stock. Based on the comparison, what conclusions do you draw about the market valuation of your company? Does this conclusion agree with your answer to part g(3) of C16-1?

C16-3 Perrigo

Perrigo is a private manufacturer and marketer of generic drugs and vitamins. In early 1986 the owner/managers of Perrigo sold the company to Grow Corporation for $85 million. Perrigo management continued to run the company. Three years later, early in 1989, Grow was in financial difficulty and badly needed to raise cash. It tried various strategies, including a failed plan for a public offering of Perrigo stock. As a last resort, Grow entered into negotiations with Perrigo management, who offered to repurchase the company. Grow retained Paine Webber to provide financial advice on the value of Perrigo.

Relying on Perrigo management's projections of future profitability and cash flows, Paine Webber estimated the value of the company to be between $80 million and $113 million. Grow and Perrigo management finally agreed on a price of $106 million for Perrigo, and Perrigo management bought the company in April 1989.

Perrigo's owner/managers operated it as a private company for a little less than three years. Then, in December 1991, the owner/managers of Perrigo decided that the time was right to take the company public. Part of the process required filing financial statements for previous periods. The financial statements showed that Perrigo had done *much* better than management projected during the 1989 buyout negotiations. So much better, in fact, that the market valuation of Perrigo in December 1991 was *$1.2 billion.*

Grow became aware of the amount raised by the stock offering, and examined Perrigo's financial statements. Grow then sued Perrigo management, claiming they had misrepresented the future prospects of the company when they repurchased it in 1989.

Discovery in the legal process found projections that Perrigo management made in May 1989, less than one month after they reacquired the company, that were much different than the projections that had been given to Grow and Paine Webber. These May projections were much more optimistic about the future than the ones that supported Paine Webber's valuation. Based on the May projections, Paine Webber's valuation approach would have estimated the value of Perrigo in April 1989 to be somewhere between $172 million and $232 million.

Exhibit A:

Comparison of the sale price with ranges of value estimates

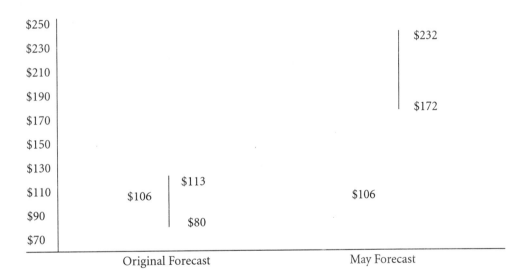

The Trial Testimony

The lawyers for Grow hired a well-known academic to testify that on the basis of the May projections, $106 million was an unfairly low price for Grow to have received. The price should have been between the upper and lower limits that would have been attained by the application of Paine Webber's valuation approach using the May projections; that is, a fair price was somewhere between $172 million and $232 million. Perrigo management lawyers argued that, even if Paine Webber had been given the May projections and estimated a value between $172 million and $232 million, Grow might still have sold the company to Perrigo management for $106 million. Their contention was that transactions do take place outside of the range of net present values of projected future cash flows. The academic strongly disagreed. He had seen and been an advisor on many transactions, and he had never seen one executed for a price outside the range of estimated present values. "Are you *sure* transactions are never executed outside the range of present value estimates?" the lawyers pressed. "I have *never* seen it," the academic replied.

Perrigo management lawyers then introduced cash flow projections they said were made at the time Perrigo initially sold the company to Grow in 1986 for $85 million. They claimed the discounted cash flow analysis resulted in a range of valuations between $120 million and $137 million. Thus, the $85 million price that Grow paid when it purchased Perrigo was outside the range of present values. So, they would argue, not only do transactions occur outside the range of present values, but Grow *itself* paid less for *Perrigo* than the minimum of such a present value range!

Exhibit B: Cash flow projections that were claimed to be the basis for the 1986 sale

	1986	1987	1988	1989	1990	1991	1992	1993	1994	1995*
EBIT***	10,000	12,000	14,856	18,213	24,351	31,535	39,912	41,908	44,003	46,203
Taxes	(4,850)	(6,220)	(7,205)	(8,833)	(11,810)	(15,294)	(19,357)	(20,325)	(21,341)	(22,409)
Net Income	5,150	5,780	7,651	9,380	12,541	16,241	20,555	21,583	22,662	23,794
Depreciation	3,351	3,925	3,885	3,885	3,885	3,885	3,885	3,885	3,885	3,885
Changes in working capital	(1,758)	2,912	4,089	4,958	6,604	4,965	5,461	5,461	5,461	5,461
Cash flows from operations	6,743	12,617	15,625	18,223	23,030	25,091	29,091	30,928	32,008	33,141
Capital Expenditures	(5,000)	(5,000)	(3,200)	(3,200)	(3,200)	(3,200)	(3,200)	(3,200)	(3,200)	(3,200)
Cash flow	$1,743	$7,617	$12,425	$15,023	$19,830	$21,891	$26,701	$27,728	$28,808	$29,941

***EBIT stands for Earnings Before Interest and Taxes.
*At the end of the tenth year (1995), it is estimated that the company could be sold for four times EBIT, or $184,812 (4 × 46,203).

Exhibit C: Perrigo Financial Information behind the Cash Flow Projections

	1986	1987	1988	1989	1990	1991	1992	1993	1994	1995
Revenues	129,600	147,800	165,580	187,138	215,852	237,437	261,181	280,000	300,000	325,000
Expenses*	119,600	135,800	150,724	168,925	191,501	205,902	221,269	238,092	255,997	278,797
EBIT	10,000	12,000	14,856	18,213	24,351	31,535	39,912	41,908	44,003	46,203
Current assets (excluding cash)	43,876	47,461	53,755	61,387	71,550	79,192	87,598	96,059	105,620	116,060
Current liabilities	17,188	17,861	20,066	22,740	26,299	28,976	31,921	34,921	39,021	44,000
Working Capital	26,688	29,600	33,689	38,647	45,251	50,216	55,677	61,138	66,599	72,060

*Expenses listed here do not include interest or taxes.

Required

a. Even experts make errors in important computations. Recall what you know about how increases and decreases in current assets and current liabilities affect the calculation of cash flows. Recall that working capital is current assets minus current liabilities. What fatal mistake did the Perrigo lawyers and accountants make in Exhibit B? Correct the cash flow numbers for the mistake.

b. Assume exactly three years elapsed between the time Grow purchased Perrigo for $85 million and resold it to Perrigo management for $106 million. What was Grow's compounded annual rate of return on this investment?

c. Grow and Perrigo agreed that the relevant interest rate to discount cash flows in the original 1986 transaction was somewhere between 13.5% and 15.5%. Discount the uncorrected cash flows in Exhibit B by each of these interest rates to verify the range of values between $120 million and $137 million is correct. Use a terminal value of $184,812 at the end of the tenth year.

d. Discount the corrected cash flows by the 13.5% and 15.5% interest rates. What is the new range of values? Does the original $85 million transaction price fall between the range of the present values?